"In a battle of ideas, unlike a battle between nations, the goal is not to vanquish the opponents but to win them. Making that challenge even more difficult is that oftentimes, what we win them with is what we win them to. The art and science of dialoguing and debate must bring together the message and the method in concert. No one does this better than my colleague Os Guinness. For years I have benefited from his incisive thinking and carefully studied presentations. Here, he wisely observes that 'Our urgent need today is to reunite evangelism and apologetics, and make sure that our best arguments are directed toward winning people and not just winning arguments.' In this landmark work, I am thrilled to see his unique thinking on these crucial subjects, co-extensive with a lifetime of doing apologetics. It is a must-read for anyone interested in engaging the skeptic or seeker. Few thinkers today rise to the level that Os does, even as he plumbs the depth of vital issues in defense of the historic Christian faith."

Ravi Zacharias, author and speaker

"*Fool's Talk* is a direct exposition of the inner logic and rhetoric of persuasion, showing how hearers are moved from unbelief and doubt to conviction of the truth of the Christian faith. Guinness's focus is not only on the nature of effective argument but the character, ethics and faith of the apologist. Intellectually profound and immensely practical. I loved the book. So will you."

James W. Sire, author, *The Universe Next Door*, *Echoes of a Voice* and *Apologetics Beyond Reason*

"There is no doubt about it, Christian apologetics is having a renaissance. Oddly though, precious little of it addresses the art of persuasion. Who better to redress this lacuna than the preeminent apologist of our times, Os Guinness. Among the many virtues of *Fool's Talk* is the presentation of a robust Christian faith that is not predictable. Many people are so sure they know what Christians are going to say that they don't actually listen. Guinness keeps them off-balance, much in the way Jesus' parables caught his audiences off-guard. Faced with a plethora of modern challenges, from technology to globalization to political sales talk to moral relativism, we are tempted to develop a single, safe, reactionary method, ten steps to the punch line. Guinness does the opposite. Like G. K. Chesterton in an earlier age, Guinness reminds us that truth is quite unlikely, that is, dubious to unaided reason. He advocates a broad range of arguments, all of them imaginative, but all of them pointing to the surprising truth—the unpredictable love of God."

William Edgar, professor of apologetics, Westminster Theological Seminary

"A remarkable book. Written with the benefit of decades of experience and reflection—this is one book on apologetics you will not want to miss. I wholeheartedly recommend it."

Michael Ramsden, joint director, Oxford Centre for Christian Apologetics, international director, RZIM for Europe, the Middle East and Africa

"In a day when Christian apologetics seems to win battles but loses wars, evangelism is abandoned by the church and biblical strategies are ignored, *Fool's Talk* by Os Guinness is necessary and vitally important. Insightfully, he guides in the use not only of wit and weightiness, but also restores winsomeness to the art of communicating Christ. He teaches the reader to 'relativize the relativists' and build on the 'signals of transcendence' with brilliance. He acknowledges his debts to Peter Berger, C. S. Lewis, Francis Schaeffer, G. K. Chesterton and many others. Readers will be indebted to him for the syntheses and wisdom we have come to expect from Guinness. The benefits of the past are freshly and insightfully applied to the present. All people need to know they are deeply loved and forgiven by God. *Fool's Talk* will better equip us to tell them. I heartily endorse this book."

Jerry Root, associate professor of evangelism, Wheaton College

FOOL'S TALK

RECOVERING THE ART OF
CHRISTIAN PERSUASION

◆ ◆ ◆ ◆ ◆ ◆ ◆ ◆ ◆ ◆

OS GUINNESS

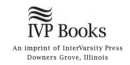

IVP Books
An imprint of InterVarsity Press
Downers Grove, Illinois

InterVarsity Press
P.O. Box 1400, Downers Grove, IL 60515-1426
ivpress.com
email@ivpress.com
©2015 by Os Guinness

InterVarsity Press® is the book-publishing division of InterVarsity Christian Fellowship/USA®, a movement of
students and faculty active on campus at hundreds of universities, colleges and schools of nursing in the United
States of America, and a member movement of the International Fellowship of Evangelical Students. For
information about local and regional activities, visit intervarsity.org.

All Scripture quotations, unless otherwise indicated, are taken from the New American Standard Bible®, copyright
1960, 1962, 1963, 1968, 1971, 1972, 1973, 1975, 1977, 1995 by The Lockman Foundation. Used by permission.

Every effort has been made to credit all material quoted in this book. Any errors or omissions brought to the
publisher's attention will be corrected in future editions.

While any stories in this book are true, some names and identifying information may have been changed to protect
the privacy of individuals.

Published in association with the literary agency of Wolgemuth & Associates.

Cover design: Cindy Kiple
Interior design: Beth McGill
Images: Dance of fools, from "Le Moyen Age et La Renaissance" by Paul Lacroix, Private Collection, Ken Welsh,
*   Bridgeman Images*

ISBN 978-0-8308-3699-4 (print)
ISBN 978-0-8308-9850-3 (digital)

Printed in the United States of America ∞

g green
press
INITIATIVE
As a member of the Green Press Initiative, InterVarsity Press is committed to protecting
the environment and to the responsible use of natural resources. To learn more, visit
greenpressinitiative.org.

Library of Congress Cataloging-in-Publication Data
Guinness, Os.
 Fool's talk : recovering the art of Christian persuasion / Os Guinness.
  pages cm
 Includes bibliographical references.
 ISBN 978-0-8308-3699-4 (hardcover : alk. paper)
 1. Influence (Psychology)—Religious aspects—Christianity. 2. Persuasion (Psychology)
3. Communication—Religious aspects—Christianity. 4. Persuasion (Rhetoric) I. Title.
 BV4597.53.I52G85 2015
 248'.5—dc23

                                                                        2015013532

P 23 22 21 20 19 18 17 16 15 14 13 12 11 10 9 8 7 6 5

Y 34 33 32 31 30 29 28 27 26 25 24 23 22 21 20 19 18 17 16

DOM,

And to Peter L. Berger,

scholar, mentor, friend, Grand Master of Comedy

and so much more besides.

In addition to being a wise man, the Preacher also taught the people knowledge; and he pondered and searched out and arranged many proverbs. The Preacher sought to find delightful words and to write words of truth correctly. The words of wise men are like goads and masters of these collections are like well-driven nails.

Ecclesiastes

When one is wise, it's wisest to seem foolish.

Aeschylus, *Prometheus Bound*

Do you know how you can act or speak about rhetoric so as to please God best?

Socrates in Plato's *Phaedrus*

There is nothing so pliant, nothing so flexible, nothing which will so easily follow whithersoever you incline to lead it, as language.

Marcus Tullius Cicero, *De Oratore*

In the beginning was the Word, and the Word was with God, and the Word was God.

St. John, Gospel of John

For Christ did not send me to baptize, but to preach the gospel, not in cleverness of speech, so that the cross of Christ would not be made void. For the word of the cross is foolishness to those who are perishing, but to us who are being saved it is the power of God. For it is written, "I will destroy the wisdom of the wise, and the cleverness of the clever I will set aside."

Where is the wise man? Where is the scribe? Where is the debater of this age? Has not God made foolish the wisdom of this world? *For since in the wisdom of God the world through its wisdom did not come to know God, God was well-pleased through the foolishness of the message preached to save those who believe.*

For indeed Jews ask for signs and Greeks search for wisdom; but we preach Christ crucified, to Jews a stumbling block and to Gentiles foolishness, but to those who are called, both Jews and Greeks, Christ the power of God and the wisdom of God, because the foolishness of God is wiser than men, and the weakness of God is stronger than men.

ST. PAUL, LETTER TO CORINTH

God, after he spoke long ago to the fathers
in the prophets in many portions and many ways,
in these last days has spoken to us in his Son.

LETTER TO THE HEBREWS

Joking often cuts through great obstacles better
and more forcefully than being serious would.

HORACE, SATIRES

Reason, even when supported by the senses, has short wings.

DANTE, PARADISO

What else is the whole life of mortals but a sort of comedy, in which the various actors, disguised by various costumes and masks, walk on and play each one his part, until the manager waves them off the stage.

ERASMUS, THE PRAISE OF FOLLY

The world is full of rage, hate and wars.
What will be the end if we employ only bulls and the stake? . . .
It is no great feat to burn a little man. It is a great
achievement to persuade him.

ERASMUS, LETTER

Jesters do oft prove prophets.

WILLIAM SHAKESPEARE, *KING LEAR*

The usefulness of comedy is that it corrects the vices of men.

MOLIÈRE, PREFACE TO *TARTUFFE*

Nothing produces laughter more than a surprising disproportion
between that which one expects and that which ones sees.

BLAISE PASCAL, *PENSÉES*

Who are a little wise the best fools be.

JOHN DONNE, "THE TRIPLE FOOL"

Out of the crooked timber of our humanity
no straight thing can be made.

IMMANUEL KANT, *IDEA FOR A GENERAL HISTORY*

Man is the only animal that laughs and weeps;
for he is the only animal that is struck with the difference
between what things are, and what they ought to be.

WILLIAM HAZLITT

One should not always so exhaust a subject that one leaves the reader with
nothing to do. The point is not to make men read, but to make them think.

MONTESQUIEU, *THE SPIRIT OF THE LAW*

Longing! Longing! To die longing and through longing not to die!

FRIEDRICH NIETZSCHE, *THE BIRTH OF TRAGEDY*

The opposition which Christianity has to encounter is no longer confined to special doctrines or to points of supposed conflict with the natural sciences, . . . but extends to the whole manner of conceiving the world, and of man's place in it, the manner of conceiving the entire system of things, natural and moral, of which we form a part. It is no longer an opposition of detail, but of principle. This circumstance necessitates an equal extension of the line of defense. It is the Christian view of things in general which is attacked, and it is by an exposition and vindication of the Christian view of things as a whole that the attack can most successfully be met.

JAMES ORR, *THE CHRISTIAN VIEW OF GOD AND OF THE WORLD*

Alone among the animals, he [the human being] is shaken with the beautiful madness called laughter; as if he had caught sight of some secret in the very shape of the universe hidden from the universe itself.

G. K. CHESTERTON, *THE EVERLASTING MAN*

Every joke is a tiny revolution.

GEORGE ORWELL, "FUNNY BUT NOT VULGAR"

The intimate relation between humor and faith is derived from the fact that both deal with the incongruities of our existence. Humor is concerned with the immediate incongruities of life and faith with the ultimate ones. Both humor and faith are expressions of the freedom of the human spirit, of its capacity to stand outside of life, and itself, and view the whole scene. . . . Laughter is our reaction to immediate incongruities and those which do not affect us essentially. Faith is the only possible response to the ultimate incongruities of existence which threaten the very meaning of our life. . . . Faith is the final triumph over incongruity, the final assertion of the meaningfulness of existence.

REINHOLD NIEBUHR, "HUMOR AND FAITH"

Laughter has a deep philosophical meaning; . . . the world is seen anew, no less (and perhaps more) profoundly than when seen from the serious standpoint. . . . Certain essential aspects of the word are accessible only to laughter.

MIKHAIL BAKHTIN, RABELAIS AND HIS WORLD

Sometimes we must laugh in order to perceive. . . . Comedy is more profound than tragedy.

PETER L. BERGER, REDEEMING LAUGHTER

I pray earnestly that God will raise up today a new generation of Christian apologists or Christian communicators, who will combine an absolute loyalty to the biblical gospel and an unwavering confidence in the power of the Spirit with a deep and sensitive understanding of the contemporary alternatives to the gospel.

JOHN R. W. STOTT, YOUR MIND MATTERS

Contents

Introduction

RECOVERING THE LOST ART

W̲E̲ A̲R̲E̲ A̲L̲L̲ A̲P̲O̲L̲O̲G̲I̲S̲T̲S̲ N̲O̲W̲, and we stand at the dawn of the grand age of human apologetics, or so some are saying because our wired world and our global era are a time when expressing, presenting, sharing, defending and selling ourselves have become a staple of everyday life for countless millions of people around the world, both Christians and others. The age of the Internet, it is said, is the age of the self and the selfie. The world is full of people full of themselves. In such an age, "I post, therefore I am."

To put the point more plainly, human interconnectedness in the global era has been raised to a truly global level, with unprecedented speed and on an unprecedented scale. Everyone is now everywhere, and everyone can communicate with everyone else from anywhere and at any time, instantly and cheaply. Communication through the social media in the age of email, text messages, cell phones, tweets and Skype is no longer from "the few to the many," as in the age of the book, the newspaper and television, but from "the many to the many," and all the time.

One of the effects of this level of globalization is plain. Active and interactive communication is the order of the day. From the shortest texts and tweets to the humblest website, to the angriest blog, to the most visited social networks, the daily communications of the wired world attest that *everyone is now in the business of relentless self-promotion—presenting themselves, explaining themselves, defending themselves, selling themselves or sharing their inner thoughts and emotions as never before in human history.*

That is why it can be said that we are in the grand secular age of apologetics. The whole world has taken up apologetics without ever using or knowing the idea as Christians understand it. We are all apologists now, if only on behalf of "the Daily Me" or "the Tweeted Update" that we post for our virtual friends and our cyber community. The great goals of life, we are told, are to gain the widest possible public attention and to reach as many people in the world with our products—and always, our leading product is Us.

Are Christians ready for this new age? We who are followers of Jesus stand as witnesses to the truth and meaning of the life, death and resurrection of Jesus as a central matter of our calling. We are spokespersons for our Lord, and advocacy is in our genes. Ours is the apologetic faith par excellence. But regardless of the new media, many of us have yet to rise to the challenge of a way of apologetics that is as profound as the good news we announce, as deep as the human heart, as subtle as the human mind, as powerful and flexible as the range of people and issues that we meet every day in our extraordinary world in which "everyone is now everywhere."

What does "the grand age of apologetics" mean for us as followers of Jesus? The full scope of this overall task is far larger than my particular concern in this book. But on the one hand, our age is quite simply the greatest opportunity for Christian witness since the time of Jesus and the apostles, and our response should be to seize the opportunity with bold and imaginative enterprise. If ever the "wide and effective door" that St. Paul wrote of has been reopened for the gospel, it is now.

On the other hand, we have to face up to the many challenges of the new age of communication with realism, for there are oddities in the age of communication that make it actually harder to communicate well today, rather than easier. And we also have to face the fact that the global era has shown up weaknesses in our present approaches to sharing the faith that must be remedied—above all because many attempts at Christian apologetics have been caught in the turbulent wake of the massive crossover between the grand philosophies of modernism and postmodernism.

This book is therefore about an issue that is timely and urgent—remedying a central and serious shortcoming in Christian communication today, and about a broader vision of advocacy to help us go forward to make the most of this new moment. For those who want to explore the wider issues of apologetics, there are many excellent books available. *Christian Apolo-getics Past and Present*, edited by William Edgar and Scott Oliphint, presents a magisterial anthology of the best of apologetics down the centuries. *A History of Apologetics* by Avery Cardinal Dulles provides a superb overview of the discipline. Among the best grand summaries of contemporary apolo-getic issues by Christian philosophers are the *Handbook of Christian Apolo-getics* by Peter Kreeft and Ronald Tacelli, and *Christian Apologetics* by Douglas Groothuis. And the *New Dictionary of Christian Apologetics* repre-sents a goldmine of an encyclopedia on the topic.[1]

This book focuses on a narrower issue and a simple problem: *We have lost the art of Christian persuasion and we must recover it.* Evangelism is alive and well in the rapidly growing churches of the Global South, where the challenge is to recover an ardor for discipleship and a discernment of the modern world to match the zeal for evangelism. But in the advanced modern world, which is both pluralistic and post-Christian, our urgent need is for the recovery of persuasion in order to address the issues of the hour. Some branches of the Western church have effectively abandoned evangelism, for various reasons, and others speak as if Christian truths and beliefs are always and readily understandable to everyone, whatever the state of their listeners' hearts and whatever the character of their audience's worldview and culture. Others again have come to rely on formulaic, cookie-cutter approaches to evangelism and apologetics as if all who hear them are the same.

This combination of the abandonment of evangelism, the divorce be-tween evangelism, apologetics and discipleship, and the failure to appreciate true human diversity is deeply serious. It is probably behind the fact that many Christians, realizing the ineffectiveness of many current approaches and sensing the unpopularity and implausibility of much Christian witness, have simply fallen silent and given up evangelism altogether, sometimes relieved to mask their evasion under a newfound passion for social justice that can forget the gaucheness of evangelism. At best, many of us who take the good news of Jesus seriously are eager and ready to share the good news when we meet people who are open, interested or in need of what we have to share. But we are less effective when we encounter people who are not open, not interested or not needy—in other words, people who are closed, indifferent, hostile, skeptical or apathetic, and therefore require persuasion.

In short, many of us today lack a vital part of a way of communicating that is prominent in the Gospels and throughout the Scriptures, but largely absent in the church today—persuasion, the art of speaking to people who, for whatever reason, are indifferent or resistant to what we have to say. They simply do not agree with us and are not open to what we have to say.

Loss of persuasion? It might seem bizarre, almost unimaginable, that Christian communication has lost something so central to its mission. Yet in profound ways it has, and that is why our challenge is to think about apologetics in ways that are not only fresh but faithful and independent—faithful in the sense that they are shaped by the imperatives of Christian truths, and independent in the sense that they are not primarily beholden to ways of thinking that are alien to Christian ways of thinking. That is why this book is not only about the lost art of Christian persuasion. It is also about an "advocacy of the heart," an existential approach to sharing our faith that I believe is deeper and more faithful as well as more effective than the common approaches used by many. Christian advocacy has had many conversation partners down the centuries—particularly the great tradition of classical rhetoric established by the Greeks and the Romans. It has also had many opponents and sparring partners—most recently the bracing challenge of the new atheists. But for all the undoubted benefits of these challenges, one of the more unfortunate side effects is that much apologetics has lost touch with evangelism and come to be all about "arguments," and in particular about winning arguments rather than winning hearts and minds and people. Our urgent need today is to reunite evangelism and apologetics, to make sure that our best arguments are directed toward winning people and not just winning arguments, and to seek to do all this in a manner that is true to the gospel itself.

The fact is that much contemporary advocacy ignores the deeper understandings of the spiritual and philosophical ways in which people think through their faiths, change their faiths, and the impact of their cultures and their ways of life on their thinking and beliefs. Even more importantly, today's advocacy often ignores the crucial biblical understanding of the anatomy of human unbelief, how God addresses those who ignore or reject him, and how we too are to learn to address people wherever they are and whatever they think about God or the church or us. The heart of the problem is quite literally the problem of the heart.

My own journey to faith was more than intellectual, but it included a long, slow, critical debate in my mind during my school years. On one side, I listened to the arguments of such famous atheists as Friedrich Nietzsche, Jean Paul Sartre and Albert Camus, and on the other side to such Christian thinkers as Blaise Pascal, Fyodor Dostoevsky, G. K. Chesterton and C. S. Lewis. But if the approach advocated here is rare today, it is definitely not unique to me. I merely sit on the shoulders of certain giants of the faith who have gone before. My debts to these giants will become clear as we proceed, and I am equally clear about my own inadequacies in following their example. But together we must rise to the challenge of our time: How can we speak for our Lord in a manner that does justice to the wonder of who God is, to the profundity of the good news he has entrusted to us, to the wily stubbornness of the human heart and mind, as well as to the wide-ranging challenges of today's world and the mind-boggling prospects of tomorrow's? In short, how can we as followers of Jesus be as truly persuasive as we desire to be? Nothing less than that is the goal of our exploration.

1

CREATIVE PERSUASION

THE COLORFUL AND CONTROVERSIAL NOVELIST Norman Mailer was once invited to speak at the University of California Berkeley. It was at a time when he was notorious for his scathing dismissals of the women's movement and had bragged publicly that he was a "champion male chauvinist pig." Many women students were incensed at the brazen way he flaunted his bigotry and the fact that he had been invited in the first place, so a large group of feminists decided to come to the lecture and give him such a roasting that he would regret accepting the invitation. In their view Mailer was a rank and shameless misogynist, and he needed to be put in his place.

As several accounts of the incident go, the air was crackling as Mailer entered the lecture room. He had been warned in advance that the feminists would be hostile and were lying in wait for him. Mailer strode confidently through the crowd, stepped up to the podium and announced that he had important things to say, so those who wished to hiss and boo should get it out at once. He then threw down the gauntlet: "Everybody in this hall who regards me as a male chauvinist pig, hiss."

As if perfectly on cue, the feminists broke out at once in loud, derisive hissing and booing, which rose to a crescendo of long, sustained jeering and barracking, punctuated with derisive cat calls and wolf whistles from men in other parts of the lecture room. For a while there was pandemonium, but inevitably it had to die down. The feminists could not keep up the booing forever, and the hubbub subsided. Mailer stepped back to the microphone, looked over to them, paused just a second or two, and said, "Obedient little women, aren't you?" (To sanitize his words somewhat.)

For a second or so the outcome hung in the balance. The ploy could have bombed and set off chaos, but it worked. The hostile tension collapsed. Mailer had shown a canny mastery of his audience, and many laughed and applauded. By all accounts, even some of the hardcore feminists were so stunned at falling for his ploy that from then on they listened in a rueful silence.

Mailer, of course, was as scathing and dismissive of the Christian faith as he was of women and anyone else with whom he disagreed, and his misogyny was inexcusable. His arrogant chauvinism toward women, amplified by the stories of his six marriages, was light years away from the example and teaching of Jesus. Our Lord always treated women with a respect and dignity that stands out from his own age and shines across all ages. But we who are followers of Jesus should consider one thing: Mailer's bigotry and the substance of his argument was as far from Jesus as anyone could be, but the *style* in which he communicated was closer to Jesus than many of us who are followers of Jesus.

What Mailer did was what I call creative persuasion or subversion through surprise. *To people predisposed to reject what he had to say, he communicated in a way that made them see his point—despite themselves.*

Such creative persuasion, conducted according to the way of Jesus and the Scriptures, is critical for the church today because we who are Western Christians suffer from a glaring weakness that we need to face candidly. Let me state the problem again: *Almost all our witnessing and Christian communication assumes that people are open to what we have to say, or at least are interested, if not in need of what we are saying. Yet most people quite simply are not open, not interested and not needy, and in much of the advanced modern world fewer people are open today than even a generation ago. Indeed, many are more hostile, and their hostility is greater than the Western church has faced for centuries.* Through the explosion of pluralism in the last fifty years, our world has grown dramatically more diverse, and through the intensification of the culture warring in many Western countries, our world has grown far more dismissive of our faith. In short, the public squares in many of our nations are more secular and the private spheres are more diverse. We therefore have to speak many languages, and not just "Christian," and we have to be persuasive when we address minds and hearts that often listen to us with a default position of prejudice, scorn, impatience and sometimes anger.

To be sure, every single human being on God's earth is open, interested and needy at some point in their lives—and when they are, we should always be ready, willing and able to speak and point them to the one who is the center and soul of all that makes life meaningful and worthwhile for us. But there are profound theological reasons why most people are not open and interested most of the time, and there are historical and cultural reasons why more people are more closed, hostile or indifferent in the West today than they were in the time of our grandparents. In the world of today we again and again have to face the fact that the world that earlier generations knew has gone, and gone for forever.

HOIST BY HIS OWN PETARD

Our guiding inspiration for Christian advocacy can hardly be Norman Mailer's prejudice, craftily defended though it was. So consider a biblical example of the same creative persuasion—the story of the prophet Micaiah, recounted in 1 Kings 22:1-28. At some unspecified year in the history of Israel after the division of the kingdom, King Jehoshaphat of Judah went up from Jerusalem to Samaria to confer with his royal cousin, King Ahab of Israel. They were forging an alliance to recapture some disputed territory taken by the Syrians. The questions before their Joint Council of War were simple. Should they forge an alliance and attack the Syrians with their combined forces? And would such a campaign have the backing of God and end in victory?

The natural step was to call out Samaria's court prophets and enlist God's backing for their plan. What else are clergy for, it seems, in times of conflict? Blessing the bombers is surely central to being a bishop. In this instance the court prophets were obliging, and they offered a unanimous opinion that just happened to be exactly what the two kings were hoping to hear. With one voice, all four hundred prophets declared that the two kings should "Attack and win!" To reinforce their message, some of the prophets—skilled communicators in a manner that would delight modern communication aficionados—created visual aids to illustrate their message. One prophet, a certain Zedekiah, brought ox horns that he brandished to show how the two noble kings would gore the enemy and drive everything before them.

Doubtless, it was an impressive performance and had its intended impact on its royal listeners. Yet for some reason, King Jehoshaphat, who unlike Ahab was loyal to the God of Israel, was not satisfied by this unanimous vote from Ahab's court prophets. He therefore asked his royal ally if he had any other prophets from whom they might inquire.

"Yes," Ahab replied, "there is one other, but he always prophesies negatively about me."

Strike one against the prophet Micaiah: he was always negative about Ahab. But when King Ahab sent the royal servant to collect Micaiah, the strike count quickly got worse. "Everyone else has prophesied victory, so mind you say the same thing too," he was told in effect. In other words, Micaiah was brought to the war council and found himself hopelessly out of line with all the other prophets, but under strict orders to fall in line and say exactly what the others had said—in short, to prophesy falsely.

Stunningly, that is exactly what Micaiah did as he began. He prophesied falsely like the others. "As the LORD lives," he had told the king's servant, "what the LORD says to me, that I will I speak." But despite that, or perhaps even inspired directly by the Lord to prophesy falsely as other prophets had done earlier in Israel's history, he went along with the other prophets, and echoed what they had said precisely: "Attack and win!"

It was then Ahab's turn to be suspicious. Could Micaiah really be agreeing for once with his own court prophets? Was there a hint in the way Micaiah was speaking that he was being tongue-in-cheek? Was his answer on this occasion so out of line with what he normally said that the king was put on the alert? Or was there somehow the suggestion that Micaiah was telling the truth but leaving out a vital part of the answer that would change everything—that their forces would in fact win, for example, but that one of the kings would die in the battle, perhaps even Ahab himself?

Whatever it was that troubled Ahab, he broke into Micaiah's pronouncement before the prophet had finished. "How many times shall I make you swear," Ahab thundered with a hypocrisy that must have been comic to everyone present, "that you speak to me nothing but the truth in the name of the LORD?"

To which Micaiah answered simply, "I saw all Israel scattered on the mountain as sheep that have no shepherd." In other words, "The truth is, your Majesty, that your people will be leaderless because you are about to die."

The effect must have been stunning. King Ahab had walked into Micaiah's knockout punch as unwittingly as the feminists had walked into Norman Mailer's. To be sure, the king was no more inclined to accept Micaiah's word than the feminists were to acquiesce to Mailer. But Ahab had been hoist by his own petard. He had asked for the word of the Lord and he had been given it, straight from the shoulder. At his own insistence, Ahab was confronted with a true prophecy that was now on public record as a counter to the false prophecies. Truth had spoken to power. Ahab could go forward and do what he wanted, presumably what he had intended to do all along. But from that moment on, he was without excuse, and it was his life that was at stake in the outcome of the prophet's word from God.

IN YOUR OWN WORDS, YOUR MAJESTY

Consider another example from the prophets (1 Kings 20:26-43), this time an acted parable—another story on an earlier occasion when King Ahab found himself on the receiving end of a devastating punch line (the term is apt). This time he had been attacked by a massive and arrogant campaign launched against Samaria by King Ben-hadad of Syria along with thirty-two allies (see 1 Kings 20:1). God had spared Israel mercifully, but with a rash complacency born of his own presumed brilliance in the victory, Ahab had spared his royal enemy after defeating his army. He was at once called to account by one of Israel's band of prophets in a curious but dramatic episode.

The unnamed prophet assigned to be God's messenger asked another prophet to strike him on the head and wound him. He then went to the road by which King Ahab was to return from the battle, and waited for him with a bloody bandage over his eyes, disguising who he was.

When the king passed by and inquired how he had been wounded, the prophet told him the following story. It was of course purely fictitious, but quite credible in the aftermath of the battle. In the heat of the fight, he said, someone had brought a prisoner to him and ordered him to guard the man with his life. If he were to let his captive escape, he would either forfeit his life or pay a steep ransom of a silver talent.

Unfortunately, the disguised prophet said, his captive did escape—to which Ahab broke in with his usual summary heartlessness: "So shall your judgment be. You yourself have decided it."

Whereupon the prophet dramatically tore the bandage from his eyes and let the king see who he was: one of his own prophets. "Thus says the LORD," the man of God declared, "'Because you have let out of your hand the man I devoted to destruction, therefore your life shall be for his life and your people for his people.'"

"In your own words, your majesty." Ahab had judged himself. In full view of his noisily celebrating bodyguards and his sycophantic courtiers, he had once again been hoist by his own petard. The prophet's judgment was far more effective than a tongue-lashing. The word of God had been acted out in public, and the king himself had chosen to enter in and play the role of his own prosecutor and judge.

CROSS-CENTERED AND CROSS-SHAPED

These stories are only two of many such examples scattered throughout the Bible, and, as we shall see, this approach was demonstrated most brilliantly of all by Jesus. There are obviously wider considerations behind their telling, and these we shall explore. But at their heart is a brilliant style of creative persuasion—one might say "prophetic persuasion"—and behind them a rich understanding of why such persuasion is needed and how it works. Together they represent a model of Christian persuasion that revives a way of persuasion that was powerful in the Bible and persistent down the Christian centuries, but largely forgotten today. For no one who reads the Bible carefully or who reflects on their own experience of seeking to share the gospel of Jesus today can avoid a blunt conclusion: *There are all too many people who do not want to believe what we share or even to hear what we have to say, and our challenge is to help them to see it despite themselves.*

This lost art of Christian persuasion stands in stark contrast to many Christian ways of communicating in the West today, ways that are prosaic, one-dimensional and ineffectual to a fault. More importantly, recovering the art of Christian persuasion helps us in two practical ways. First, it shows us a way out of the tragic impasse in which much contemporary Christian communication has been caught. When people are not interested in what we have to say, whether they are hostile, prejudiced, indifferent or blasé, we often find ourselves mute and at a loss. But at such moments there is a better way, so that *there is no one anywhere and at any time to whom we cannot speak constructively.* There is an important reason why such persuasion will not and should not always lead to success, but it is a style of raising issues that challenges people to be responsible to truth and to their own consciences, and therefore leaves them without excuse.

Second, this lost art challenges us to be more decisively Christian in our communication. Contrary to the impression many Christians give today, Christian communication is not a matter of communicating the Christian faith with whatever means we find handy and effective. "If it works, use it" is a naive contemporary approach that has already reduced much Christian speech to slick and smoothly delivered formulas or to garbled and mumbling impotence. By contrast, Christian communication is a communication of the gospel that is shaped by our understanding of God's communication in Christ, just as God's communication in Christ is shaped by God's understanding of the condition of our hearts that God addresses in the gospel.

Put simply: *As God saw, so he sent, and as God sent, so we share.* As God saw our sin, so he sent his Son, and as God sent his Son, so we share our faith. To be truly Christ-centered, Christian persuasion is much more than just arguments about evidence or a battle over worldviews. There is an art to the advocacy of truth. It is an art that should be true to the truths of the Christian faith itself, and therefore shaped by both the Christian understanding of truth itself and by particular truths of the faith.

To say that does not mean, as some people argue today, that we simply preach the gospel and never seek to persuade. Proclamation and persuasion must never be separated. What it means is that Christian advocacy must always be independent. It must always be consistent to itself and shaped decisively by the great truths of the Scriptures, and in particular by five central truths of the faith—creation, the fall, the incarnation, the cross, and the Spirit of God.

True to the biblical understanding of creation, Christian persuasion must always take account of the human capacity for reason and the primacy of the human heart.

True to the understanding of the fall, Christian persuasion must always take account of the anatomy of an unbelieving mind in its denial of God.

True to the incarnation, Christian persuasion always has to be primarily person-to-person and face-to-face, and not argument to argument, formula to formula, media to media or methodology to methodology.

True to the cross of Jesus, Christian persuasion has to be cross-shaped in its manner just as it is cross-centered in its message—which as we shall see, lies behind the choice of the title of this book: *Fool's Talk*.

And true to the Holy Spirit, Christian persuasion must always know and show that the decisive power is not ours but God's. For God is his own lead counsel, his own best apologist, and the one who challenges the world to "set out your case." And as Jesus tells us, his Spirit, the Spirit of truth, is the one who does the essential work of convincing and convicting.

Can the good news of Jesus be defended by means that are completely independent of that good news and therefore neutral between believers and unbelievers? Should it? No. I will argue that there is no one we cannot talk to, however hostile to and distant from the gospel, but that this is precisely because we can count on the distinctive truths of the gospel itself—and therefore that our approach is independent in the sense of being decisively Christian and not neutral between belief and unbelief. This vision of Christian advocacy as "the art of Christian truth and of Christian truths" is the core of the lost art of persuasion we shall be exploring.

For the early Christian apologists in the time of the Roman Empire, the challenge was to introduce a message so novel that it was strange to its first hearers, and then to set out what the message meant for the classical age and its sophisticated and assured ways of thinking. For much of the advanced modern world today, in contrast, the challenge is to restate something so familiar that people know it so well that they do not know it, yet at the same time are convinced that they are tired of it.

In other words, our age in the Western world today is generally post-Christian rather than pre-Christian and pluralistic rather than secular, which creates important differences and is broadly more difficult to speak to. But generalities count for only a little when we talk to individuals. The context that is the challenge for Christian apologists will always differ from person to person, from age to age and from country to country. But for all of us in any age and in any part of the world, we are followers of Jesus, for whom knowing him and making him known is life's supreme joy. Christian persuasion is therefore an inexpressible privilege, a costly challenge and a demanding lesson well worth learning.

2

TECHNIQUE

The Devil's Bait

O<small>N THE FRIDGE IN OUR HOME</small> is a little magnet that shows a flock of sheep meandering down a country road. Underneath is a caption: "Rush hour, Ireland." It reminds me of a story of a Spanish professor visiting the west of Ireland where the sense of time used to be the slowest of all. Interviewing an old gentleman he observed sitting for hours outside a pub, he asked him if the Irish had an equivalent for the Spanish word *mañana*.

The old Irishman thought for a long while, and then answered, "No, we don't have any word as urgent as that."

That, of course, was then. Ireland more recently has been Europe's "Celtic Tiger," and it is beginning to suffer from the same pressures of advanced modern time that we almost all do. In our 24/7 modern world, we say the time is five or six or seven *o'clock*, which is quite literally "of the clock," as opposed to the timing of the sun, the seasons, or the birds and the bees. We are in fact ruled and run, first by clock time as we live in our industrialized clock world, and second by electronic time and "life at the speed of light." We all know the craziness of the pressure of life's "speed, stuff and stress." Social scientists talk of "fast life," psychologists talk of "hurry sickness," and business people of "turbo-capitalism." Life fired at us point blank becomes the survival of the fastest. As a Kenyan saying goes, "Westerners have watches, Africans have time."

Perhaps saddest of all, we Westerners have been taken in by the presumptions and prejudices of our modern views of time, and nowhere is the modern church more worldly than in its breathless idolizing of such modern notions as change, relevance, innovation and being on the right side of history. The fact is that we are constantly being tempted by a radical worldliness at two key points that are at the heart of the modern world: our views of time and our view of technique.

These two seductions are actually closer than most people realize, for time is the result of accelerated technology, and when we fall for the seductions of modern time, we are vulnerable to the seductions of technique too. (I must have the next new thing, and I want it fast, and I want it now, so give me the latest app.) Conversely, when we accomplish more and more through technique, we open ourselves to the seductions of time and assume the superiority of fast life and instant immediacy everywhere.

The world of fast food has long been the place where quantity has conquered quality, efficiency has trumped excellence, and both have excelled at the expense of health. But the so-called McDonaldization of the world means that the same spirit and process have now invaded many other areas too. All of life, we are told, can be transformed by the magic touch of the McDonald's formula, so that when we copy the four secrets of "the golden arches" (calculability, efficiency, predictability and control), we can multiply quantities of any kind—whether hamburgers, computers, health clinics, new churches or new converts. ("Billions and billions of hamburgers sold"; Millions and millions of converts won.)

This mentality is bad enough when applied to church growth, and we are advised to plant churches in the same way that McDonald's, Starbucks or KFC franchise their stores. But when it comes to Christian persuasion, the result is as obscene as it is ineffective. We can learn a great deal from excellent conversation partners, such as the classical tradition of the art of rhetoric and its grand practitioners such as Socrates, Plato, Aristotle, Demosthenes and Cicero. We can learn a great deal too from our sparring partners and opponents, such as Friedrich Nietzsche and the new atheists. But we must also and always be discerning about the spirit of the age in any generation, which today means squarely facing the seductions of technique. Technique is the devil's bait for the Christian persuader today, and at point after point we must turn down its seductions point blank, just as Jesus refused the tempter in the desert. We still do not live by bread alone, even in a day when the illusion is stronger than ever that we can live by science alone—or technology, management, metrics or education alone.

WINNING THE WORLD BY TOMORROW AFTERNOON

All good thinking is a matter of asking and answering three elementary questions. What is being said? Is it true? What of it? Yet one of the curious experiences of speaking in many places in the West is an almost universal preoccupation with the last question, as if audiences were incapable of answering it for themselves. A speaker must therefore provide ready-made "take home values," "next steps," "measurable outcomes" and the like. I sometimes wonder if some audiences raise the first two questions at all, and I am far from certain that such insistence on formulas and recipes for action really leads to more decisive action in practice. But the hosts and chairpersons in many events act as if without spelling out all the next steps, audiences would be cruelly short-changed.

The reason, of course, is that we live in the grand age of technology when everything thought worthwhile must be transformed by the magic of technique. This in its turn is part of the overall spread of what Max Weber famously called "rationalization," the imperial spread of applied reason, through which we can calculate and control everything by applying numbers, rules, methods and metrics everywhere and to everything. If McDonaldization is Weber's process applied to commodities, McDisneyization is the same thing applied to experiences and entertainment, and it is significant that both first flourished in California in the 1950s.

Just as to a man with a hammer, everything is a nail, so in the age of science and technology, everything is a scientific and technical matter to be solved by scientific and technical means. Thus, ironically, our sophisticated teachers have no sooner urged us to eschew all forms of absolutes and certainties, and to be resolutely skeptical when it comes to knowledge, than they turn around and urge us to place unquestioning confidence in experts, specialists and pundits, and all their insights and techniques—and to address our ignorance through the authoritative guidance of ever-changing, ever-improving commodities such as seminars, courses, recipes, self-help books and a myriad of formulas for "life-changing results." Tied in together with the myth of progress, what we are offered is the eternal promise that the next new, new thing will always be better.

One of several results is the imperialism of technique and a major cause of the infamous disenchantment of the modern world, about which so many have written and protested. And sure enough, the temptation of the lure of technique raises its head at the very start of our exploration of creative persuasion. Surely, the temptation runs, we can master persuasion, reduce it to a surefire technique, and launch and market "a must-see, all-new school of persuasion that is guaranteed to win the world by tomorrow afternoon."

Not so fast. Christian persuasion is a vital part of the overall task of making a convincing case for the Christian faith—the task known as apologetics or advocacy. But there is no McTheory when it comes to persuasion. There is no such thing as McApologetics, though it is significant that the nearest one-size-fits-all approach—the Four Spiritual Laws—was also created at the same time and in the same place as the first flourishing of McDonald's as we know it and the first theme park run by Walt Disney: 1950s California.

With all the confusions and controversies surrounding contemporary Christian advocacy, recovering persuasion will not be easy. But if we are not to miss the way from the outset, we need to close our ears to the siren sounds of technique and take note of three reminders that are essential to our exploration.

No One Way

The first reminder is a simple point, though negative. As with almost everything worthwhile in life, there is rarely just one way to do it. The same is true of persuasion. There is no single right way it should be done. There is no one-size-fits-all approach that will work with everyone. To be sure, there are some ways that are *not* Christian and some that are not effective, but there is no single way that alone *is* Christian.

The reason for this is equally simple. Life is much more than reason, so it can never be captured and explained by reason alone—crucial and valuable though reason is. Apply reason as carefully and systematically as you like, and there will always be things it cannot explain, things that simply will not fit into its categories, however hard you push, press and pull. Then comes the Procrustean temptation. Procrustes ("the racker") was the Greek innkeeper, who insisted that all his guests had to fit his beds perfectly, so those who were too short he stretched, and those who were too tall he lopped off their limbs and surplus inches. Just so reason operates when it is made king and given the final word.

All the studies of McDonald's and Disney point this out too. Highly rationalized as they are, or carefully as reason has been applied to every part of their businesses, there is always the "unintended consequence" and "the irrationality of the rational." Automated telephone calls, for example, save time and personnel for the company that uses them, but waste time and create frustration for the customer. Equally, waiting for a ride at a theme park often takes longer than the ride itself, just as queues at a fast-food restaurant can often be long and make the food anything but fast. In each case, it is the customer, rather than the business, that suffers—though the business finds that it is easier to rationalize the process of flipping burgers than it is the process of handling customers.

The same is true of apologetic methods. No single method will ever fit everyone because every single person is different, and every method—even the best—will miss someone. There is no question that the Four Spiritual Laws have been remarkably fruitful as a way of evangelism, but they are not good for everyone. The first law, "God loves you and offers a wonderful plan for your life," may be perfect for people who believe even vaguely in God, and it even speaks to an atheist who is beginning to search for "something more." But it is meaningless and water off a duck's back for an atheist satisfied with his atheism. Worse, to a hostile atheist, mention of God at the start of a conversation is like a red rag to a bull, and invites a snort and a pawing of the ground. As we need to remind ourselves again and again, and then again, *Jesus never spoke to two people the same way, and neither should we. Every single person is unique and individual and deserves an approach that respects that uniqueness.*

AN ART, NOT A SCIENCE

The second reminder is that Christian persuasion is an art, not a science. It has more to do with theology than technology. As such, it needs to be clearly understood and carefully guarded in today's world, and I would highlight this insistence in three different ways.

Creative persuasion is a matter of being biblical, not of being either modern or postmodern. In today's climate, anyone who prizes reason and truth and makes use of them in the defense of the faith is apt to be dismissed as a modernist. Equally, anyone who uses imagination and stories is apt to be either praised or dismissed as postmodern, depending on the speaker's view of postmodernism. But the fact is that the Bible itself is the grandest of grand stories, yet it prizes truth and reason without being modernist, and it prizes countless stories within its overall story without being postmodern either. In short, the Bible is both rational and experiential, propositional as well as relational, so that genuinely biblical arguments work in any age and with any person. Modernism and postmodernism, in contrast, both have assets as well as liabilities, and postmodernism was for a time the greater danger only because it was then the current danger. Christian persuasion, by contrast, aims to be neither modern nor postmodern but biblical and holistic, and therefore faithful.

As any reader can see, the Bible has a high place for truth and rational arguments as well as for stories, drama, parables and poetry. The Bible contains the book of Romans as well as the psalms of David and the parables of Jesus. To be sure, stories are at the heart of the biblical view of creative persuasion, but not at the expense of reason or argument. In the biblical view the issue is not modern versus postmodern. Both these views are partly right, and both are finally wrong. Nor is it rational argument versus story, or reason versus imagination. In fact it is not either-or at all. The deep logic of God's truth can be expressed in both stories and arguments, by questions as well as statements, through reason and the imagination, through the four Gospels as well as through the book of Romans. This is one reason why C. S. Lewis has had such an enduring appeal. At times he was coolly rational, as in *Mere Christianity*, while at other times he engaged the imagination brilliantly, as in *The Screwtape Letters* or The Chronicles of Narnia. There is a time for stories, and there is a time for rational arguments, and the skill we need lies in knowing which to use, and when.

Put differently, creative persuasion is a matter of truth, not simply of technique. More accurately, *creative persuasion is the art of truth, the art that truth inspires.* I started in chapter one with two stories from the Bible, and we will look at many more. I shall also introduce and discuss several principles and practical tips. But if anyone is simply looking for techniques, formulas, recipes, how-to methods or for any surefire ways of persuading anyone, they will be disappointed. There are no such things. And I will not pretend that there are, or that I have any to offer.

The desire for a surefire, foolproof approach to sharing faith is understandable—if only because there are people whom we love so much that we wish them to come to faith decisively, people we love, for whom anything short of success will seem a heartbreaking failure. That is only natural. But as we shall see repeatedly, we live in a fallen world in which any thoughts are thinkable, any arguments are arguable and any doubts are dubitable. In other words, there are people for whom no amount of evidence will ever establish any claim if they have determined to deny the claim no matter what. We might say they would deny the claim "even if God makes the claim," but with some of them it would be more accurate to say "especially if God makes the claim." For they see God as the great interferer, the ultimate spoilsport they must fend off at all costs. There are therefore no foolproof methods of persuasion, and those that come closest are coercive and dangerous because they override the will rather than convince the mind. For anyone seeking surefire, foolproof methods, the techniques of brainwashing used by communists and by cults would provide a better model than the way we are exploring here.

Our modern lust for technique comes from the fact that we live in the great how-to age. The age of technology and technique is the age of endless methods, formulas, recipes, seminars, how-to manuals, twelve-step programs and the constant lure of efficiency. Our temptation then is to pursue the admirable goal of becoming more persuasive and to fall into a common trap: becoming preoccupied with technique, as if persuasion could be learned by observing the process carefully, reducing it to reason, reversing it and then repeating it ourselves.

There are certainly skills with which this approach works well—especially in the spheres of science, technology, engineering and the do-it-yourself world. Repairing a car or a computer, for example, can be done by the book— although even there most of the younger generation throw away the five-language instruction guide and just do it intuitively. In such instances the techniques can be reduced, reversed and repeated to great effect, and published in manuals designed even for "dummies." But a moment's thought shows that these techniques are generally effective only on the lower levels of life. As soon as we move to higher human skills—say, leading a team, making a high-quality wine or making love—the skills required are more an art than a science, and anything but a how-to method.

This may well be the reason why Jesus (and Socrates too) never wrote a book. The way of Jesus has to be learned from the Master, under his authority and in experience along the journey of life. Like any art, such as painting, fishing or cooking a soufflé, creative persuasion is better caught than taught, and better caught from those who are experienced rather than expounded in a book or a classroom. *With the deepest things in life, there is always more to knowing than knowing will ever know, so the deepest knowledge must be learned in life, from experience, and under a master.* Even a master cannot specify in words what, at its deepest, is beyond words. The best of teachers, lectures, seminars and books simply cannot do what it takes. The way of the disciple is a different and deeper way of learning.

That is the worst of our modern preoccupation with technique: it misses the independence of the biblical way of thinking and the depth and brilliance of the way of Jesus. To be sure, the vogue for technique has problems of its own. For one thing, it is highly rationalistic, for all technique is reason writ large, as if everything in life could be reduced to reason and spelled out in simple, specifiable steps. John von Neumann, the mathematician and father of game theory, was one of the most brilliant men who ever lived. Even Edward Teller, the great physicist, was in awe of Neumann's mind, and some wondered if it indicated a species superior to that of human beings. It was von Neumann who conceived the idea of programming that led to the computer—the notion that you can break down a problem into a series of simple steps that can be manipulated as numbers are manipulated. But what works for a machine does not work for a human being. If only we humans were more logical, or were *only* logical.

For another thing, our preoccupation with technique condemns us to a culture in which we are increasingly dependent on experts and cowed by expertise. But there are simply no experts in many of the deepest areas in life that matter most to us. Who, for example, would claim to be an expert in facing suffering? And when we start seeing every problem in terms of experts and consultants, problems and solutions, we condemn ourselves to dependency. After all, we ordinary folk have problems, and experts, by definition, are "people with answers." The expert "knows best" so that "we can do better." Thus the mystique of the experts' power to prescribe becomes a means to their power and our dependency, and the age of "disabling professions" gains another victim: the ministry of *all* believers. Christian persuasion is for all Christians, not just for experts and certainly not just for so-called intellectuals.

God forbid that we ever see the day when we have a guild of apologist experts to provide all our public answers for us, and who will prescribe every argument we must use or not use—if only we knew how to do it as skillfully as they do. Christian persuasion is a task for all Christians, not just the expert few; and a task to be done, not merely talked about. Yet at both the popular and the academic level, the ratio of talking to doing is grotesquely out of line today, and one danger of our specialized times is that apologetics will become the art of apologists talking to other apologists about apologetics, but never doing it.

Undoubtedly some people are better advocates and persuaders than others, and we can all learn most by modeling ourselves on the best. My own apologetics owes more to C. S. Lewis, Francis Schaeffer and Peter Berger than to anyone else alive in my lifetime. They did not know each other, they were all very different, they might not have got on well with each other, and Berger even had strong reservations about the enterprise of apologetics as much of the twentieth century understood it. But as I hope to show, the combination of their ideas is potent, and it has been extremely fertile for me. Reading Lewis was the capstone of my journey to faith, although I never had the good fortune of meeting him, whereas Peter Berger has long been my principal mentor in thinking about the modern world. And Francis Schaeffer was quite simply the most brilliant and compassionate face-to-face apologist I have ever met. I often watched him when I was younger, but his modeling the art was always far greater than his teaching on it. Many of those who did not know him but look to his books alone have either been wooden in their application or have become so engrossed in discussions about the theory of apologetics that they rarely get round to doing what he did so well—actually leading people to faith, some of them starting a long, long way from faith.

Put differently, we always need to beware the drive toward an arid scholasticism in apologetics. We should always give honest answers to honest questions, but we should know from the start that we can never give complete and convincing answers to every question. On the one hand, there will always be questions to which we as individuals have no answer, because of our ignorance or because of the limits of our present knowledge and interests. On the other hand, there will always be questions to which there is presently no answer at all, because they are part of the inescapable mystery of life. Why, for instance, did God create the world, knowing that (in the case of my own little life) such a world would lead to the horrendous rape of Nanking, where I grew up as a boy, to my brothers' premature deaths through the terrible Henan famine in which five million people died in a few months, or (a long time later) to my wife's cancer (which she fortunately survived)? To me such questions will always be unanswered and unanswerable—unanswerable, that is, until I see God face to face, and that inability will be true for all of us in our different journeys.[1]

Just as no two painters or sculptors are alike, so each person's apologetics will be refracted through their own personalities and life experiences. People who forget this tend to present apologetics as a chess game in which our task is to figure out all the moves, countermoves and counter-countermoves that would help us checkmate all objections and make us invincible Grand Masters in argument. But if Christian advocacy is an art, it is also like philosophy and not science. There is no completeness, finality or scientific level of proof in any philosophical argument, and those who have claimed to find one have always fallen on their faces. All philosophical claims can be countered with refutations. All positions can be ridiculed and rejected. And in a fallen world, God can always be disobeyed, truth can always be rejected and apologetic arguments can always be countered—however weak the objections and however transparently poor the motive. Therein lies one reason for the humility of the Christian advocate, and we will encounter others as we proceed.

This book is of course a book, and it contains arguments. It is an attempt to capture in writing a forgotten side of persuasion. But for all the reasons stated here, I have waited nearly forty years to write this book because of a promise made to God. When I was leaving university, I promised that I would always *do* apologetics rather than simply write about it, that I would do it *before* writing about it, and that I would do it *more* than writing about it. With Christian persuasion, doing it must always outweigh talking about it.

CROSS TALK, NOT CLEVER TALK

Far worse than these two problems is the way the seduction of technique lures us away from learning from our master Jesus in the way he communicated, and from thinking independently in ways that are shaped by Christian understanding rather than the understanding of the world. When we fall for this temptation, we are neither as faithful nor as creative as we should be.

Put differently again, Christian persuasion is a matter of cross talk, not of clever talk. To be sure, it is important to acknowledge the immense debt that apologetics owes to other sources such as classical rhetoric. As Jaroslav Pelikan noted, "It remains one of the most momentous linguistic convergences in the entire history of the human mind and spirit that the New Testament happens to have been written in Greek—not in the Hebrew of Moses and the prophets, nor in the Aramaic of Jesus and his disciples, nor yet in the Latin of the imperium Romanum, but in the Greek of Socrates and Plato, or at any rate in a reasonably accurate facsimile thereof," the common Greek of the New Testament.[2]

That convergence was indeed momentous. The Jewish and Christian faiths differ decisively from the classical civilization of Greece and Rome at many points, but they overlap in their common love of language and the supreme place they all give to reason, to words and to the art of communication. The opening words of the Gospel of John are therefore titanic in their significance as well as inexpressible in their profundity: "In the beginning was the Word, and the Word was with God, and the Word was God" (Jn 1:1).

But that said, it would be as bad a mistake to shape apologetics solely according to the criteria of classical rhetoric as it would be to tailor it to the insights of the world's latest communications theory or the strident attacks of the noisy atheists. Such basic categories as logos, ethos and pathos may be universal in application, but our gold standard is neither the best of the classics nor the most brilliant or brazen of the modern theorists, but the way in which God himself has spoken to us—supremely as we see it and hear it in the life of Jesus, the death of Jesus on the cross and the stunning turnaround of the resurrection. As Robert Louis Wilken, the eminent historian of early Christian thought, reminds us, Christian faith and thinking is too independent to be shaped by its responses to its critics and its conversation partners in any age. "It is instructive to hear the voices of the critics of Christianity, . . . but the energy, the vitality, the imaginative power of Christian thought comes from within, from the person of Christ, the Bible, Christian worship, the life of the church."[3]

Sad to say, we are more likely to find that recent forms of evangelism are modeled not on classical rhetoric or even on good communications theory, but on handbooks for effective sales techniques. A laudable goal, and one secret of the powerful influence of Francis and Edith Schaeffer's L'Abri community, was its desire always to "give honest answers to honest questions." But one recent evangelistic approach roundly rejected this aim. Rather, it taught that in working to "close the deal" (whether a commercial sale or a "decision for Christ"), we should always refuse to stop and answer questions, as questions are said to be nothing but a moral smokescreen and therefore a distraction and a delay as we drive toward the desired conclusion.

I have often been advised that sales strategies are a rich quarry for Christian advocates to mine, for today's marketers and retailers are highly sophisticated in knowing how to use science to get inside our heads and persuade us to buy. When we shop, most of us are notoriously irrational and easily duped, and retailers count on it. One current study, for instance, tells us that a buyer's happiness depends on the manner in which goods are presented—logically rather than aesthetically—and then sets out the best three approaches for showcasing goods. Research tells us that buyers' happiness has little or nothing to do with the quality and real value of the product. It all goes back to how the product is presented logically.

If this is so, then all we have to do in order to be savvy apologists is to read up on the latest techniques, mimic the same logic in presenting the gospel, and then count on the same surefire results. After all, if all truth is God's truth, it is surely legitimate to use the best tricks of the trade, but this time use them in the service of truth.

Not so. All truth is indeed God's truth, and it was God himself who commanded the people of Israel to "plunder the Egyptian gold" when they left Pharaoh and escaped from Egypt. But not long afterward, God condemned them for using that same gold to "set up the golden calf" (compare Ex 3:21-22 and 32:7-8). The Lord's work must always be done in the Lord's way. The method must serve the message. Technique is never neutral. It can be positive and useful, and it can also be harmful. Sometimes it can even be so brilliantly effective that its danger lies in its weaning us away from needing God at all. True apologetics is the art of truth, and its art must be shaped by the distinctiveness of the truth it proclaims.

This contrast between cross talk and clever talk lies at the heart of the apostle Paul's preaching of the gospel as he explains it to the Christians in Corinth (1 Cor 1:17-31). He juxtaposes "the word of the cross" and the message of "Christ crucified" with what he calls "cleverness of speech" and "superiority of speech." The former may look foolish to those who have become lost, but in fact it is power and wisdom. Conversely, human wisdom may look wise, but God's folly is wiser than human wisdom and the human clever talk actually empties the cross of its power and leaves people lost and floundering.

This is the deepest reason why Christians must never leave persuasion at the level of technique: Christian advocacy must be faithful. At the end of the day, when all the debts to Greece, Rome, moderns, postmoderns and others have been acknowledged, Christian persuasion must be decisively Christian and true to itself. As I said earlier, Christian advocacy must be true to its own truths and to its own understanding of truth. In particular, as I said in the first chapter, our persuasion must be shaped above all by the truths of creation, sin, the incarnation, the cross and the Holy Spirit. That is certainly my aim, and it will shape our exploration in two ways that may be different from some approaches to apologetics.

First, Christian persuasion, while always addressing the human mind and therefore focusing on the act of knowing, must also address the human heart and what the Bible views as the anatomy of belief and unbelief. Sometimes we must do this negatively, as when we assume the biblical understanding of the human resistance to truth and hatred of God. And sometimes we must do it positively, as when we assume the biblical understanding of the conscious and unconscious desire for God that is fulfilled only in the knowledge of God who is love.

Second, Christian persuasion, while addressing the mind, must be faithful to address the heart, including the passions or emotions. From Aristotle on, it has been recognized that the passions have an important role in our human lives—for better or worse they move us to thought and to action. Sometimes, for example, we can address the passions to move people to seek God through desire—the longing to possess something they do not

have, or through joy—the yearning to possess what they desire. And sometimes we can address the passions to move people to seek God through the
equally powerful passion of fear—the aversion to what they do not want, or
through grief—the deep realization of where they have gone wrong or what
they have lost in their rejection of God.

To see apologetics only as technique is an insult to the gospel and to the
high importance of what God is saying and doing in Jesus. From the humblest pun to the greatest *double entendre* of all time—the incarnation—the
Bible is full of stories, parables, drama, ploys and jests that serve the ultimate
purpose of the gospel and are shaped by the truth and logic of the message
of the birth, life, death and resurrection of Jesus the Christ. Apologetics must
always be wise in knowing the best and the worst of the thinking of the
world, but at the same time it must always be true to the One we know and
the One whom we want others to know.

The Ultimate Paradigm Shift

To be sure, many forms of creative persuasion make their point by turning
on a pair of creative tensions, and this is the level where technique may be
appreciated. One dimension of creative tension works at the surface level,
the level at which technique is most obvious. As the speaker asks a question,
unfolds a story or plays out a drama, an *expectation* steadily builds up in one
direction until, suddenly—through the wham of the punch line—an *effect*
is brought about in an entirely different direction. The method acts like a
spring-loaded trap that promises cheese but delivers a *coup de grâce* to the
unsuspecting mouse. The sudden switch between the expectation and the
effect triggers a complete revolution in seeing that both *reverses* the original
way of understanding and *reveals* an entirely new way of understanding. The
effect of this revolution in thinking is a paradigm shift, or a complete turn-
about of mind and heart.

That surface play of creative tension points beyond itself to another dimension. The term *paradigm shift* is common currency today, and there are
similar terms in other fields—for example *gestalt switch* in psychology or
alternation between realities in sociology. They are broadly used to describe
a revolutionary change in the pattern or framework of people's thinking.
Paradigm shift is undoubtedly the most popular term, but many who bandy

it around forget its background. Thomas Kuhn first introduced it to describe complete revolutions in scientific thinking, but he acknowledges that he borrowed the idea from the language and experience of Christian conversion. A paradigm shift, in other words, describes the ultimate reversal: the complete change of heart and mind that the New Testament calls *metanoia*, the biblical term for repentance. It signifies the complete about-face of heart, mind, thought and life that that triggers conversion and initiates the migration from one reality to another—from the kingdom of darkness to the kingdom of light.

Importantly, as the terms are used today, *paradigm shift* and *alternation* are morally neutral. They describe a migration from one way of seeing to another, but with no moral judgment that one is better than another. The new way is merely the current choice that supersedes the previous one. That is not so with the Christian understanding. The Greek word *metanoia* literally means "to perceive afterwards," in contrast to the related term for "perceiving ahead." In other words, "to see afterwards" is to repent because we see that the way we thought or lived before was wrong and needed changing.

"Repent" is the commanding imperative at the heart of the opening message of Jesus in the Gospels and also of his disciples as he sent them out with his message. Repentance speaks of the challenge to a change of mind and purpose that is for the better, but that turns on a frank acknowledgment of being previously wrong and for the worse. In the same way, the Latin word used for *metanoia* is *resipisco*, which means "to recover one's senses" and "to come to a right understanding"—as opposed to a wrong one. When we repent, we are saying that we know what we thought or did before was wrong. Like Nebuchadnezzar, whose hubris had felled him, or the prodigal son, whose rebellion had driven him to the pigsty, we have to come to our right mind and turn around. We have sinned, and we need to repent and to be forgiven and put right.

The effect of creative persuasion is therefore spiritual and moral, and not simply intellectual. It triggers a profound intellectual, spiritual and moral conviction of being wrong that acts to switch people between two realities—from the unbeliever's way of seeing to God's way, and so from unbelief to truth and from complacency to conviction. Like a trapdoor sprung open to drop someone into a room they did not imagine existed below them, creative Christian persuasion works to catapult someone from one plane of reality to another, and thus from people's own imagined reality to truth or reality as God sees it and as God sees them.

Technique, in other words, is certainly there, but when it is used to communicate God's truth, the mere technique is swallowed up in the larger truth, and the truth it serves is the truth and dynamic of the subversive gospel of the cross. So it is legitimate to recognize the place of technique and to appreciate other arts such as humor that share the same technique. But in the end, we are trying to shape our persuasion not so much by a modern understanding of technique as by the timeless, subversive dynamic action of the gospel itself. At times other people may appear to overlap with us when they use the same or a similar technique for their own ends. But our focus is not the technique itself but the deepest, fullest truths of the gospel that the technique serves, truths such as creation, sin, the incarnation, the cross and the Holy Spirit that are at the heart of the Christian faith. Technique by itself is essentially soulless, whereas apologetics is essentially soulful.

AN ART FOR LOVERS

The third reminder is that Christian persuasion is for those who love God, who wish to make the best possible case for the one they know and love, and who appreciate that love is an essential part of the knowledge that stems from true seeking and finding. Persuasion is for followers of Jesus who love him because they know him, and therefore need no convincing of their unspeakable privilege of knowing him and making him known. It is true that all Christians have an obligation to spread the gospel, that classical rhetoric and modern theory offer us a thousand tips for being more effective communicators, and that there are cultural and demographic pressures that challenge us to share our faiths or wither and die.

Yet the Christian persuasion we are exploring here is not for salesmen, propagandists, proselytizers, PR consultants, lobbyists, press officers, spin doctors, damage control experts and the like. It is not enough to share our faith out of guilt or social pressure or a desire to compete with rivals for cultural influence in today's world. There are more than enough consultants to cater to those with such motives. This book is for those who desire to share the way of Jesus because of their love for Jesus, and who know that love is also a key part of any human being's search for knowledge and truth. It is for those whose hearts resonate with the prophet Isaiah's words about the beauty of the sight of the herald running on the mountains announcing good news, or those who know something of what the great French apologist Blaise Pascal experienced in his mystical "night of fire" when he came to know the presence of God directly:

Fire

"God of Abraham, God of Isaac, God of Jacob," not of

philosophers and scholars.

Certainty, certainty, heartfelt joy, peace.

God of Jesus Christ.

God of Jesus Christ.

My God and your God.

"Thy God shall be my God."

The world forgotten and everything except God.[4]

The lost art of Christian persuasion certainly includes a method, but a method that is overwhelmed and utterly lost in the message that shapes it and the Master whom it serves. In other words, whatever little of apologetics is method must come from our experience of God and his love, his truth and his beauty, which are the heart of faith. When the message of Jesus comes to the foreground, method must be left in the background, where it belongs. It is said rightly that love is "the final apologetic," in the sense that our best argument is our love for the people we talk to. But that is not the end of the insistence on love. Love is "the alpha and the omega of apologetics," in the sense that all we say must come from love, and it must lead to love and to the One who is love—in other words, Christian advocacy must move from our love for God and his truth and beauty, to our love for the people we talk to and work right up to their love for God and his truth and beauty in their turn.

Persuasion is ultimately about the way we witness to the reality of the ultimate Presence in the universe. It is our witness to the story that invites people to come to know the Great "I AM," "He who is," the one who comes down to earth in the person of Jesus of Nazareth, before whom the only legitimate response is "My Lord and God." Christian advocacy therefore turns on a truly revolutionary method for a truly revolutionary message on behalf of a truly revolutionary experience. The good news of Jesus is the best news ever, God's foolishness that is God's Grand Reversal, which subverts the wisdom of the world to show true wisdom and display real power. Recovering the lost art of persuasion is urgent, timely and supremely practical, but it is always an art and not a science, and it is not for cheap salespeople but for genuine lovers of Jesus and lovers of truth, beauty and a knowledge that is more than facts and information. Technique has its place, but it is time to challenge the imperialism of technique and keep technique in its place.

3

The Defense
Never Rests

FOR READERS OF DOROTHY SAYERS'S NOVELS, Harriet Vane is an important character because in many ways she is the author's double. Like Sayers, she is a mystery writer. Like Sayers, she gained a first-class degree at Oxford University, and like Sayers, she has a formidable mind. (Sayers was one of the first woman graduates in Oxford history.) And like Sayers too, she had affairs. In Harriet's case, she frequented artists' circles in Bloomsbury, where she lived with her lover for a year—a less successful writer, Philip Boyes. He claimed not to believe in marriage, so she was persuaded to live with him without marrying.

Sayers's own affairs were not publicly known during her lifetime, and there are key differences between her life and that of her fictional stand-in. But the public was aware of some of the similarities, and they engaged in a lively correspondence with Sayers about the advisability of that "horrid girl" having such a place in the life of Sayers and their real hero, the debonair and aristocratic Lord Peter Wimsey.

It would be several books and many adventures before Harriet accepted Peter's proposal and became Lady Wimsey. But the novel in which they are brought together closely is *Strong Poison*, published in 1930, and the reason hinges on a key part of the logic of the Christian faith that meant so much to Dorothy Sayers. After Boyes and Harriet had lived together for a year, he asked her to marry him, now assured that she loved him. Her reaction, however, was indignation. Furious with him, she broke off the relationship altogether—outraged at his hypocrisy and at being offered a wedding ring as what she considered a "bad-conduct prize" for living with him.

Soon after the breakup, Boyes was found dead through arsenic poisoning, which was the very murder method Harriet had researched for the book she was writing. She at once became the prime suspect, with a strong and obvious motive, and all the circumstantial evidence against her. So she was arrested, tried for murder and looked to be staring at the hangman's noose.

Harriet's prospects were grim. The case against her looked watertight, and the prosecution pressed for a guilty verdict. She had the motivation to kill her former lover, and she had the opportunity. All the known facts of the case were against her, and there were no other suspects. She should obviously hang. When conclusive evidence appears to lock hands with justice, even a rush to judgment seemed appropriate. Harriet Vane had committed a horrible crime, and she would pay the supreme price.

But into that grave situation steps the fearless hero, Lord Peter Wimsey. He knows Harriet, so he believes in her innocence, and his logic has a steel to match the prosecutor's case: *The known facts may be against her, but because he knows her, he knows that the known facts cannot be all the facts. The challenge is to find the missing facts that change the picture entirely.* The police had jumped to the wrong conclusion on watertight-seeming evidence that was actually incomplete. Harriet had been unjustly framed. She was innocent, and she did not deserve to die.

Lord Peter argues with his colleagues, "There must be evidence somewhere, you know. I know you have all worked like beavers, but I am going to work like a king beaver. And I have one big advantage over the rest of you . . . I do believe in Miss Vane's innocence."[1]

FAITH'S HALL OF FAME

This daring style of trust turns on a logic that lies at the core of Christian faith and of Christian advocacy. If we truly know why we trust God—and that crucial *if* must be answered with full intellectual and spiritual assurance—if we truly know why we trust God, then God is greater than all, and God may be trusted in all situations, despite everyone and everything. At an obvious level, the logic in that trust fuels the soaring dynamism of the visionary and history-changing faith that we find in Hebrews 11, the inaugural roll call of Faith's Great Hall of Fame. Abel, Enoch, Noah, Abraham, Sarah, Isaac, Jacob, Joseph, Moses—"all these died in faith, without receiving the promises, but having seen them and having welcomed them from a distance" (v. 13). Such men and women of faith defied their circumstances and their times because they knew God. They knew why they trusted that God is there and God is good. So as entrepreneurs of life they rose to life callings and to tasks that set them against the grain of the world of their day, and that tested to the limits the obedience and enterprise of their faith.

Knowing why they trusted God, they knew why the known facts were never all the facts. So even when the known facts were against God, they trusted and they waited, they waited and they worked, and in this way they called into question the ways of the world of their time and challenged even the impossible. The conclusion of the writer to the Hebrews is that such faith was the very reason God was not ashamed to be their God. Their lesson is a challenge to us: time after time the known facts of our lives and of the world may be against God, but one day all the missing facts will be known too, so our task as his people is to trust and prove him now, in the meantime, whatever the odds, whatever the opposition and however agonizing the suffering at the present moment.

When God Himself Was Framed

Far less obviously, the same daring logic of trust lies at the heart of Christian advocacy and provides its deepest rationale and its most passionate motivation. But where does that passion come from? We can answer that question by asking another one: Where should we ground our view of apologetics? Too few people think about that question or have a clear answer to why they are doing what they are doing.

There are many Christians, of course, who summarily dismiss apologetics altogether. They argue that evangelism, not apologetics, should be our priority. Apologetics, as they see it, is not a biblical concern. It is a narrow exercise for Christian intellectuals only, and emphatically not for the faithful or for the simple and straightforward. The former do not need it, and the latter cannot handle it. Besides, apologetics as they see it relies solely on human reason and reasoning, so it must also be a denial of the power of the Spirit. Clearly, such people are pious sounding, but in fact they are too pious by half. They quote the Scriptures, but they have yet to study the rich evidence of the place and importance of apologetics in the Scriptures.

But what of those who take apologetics more seriously? I meet many who equate all apologetics with one particular school of defending the faith, and since they have been trained in that one way, they waste no time thinking of other ways or asking how each specific way arose in its time. Again, like a man with a hammer who sees everything as a nail, they apply their favored method regardless of the situation or the outcome. And when people do not respond to their efforts as they hope, they fall back on handy theological alibis and never lose sleep over their failures or think of questioning their methods.

Still others think more deeply, and recognize that the different apologetic schools have themselves been shaped by the different conversation partners and sparring partners with which the church has engaged down the centuries. From the early Christian apologists, such as Justin Martyr, Irenaeus and Origen, down through the great church fathers who wrestled with the Greek and Roman classical tradition, to Thomas Aquinas and the scholars of the High Middle Ages, to modern and postmodern philosophies, Christian advocacy has engaged with many conversation partners, and often the dialogue has been extremely fruitful.

Equally, the church has benefitted from its many sparring partners. It has picked up the gauntlet and gone into the arena to face up to many redoubtable opponents, such as Celsus in the second century, Porphyry in the third, the Emperor Julian in the fourth, David Hume in the eighteenth, Nietzsche in the nineteenth, and Richard Dawkins and his noisy fellow pugilists most recently. Usually the effect has been to brace the defenders of the faith and to leave them in better fighting trim, but at other times it has also meant a narrowing of the defenders' range, so that they were ill-prepared to fight the wider battles of their own time or the different battles of the next generation. For example, it appeared for a while that long centuries of debating the theistic proofs had narrowed apologetics to a rarified conversation for philosophers, with next to no significance for ordinary people. It then took the brilliance and originality of Blaise Pascal to steer it back to matters of the human heart and to issues of real life such as "diversion."

Others concerned about Christian advocacy go further back still and trace its source to the Bible itself. But many who do this limit their exploration to the New Testament. Some cite Peter's speech on the day of Pentecost, which led to the conversion of three thousand people, some cite Stephen's ringing defense of the gospel that precipitated his stoning, some cite Paul's great speech to the Athenian philosophers on the Areopagus, and some cite the apostle Peter's famous admonition: "Always [be] prepared to make a defense to anyone who asks you for a reason for the hope that is in you" (1 Pet 3:15 ESV).

All these New Testament sources of understanding are vital, and each adds something of great importance, but they do not exhaust the Bible's view of the heart of apologetics. For that we must go further back to the Old Testament. In doing so, there are rich themes to be mined that many have overlooked. A few have looked at the specific covenant lawsuit language used by the Hebrew prophets, but most apologists have yet to unpack the remarkable range of the prophets' appeals—to reason and logic, to history and its grand events, to the lessons and warnings of ruined cities, to shared memory and common political sentiments, to nature and creation, and to the follies and madness of relying on such forces as superpower nations and idols.

Above all, the great Hebrew prophets introduce us to the unsurprising but radical theme that apologists too often forget in practice: God is his own best apologist. At our best, we are humble junior counsels for the defense, and no more. At worst, we can behave like Job's friends, the well-meaning ones who darken rather than enlighten the spiritual situation. All in all, it is embarrassing to compare ourselves as apologists today with the powerful and majestic sweep of the Hebrew prophets. In their mighty shadow, much of our contemporary apologetics is timid in its authority, puny in its reach and limited in its range.

The prophet-apologists, then, offer a rich and largely unexplored territory that opens up vast new vistas for contemporary Christian advocacy. It would be a mistake to call their work "cultural apologetics," as some do, as if they were merely using culture to make their case as some modern apologists try to do—proving their relevance by quoting the latest films and the changing hit parade of music. Rather, the prophets were addressing the world of their day with the word of their Lord, and so confronting everything in their day that allowed their contemporaries to refuse the claims of God. We must do the same today in an equally radical way, but even that is not enough. We must learn from the prophets and address not just individuals but whole institutions, societies, nations and even the spiritual powers that are behind them. Yet we must also gather up all these different motivations, such as our conversation partners, our sparring partners and the precedents of the New Testament and the prophets, and then go back to the very opening chapters of Genesis and in particular to the story of the fall. That is where apologists find their earliest and deepest motivation of all.

The opening words of the serpent's seduction of Eve were a question, "Has God said, 'You shall not eat from any tree of the garden'?" (Gen 3:1). Introduced as "more crafty" than any other creature, the serpent knew that Eve's trust in God was complete, if innocent and untested. The entire framework of the way she viewed God and life was the framework with which she had been created and by which she and Adam lived. She saw God as he was and life as it was under God. Her faith in God and her view of God's world was a perfect match, a one-to-one fit between truth as it was before God, reality as she saw it and the view of the world in which she trusted.

If the serpent had contradicted her outright, the result would have been a head-on collision and an unequal contest. It would have meant the serpent's word pitted against God's word, and the serpent would have been the instant loser.

Instead, the serpent makes no statement of any kind, but craftily (in character) asks a question, "Did God say?" Questions are always more subversive than statements. For one thing, they are indirect. Whereas it should be crystal clear what a statement is saying and where it is leading, a good question is not so obvious, and where it leads to is hidden. For another thing, questions are involving. Whereas a statement always has a "take it or leave it" quality, and we may or may not be interested in what it tells us, there is no standing back from a well-asked question. It invites us, challenges us or intrigues us to get into it and follow it to see where it leads. In short, even a simple question can be a soft form of subversion.

That, of course, was the design of the evil one in tempting Adam and Eve. To mount a frontal attack on what God had said would have courted disaster and doomed his plans before they were launched. But to raise a polite and innocuous-sounding question was to gain just the tiniest toe-hold on his enemy's ground, which could be slowly and subtly expanded. The thrust of the question may have been factual: "Did God *actually* say?" (as some translations have it). More likely it was a challenge to the facts that slyly carried a subversive twist about motives too: "Don't you see," the serpent hints, "what God was saying in what he said?" Speculate about what God may have had in mind—in fact, almost certainly had in mind—and you see how his command is in the interests of his control. In short, God's command is a power play. There are no free lunches, and there is no free obedience. God does nothing for free.

Only then, once Eve has swallowed the bait and turned the question around in her mind, does the evil one dare to contradict God flatly: "You will not surely die. For God knows that when you eat of it your eyes will be opened, and you will be like God, knowing good and evil" (Gen 3:4-5 ESV). Come on, he says, eat the fruit you have been forbidden to eat and your eyes will actually be opened. "Dare to know," as Immanuel Kant and eighteenth-century thinkers were to express it later, and you will be enlightened and liberated from your tutelage.

By the end of this little exchange Eve's trust was no longer absolute and implicit, a perfect match with the truth God had spoken. Instead, she had risen to the bait, first, to suspect God, and then to put herself forward as the arbiter between God's word and the serpent's word, and so to be a deciding, independent viewpoint capable of judging between them. Intoxicated by the heady freedom of this position, she decides there can be no harm in eating the fruit she was forbidden to eat. Surely she needed to experiment in order to know, and so to be able to decide between God's word and the serpent's. Without stating it so baldly in words, her action says that she is right and God is wrong. His word can be ignored with impunity.

Were Adam and Eve aware of what they were doing? The thrust of the biblical account of the fall is powerful. Their disobedience entailed two things that are now characteristic of all of us as humans. On the one hand, for each of us, sin is the claim to the right to myself, and so to my way of seeing things, which—far more than class, gender, race and generation—is the ultimate source of human relativity. On the other hand, sin is the deliberate repudiation of God and the truth of his way of seeing things. If my way of seeing things is decisive, anyone who differs from me is wrong by definition—including God. No, especially God, because his way of seeing things is more powerful and therefore more threatening than anyone else's. His word, our interference.

This last point means, in turn, that sin, and the mistrust of disbelief in which it issues, does not, will not and cannot see God as he truly is. Still knowing God, it must now always refuse to face the responsibility of its knowledge of God and of its own guilt. It must therefore pass the buck. So when God asks Adam what he has done, he ducks the question by blaming Eve, just as Eve in her turn deflects the question by blaming the serpent.

No doubt if God had asked the serpent what it had done, the serpent would have slithered and ducked it too, and pointed the finger back to the one who created him—God. And so it goes. All roads lead to Rome, and all fingers point at God. So long as the world's last sin remains unconfessed, the buck will keep on passing and passing, and the final finger always points at God. "Why does God allow?" is often the hurt and angry cry of those who say they do not even believe in God.

Jean-Baptiste Clamence, in Albert Camus's *The Fall,* is a literary example of this buck-passing. He cries out that everyone needs to be innocent at any price, even if "one must accuse humankind and the sky."[2] Examples in real life are even more brazen. When Lieutenant William Calley was tried for his part in the My Lai massacre in the Vietnam War, his psychiatrist defended him with these words: "I do not believe we should make any one person responsible for My Lai. . . . I do not believe we should make any one person or even the nation responsible for My Lai. If you want to hold someone responsible, I think the only one you can point to would be God."[3]

Like the prosecutor falsely pinning the murder charge on Harriet when she was innocent, sin must always end in justifying itself by framing God. God is in the dock. To excuse ourselves, we have to accuse him. In short, *sin frames God falsely*.

Here at this precise point lies the core reason for Christian advocacy, as well as its motivating passion. Apologetics (from *apologia* in Greek) is a "word back," a reasoned defense mounted on behalf of the one we love who is innocent but has been falsely and unfairly accused. *Faith desires to let God be God. Sin has framed God, whether by the ultimate insults that he, the creator of all things, does not exist, or that he, the white-hot holy One, is responsible for the evil and suffering that humans have introduced into his good creation. So God's name must be cleared and his existence and character brought to the fore beyond question.* Thus "Hallowed be thy name" is our prayer, and the defense of that name is our burning motive in apologetics. Those who love God and desire that he should be known for who he is are outraged when he is unjustly framed and are therefore eager to defend his honor, clear his name and vindicate his character.

In short, so long as sin frames God, those who love God have a job to do in the world. We are defenders of the one we know and love. Not until the last judgment itself has concluded, and the great assize of history is finished, the books are balanced and justice is both done and seen to be done, can it ever be said, "The defense rests."

It is true that each time we, or anyone, make a genuine confession, we step up to accept our own responsibility for what we have done. Confession therefore stops the passing of the buck, calls off the outrageous (and absurd) attempt to frame God, and clears God's name. King David recognized this when he confessed his adultery and murder.

> Against You, You only, I have sinned . . .
> So that You are justified when You speak
> And blameless when you judge. (Ps 51:4)

In stark contrast to our ceaseless human buck passing, the Day of Judgment will be the day when all passing of the buck will end and all chickens will come home to roost. The apostle Paul describes how on that day God will be vindicated, his name cleared and "every mouth will be stopped." The word Paul uses literally means that people will be "apology-less." They will have no legal defense and no legal counsel to defend them (Rom 3:19). When the books are opened and the secrets of every heart are revealed, there will be no ducking, dodging, denial or deflecting. We will all be naked before God and the truth, and have no one to blame but ourselves. None of us will have a leg to stand on. There will be no apologist or defense counsel to speak for us, so we will all face up to who we really are and what we have really done—which of course is when grace will be seen at its most amazing.

Until that great day, however, the game goes on, the music keeps playing, the buck passes around without stopping and the fingers always finally point at God—wrongly. The medieval rabbi Rashi wrote, "As long as idolatry exists in the world, God's fierce anger will exist in the world."[4] So too for apologists as lovers of God, as long as God is deliberately framed by sin and not seen as he is, there is no letting up. Until that Last Day, Christian advocacy will always be in business, and its business will be the honor of God's name. Until that moment in the grand assize of history, the defense *never* rests.

QUITE THE OPPOSITE

Major consequences flow from this fact. First, it means that apologetics is all about the Lord, and not about us. Lesser and darker factors always threaten to intrude into the enterprise of course, such as the potential blow to our pride if we are tongue-tied in the face of the devastating objections thrown at our faith, or we feel that our comfort and social standing are shamed if we have no answer to a withering barrage of scorn leveled against us. But compared with the honor of the Lord, these factors are utterly and overwhelmingly irrelevant. Christian advocacy is not about us but about him.

The striking term *living God* always comes in the Bible when the Lord is contrasted with idols and his honor is at stake. The account of young David's slaying of Goliath shows that he was well aware of the giant's sword, spear and javelin as he went out to face the Philistine champion. But that was not what concerned him. His greater concern was the pagan taunts against the living God, so he fought that "all the earth may know that there is a God in Israel" (1 Sam 17:46).

King Hezekiah showed the same attitude when he faced the over-whelming forces of Sennacherib, the all-conquering king of Assyria. He knew well the cruel fate of other kings conquered before him who had been captured and skinned alive, but he was more concerned for the vindication of God's name than for his own and his people's deliverance. "Now, O LORD our God," he prayed, "deliver us from his hand that all the kingdoms of the earth may know that You alone, LORD, are God" (Is 37:20).

Second, this motivation reminds us that Christian advocacy always goes wrong when we become the focus of our efforts, rather than the Lord. For when we are the focus, we subtly come to believe that God is no more certain than our defense of him. Argue and defend God well, and the world of faith appears unshakable. Defend him badly, and doubts creep in or crash down on top of us.

Put these two points together and you can see why the danger for apologists is exactly the opposite of what many people think. There are two widespread misconceptions about apologists and apologetics, and they are sometimes linked. One is that apologetics is a minority sport, something for intellectuals only. The other is that it is only a theoretical exercise—dry, bloodless and sterile, as all intellectuals are presumed to be.

Far from it. I strongly prefer the simple word *thinker* to *intellectual* because of the fog of bad connotations that surround the latter. But both thinkers and intellectuals are unfairly maligned today, when many people fail to see that both are much more passionate and engaged in their thinking than people realize. The next time you see Auguste Rodin's famous statue *The Thinker*, or a copy of it, look at it closely. Rodin described his great figure in these terms: "What makes my Thinker think is that he thinks not only with his brain, but his distended nostrils, and compressed lips, and with every muscle of his arm, back, and legs, with his clenched fist and gripping toes."[5]

Passion even in his toes? If such intensity is true of Rodin's *Thinker*, how much more is it true of the Christian persuader and defender. Christian advocacy is a lover's defense, a matter of speaking out and standing up when God is framed unjustly and attacked wrongly. It is therefore anything but dry and far from sterile. The New Testament describes it as a task for all followers of Jesus, not just for some, and certainly not for intellectuals only. Peter's admonition, "Always [be] prepared to make a defense to anyone who asks you for a reason for the hope that is in you; yet do it with gentleness and respect" (1 Pet 3:15 ESV), was written to young Christians in all the first-century churches, and not just to church leaders, let alone intellectuals.

The real problem is that when we feel that Christian advocacy is all up to us, we lay on ourselves the impossible burden of being the "great boxing hope" who is expected to knock out of the ring all comers. We are expected to be the fearless David who ventures out to slay all Goliaths, the intrepid Elijah who exposes all false prophets, and the confident Luther who vouches for the truth with ringing convictions before all the powers of the day.

To be sure, David did slay Goliath, Elijah did triumph over the prophets of Baal, Hezekiah and his tiny kingdom were delivered from the armies of the greatest empire of his day, and Luther did prevail against the princes and prelates of his day. But faith in God is true because it is true—not because we, or David, Elijah and Luther defend it successfully. *If the Christian faith is true, it is true even if no one believes it, and if it is not true, it is false even if everyone believes it. The truth of the faith does not stand and fall with our defense of it.*

A good or bad defense of the faith may be helpful or unhelpful, but in each case that is only corroborative. The Christian faith is not true because someone argues for it brilliantly, nor is it false because someone defends it badly. Christian faith is true or false regardless of anyone's defense of the faith. Faith's certainty lies elsewhere than in the rapier sharp logic or the sledgehammer power of the apologist. At the end of the day, full certainty comes from the conviction of the Holy Spirit.

That is often the problem with the public debate format so loved by Christians today. Some Christians are superbly gifted in using this format. Others are less so, but the problem lies in the assumptions of the format itself. The expectation is that the apologist is brought in to trounce the enemies of the gospel publicly. Yet in such a win-lose situation, the danger is that some apologists are tempted to speak so as to win the debate but lose the audience, or to lose the debate and appear to let down the faithful—as if the faith were no more certain than one particular defense of it.

His Own Best Counsel

An even stronger way of expressing the point is that God is his own supreme counsel for the defense. If the effect of sin is to frame God, then God himself is the one who actively counters the outrage. Our work is important, but at best our part is to bring the presence of God into the debate through the power of the Holy Spirit, and to remember that we are no more than junior counsels for the defense. Read the Bible with this in mind, and again and again you see a law court scene with God himself as the lead prosecutor indicting the sins of his people and others.

"Who is this," he asks Job,

> whose ignorant words
> cloud my design in darkness?
> Brace yourself and stand up like a man;
> I will ask questions and you shall answer. (Job 38:2-3 NEB)

"Come now, let us argue it out," God says in the opening message of the prophet Isaiah, who describes the arraignment graphically,

> The LORD comes forward to argue his case
> and stands to judge his people.
> The LORD opens the indictment. (Is 1:18; 3:13 NEB)

> Hear the word of the LORD, O Israel,
> for the Lord has a charge to bring against the people of the land. . . .
> [I]t is not for any man to bring a charge,
> it is not for him to prove a case;
> the quarrel with you, false priest, is mine. (Hos 4:1, 4 NEB)

Sometimes this prosecuting role is surprising, as it is when used of the coming Servant predicted in Isaiah, who will eventually be the Suffering Servant.

> Here is one who will speak first as an advocate for Zion,
> here I appoint defending counsel for Jerusalem; . . .
> Here is my servant. (Is 41:27; 42:1 NEB).

Supremely the same prosecuting role can be seen in the self-awareness of Jesus and his promise of the Holy Spirit, who will come when he has left. "It is for your good that I am leaving you," he says to the disciples.

> If I do not go, your Advocate will not come, whereas if I go, I will send him to you. When he comes, he will confute the world, and show where right and wrong and judgment lie. He will convict them of wrong, by their refusal to believe in me; he will convince them that right is on my side, by showing them that I go to the Father when I pass from your sight, and he will convince them of divine judgment, by showing that the Prince of this world stands condemned. (Jn 16:7-11 NEB)

In strong contrast to this insistence on God's initiative, our human role is always a humble, supporting and subservient part. With the Holy Spirit resting upon us as Jesus promised, our part is to host the very presence of God wherever we are, to exercise the very power of God in every situation and to witness to the gospel and what God has done in Jesus and is doing in the world today. The call to be witnesses is central and decisive. We are not out to prove something new through the brilliance of our arguments. Our calling is to point to something old, or rather to bear witness to the established facts of the story of the gospel, though in the process clearing up anything and everything that may obscure or block a person's understanding.

We therefore speak only on behalf of God, we speak under God, and we have no authority or power apart from God. The prophet's formula is always "Thus says the LORD," and the worst indictment against the false prophets was for their presumption in claiming to speak for God when their words were entirely their own. In short, the major work in the defense of the faith is about God and by God. It is not about us, and it is not up to us.

THE PATRON SAINT OF APOLOGISTS

On the desk in front of me as I write is a tiny silver donkey, standing awkwardly with its characteristic big ears. It could hardly be more different from a thoroughbred race horse or a magnificent charger that could carry a knight in armor into battle. The donkey reminds me of the proper role of the apologist. In the apostle Peter's sequel to the letter mentioned earlier, he refers back to the book of Numbers when the prophet Balaam, en route to delivering a message that God had not sanctioned, was stopped in his tracks by the donkey he was riding. Peter described Balaam as the man who was sharply rebuked for his offence "when the dumb beast spoke with a human voice and put a stop to the prophet's madness" (2 Pet 2:16 NEB).

Balaam's ass is the patron saint of apologists. Madness, as we shall see, is an appropriate term for the unreality of unbelief. In order to counter it, we play our part, and we do the best we can. But even when our efforts are serviceable, our role is always humble and all too often inadequate and somewhat ridiculous. Christian advocates who understand their calling should never be too big for their boots. The task is not about us. It's all about him, and he may be trusted to do what matters.

· 4 ·

THE WAY OF
THE THIRD FOOL

I N WHAT SENSE ARE THE "NEW ATHEISTS" really new, and why
are they often so aggressive, strident, intolerant or just plain rude—as
Richard Dawkins appears to delight in being? The claim to newness is easily
debunked. From a historical perspective it is atheism that was old and the
Christian faith and its good news that burst on the world as new. Once commonly called "atomism," the genealogy of atheism can be traced all the way
back through the Enlightenment to Roman poets such as Lucretius and his
poem *De Rerum Natura*, and behind that to Greek philosophers such as
Epicurus and Democritus and their philosophy of atomism. It was precisely
such a philosophy that contributed to the classical world a strong sense of
fate and the futility of both life and human purpose. And it also provided
the dark setting against which the brilliance of the hope of the good news
of Jesus shone by contrast—as soon it will once again.

But why the current aggression and rudeness? One obvious reason lies
in the alarmed response from atheists to the collapse of the secularization
theory so loved by the Enlightenment. The worldwide explosion of religion
since the 1970s shows that religion is far from dying out as it was supposed
to. But there is even more to it than that. Atheists were not always so aggressive, even when religion was strong. In the late eighteenth century
Edmund Burke noted that "boldness formerly was not the character of
atheists as such. They were even of a character nearly the reverse; they were
formerly like the old Epicureans, rather an unenterprising race. But of late

they are grown active, designing, turbulent and seditious."[1] Joseph Priestly, a Unitarian, wrote in the same period that humanity was on the verge of a new era in public affairs, and therefore a new openness for the so-called free thinkers. "We are not indeed persecuted for our religious principles, and few persons have even much scruple of openly declaring what they think."[2]

What was behind that change in the eighteenth century and its milder parallel more recently? Sadly, we have to acknowledge as Christians that the new assertiveness was largely due to the ending of a bad chapter in Christian history—the oppressive intolerance of Christendom. Far from honoring truth and open debate, the orthodoxy of the previous centuries had "made truth dangerous" in the sense that when the power of orthodoxy was coercive, there was no freedom to disbelieve. When the Catholic Church claimed a monopoly of thought, when dissent was outlawed and "error had no rights," when the era of the Inquisition, the Index, and later *The Syllabus of Errors* was at its height, and when forced conversions were the order of the day, dissent was impossible and the truth was considered too dangerous to allow people to be open about what they thought. Thought control in its late medieval form was a Christian form of political correctness on steroids, and it could be life threatening.

The result of such oppressive intolerance became what was called the "age and politics of dissimulation." People who did not agree with Catholic orthodoxy did not say what they thought. Often they said the opposite of what they thought, and readers learned to read with an early version of the "hermeneutics of suspicion." Nothing was quite what was being said. Michel de Montaigne noted this feature in the sixteenth century: "Dissimulation is one of the most notable qualities of this age."[3] Living a little later, Descartes remarked that he wished to avoid Galileo's fate, so he would abide by the maxim of the Roman poet Ovid: "He has lived well, he who has remained well hidden."[4] Earlier, Cesare Cremonini, an Italian Aristotelian, admitted that he did not have a shred of piety, but he wished to be thought pious. His maxim captured the dissimulation perfectly: "Within, as you please; out of doors, as custom dictates."[5]

An extraordinary example of the politics of dissimulation was the career of Paolo Sarpi (1552–1623), the state theologian of Venice who has been hailed as "the original New Atheist."[6] In 1609, Sarpi wrote, "I am of such character that, like a chameleon, I take on the manners of those with whom I have intercourse. . . . I am forced to wear a mask. In Italy, no one can be without one."[7] Born during the Council of Trent, which cemented the dogma and tone of the Counter-Reformation for more than three hundred years, he was a friend of Galileo and rose fast in the church hierarchy to become the state theologian of Venice. As such, he actually wrote *The History of the Council of Trent*, although exposing its state-managed chicanery and becoming a hero to the Protestants in the process. Read one way, the account presents him as a faithful son of the Church and a Catholic reformer, and his friends circulated suitably devout stories about the way he died in order to protect him from Pope Paul V. But read in light of his more recently discovered private notebooks, *Philosophical Thoughts*, a completely different picture emerges. As one historian comments, "Venice's state theologian was an infidel intent on destroying the authority of the institutional church," and someone whose thought anticipates the skepticism of the Enlightenment and the anti-religious aggression of today's new atheists.[8] State theologian Sarpi was anything but what he appeared to be. The times did not allow him to be truthful.

MORE THAN MEETS THE EYE?

Such Christian oppression stands as a gigantic black mark against the church, and a foundational reason for secularist aggression whenever it was relaxed—as it was in a milder form when the previous Christian consensus collapsed in Western societies after the Second World War. Not surprisingly there were many ingenious attempts to circumvent the oppression while it lasted, but when it was relaxed the aggression reflected the determination that such a dominating Christian consensus should never happen again.

Some people have interpreted Erasmus's little book *The Praise of Folly* in light of this dark history. The tomfoolery and jesting, they say, was a matter of studied deception. Erasmus was masking his message in the interests of safety from the authorities in general and the eagle eye of the censor in particular. Others argue that Erasmus coded his message to serve the interests of the elite—the point was deliberately esoteric to make truth incomprehensible to the ignorant, as Leo Strauss and others have argued.[9] From this perspective, Erasmus was like Francis Bacon, Montaigne and Pierre

Bayle later. He was careful to camouflage his highest thoughts in case they fell on ears and minds that could not digest them properly. As Montaigne wrote, "A man must not say all that he knows, for that were follie." Or again, "I speake truth, not by belly-full, but as much as I dare."[10]

What is plain is that Erasmus wrote *The Praise of Folly* during a week's stay in England with his friend Thomas More, who himself employed a full-time jester in his household. The title of the book played on the meaning of More's first name in English (*tom*foolery) and his surname in Greek (*Morias* is the Greek for folly). Published in 1511, the book took Europe by storm and became both a classic of the Renaissance and a catalyst of the Reformation. Surely, people have said, Erasmus uses his jester Dame Folly to deflect any criticisms of his trenchant critique of the Renaissance papacy and the Church, and to mask the depths of what he really thought and felt. The vogue for court jesters in the late-medieval world was tailor-made for such a purpose. ("Jesters do oft prove prophets," Shakespeare said.)[11] After all, Erasmus finished the little classic with just such a skillful sidestep in the last paragraph: "If anything I've said seems rather imprudent or garrulous, you must remember it's Folly and a Woman who's been speaking."[12]

There is certainly far more than meets the eye in Erasmus's *The Praise of Folly.* And unquestionably there are times that will not endure the truth, or are like our own time, an age of advertising and political correctness that will put up with unbelievable levels of nonsense, but still draws the line at *some* truths it will not tolerate—in our case, ironically, Christian truths. Such times, as Bayle wrote, are enough to make an honest reader so sick that he cries out, "*Date mihi pelvim*—Give me the basin!"[13]

But Erasmus's strategy was surely not prompted by elitism and the politics of dissimulation, or merely by the Renaissance vogue for jesters. There is a deeper, Christian explanation that is both the key to the book and an important signpost to a profound element in apologetics: Erasmus was a man of deep and genuine faith, who in his use of Dame Folly as the central spokesperson is returning to the biblical notion of fools and folly. Truth was dangerous in the Renaissance world, but behind the classical view of folly that he uses lies the even deeper Christian understanding of folly and fool-making.

Consider some of the challenges Erasmus faced in standing against the Church's corruption in the Renaissance era. He had just returned from a visit to Rome, which had left him profoundly outraged by the crimes and corruptions of the Renaissance papacy and the city as a whole. Part of the problem lay in the fact that *the world of his times was radically relativistic.* Christendom was collapsing, and its unity was about to come apart completely. There was a clash between the north of Europe and the south, between the new ways of learning and the old ways, and soon the clash was to be between the forces of the Reformation and the Counter-Reformation.

Shakespeare gave a pithy expression of this relativism in the words of the Duke of Albany in *King Lear*: "Wisdom and goodness to vile seemed vile."[14] Seen that way, nothing was simple and straightforward anymore. With Christendom collapsing, there was no shared authority, and not even a shared language. Everything was a matter of perspective, and "where you are coming from," which meant that to anyone different, it could equally seem inside out, upside down, the wrong way around, and topsy-turvy. There was nothing plainly and straightforwardly good, even about the good news, and the earnest, simple style of the preacher and the sermon would no longer be effective. The result was a profound crisis of authority in the late medieval world.

Relativism was only the beginning of Erasmus's problem. The other challenge he faced was that *the church of his day was thoroughly worldly.* From the tawdry promiscuity and mumbling superstitions of the uneducated local priest to the shameless crimes and corruptions of the vicars of Rome in the Fisherman's Chair, the sickness of the Church was dire and scandalous. Erasmus himself had witnessed the return of Pope Julius in his golden armor after his victory at the battle of Bologna. Was the pope, he muttered angrily, really the disciple of Jesus of Nazareth, or was he the disciple of his famous namesake Julius Caesar?

This second part of the problem compounded the crisis of authority. The first and indispensable requirement for classical rhetoric had always been *ethos*, the moral character of a speaker that supported the power of his *logos*, his rational argument. By that standard the church of the Renaissance had no leg to stand on when it spoke, let alone the capacity to stand against the tide of worldliness and address its age with prophetic faithfulness. That in itself should make us pause, because at both these points there is probably no generation closer to Erasmus's age than our own. Postmodernism has made our own age as crazily relativistic and as worldly today as at any age since just prior to the Reformation. The result is a severe crisis of authority that leaves the church in many Western countries sounding as either a mumbler, a mute, a hypocrite or someone speaking out of several sides of his mouth however loudly he tries to speak.

How did Erasmus attempt to get around these barriers? How did he choose to speak and write when the avenues for simple and straightforward communication were so unpromising? He went back to the distinctive way of fool-making that can be found in the Bible. There are three types of fool in the Bible, and Erasmus restored the way of the third fool to recover the power of subversive persuasion in order to make his point. His point is crucial to our discussion, for the way of the third fool carries the power of the cross and contains the secret of creative persuasion that our Christian advocacy needs today.

FOOL PROPER

The first type of fool in the Bible is the character that might be called *the fool proper*. Folly in a fallen world is obviously partly relativistic, and we are always wise to say, "Says who?" Different families and different parts of the world will find some jokes funny and others not, just as different communities and different nations will admire certain heroes and despise certain villains, but not others. Heroism, villainy and folly are all relative, but there is one fool in the Bible whose folly is seen as absolutely foolish and who is pronounced a real fool—the person who is truly, objectively and actually a fool because God says so: the practical atheist who has no fear of the Lord and roundly refuses to acknowledge God in practice.

There are individuals in the Bible who are called fools in this sense, but while some were obviously so, stupid and ridiculous, others were not. The Hebrew word for "fool" is very close to the Hebrew for "noble," with only one letter different, and it is sometimes only in the outcome of their lives that the people considered noble by the people of their time are shown up as fools or pronounced as fools by God. David's wife Abigail was originally married to the more obvious type of fool, and she described her first husband as a "worthless man" who lived up to his name, Nabal, which means "son of Belial," or fool (1 Sam 25:25). By contrast, the farmer called a fool by Jesus ("You fool. This very night your soul is required of you") may well have been the much admired and industrious pillar-of-the-community business man whose sole folly was to leave God out of his reckoning and therefore to miss the one factor in his business plan that counted in the long term.

But whatever the differences between these two types of fool, the word fool is applied to the broad category of people who have no time for God. The Psalms and Proverbs are full of such fools—for example, "The fool has said in his heart 'There is no God'" (Ps 14:1). Similarly, the apostle Paul talks of humanity at large as suppressing God's truth, and therefore professing to be wise, but becoming fools (Rom 1:22). Lacking the fear of the Lord that is the beginning of wisdom, all such people, whether individuals or nations, inevitably end up in some form of social, sexual, economic or cultural folly—however noble, daring or advanced in the eyes of others. Truly they are fools, and this first type of fool offers little help to us, except to stand as a warning sign to mark off a way of life that people of faith should avoid. We are never to be "worldlings" and fools in this first sense. That sort of fool has nothing to teach us in terms of communication.

FOOL FOR CHRIST

The second type of fool in the Bible is quite different and takes us significantly closer to the secret of persuasion. This is *the fool bearer,* the person who is not actually a fool at all, but who is prepared to be seen and treated as a fool—the "fool for Christ's sake." Those last four words go back to a famous passage in St. Paul's letter to the church in the Greek city of Corinth, where he was defending his standing before the church as an apostle. Not for one moment did he consider that he and his fellow apostles were really fools, but the Corinthians thought so because they saw themselves as superior. They thought too highly of themselves, so when they disagreed with the apostles, they disparaged the apostles as fools.

The truth was that Jesus was the very wisdom of God. He did not just speak the truth. He was the truth, the truth in person, so that the wisdom of his apostles was the very wisdom of God. But Paul did not stop to quarrel with this false verdict of the Corinthians. He merely says, with a touch of irony, "We are fools for Christ's sake" (1 Cor 4:10). The apostles were anything but fools, but they were ready to be seen as fools and treated as fools. Like Dostoevsky's misunderstood and mistreated Idiot, they were even prepared to be regarded as the "scum of the world" and a "spectacle to the world." On the great day that is coming, truth will be set right and they would be vindicated. But until then, Paul would gladly bear any derision and rejection that came his way so long as he was able to preach the gospel and remain true to his calling.

Paul, as he tells us elsewhere, had faced physical hardships of many kinds, including riots, hunger, beatings, imprisonment and shipwreck. So being dismissed as "mad" by a Roman governor or as a "fool" by the Corinthian Christians was trivial. It was merely the emotional and social equivalent of these physical trials. Followers of Jesus who count the cost and are willing to take up their crosses after him must have broad shoulders. The despicable modern resort to playing the victim card or charging one's opponent with being "phobic" in one way or another was not for Paul.

If the specific words "fools for Christ's sake" go back to Paul's letter to Corinth, the idea of the fool bearer goes back earlier still. King David, for example, danced in public with such abandoned joy before the Lord that his own wife Michal thought he was a fool, and the prophet Jeremiah lamented that his stand for God had reduced him painfully to a laughing stock among his own people. Faithfulness in a fallen world carries a cost.

THE MOCK KING

All these examples fade into insignificance beside the supreme fool bearer in the Scriptures. This is of course Jesus himself, when he was made a mock king. This happened first in the house of Caiaphas the high priest, then at the hands of King Herod's guards, and last in front of Pilate and his Roman soldiers—in other words, Jesus was cruelly mocked before the highest religious leaders of his day, before the representatives of the best law of the day, and before the mightiest political and military power of his day. Conditions in most prisons in the world are rife with cruelty and degradation, and executions only heighten the dehumanization. The victim being processed for death is usually reduced to something less than a man long before the authorities cut off his life as a man. Warders, soldiers and assistants, those who elsewhere in life are normal fathers, neighbors and colleagues, feel nothing personal against the victim, but often they vent their suppressed emotions in the thick of the grisly business of processing a person for death.

So the high priest's servants played a sadistic version of blind man's bluff, and then in a mean mockery of the reputation of Jesus, they twisted the game into "Let's see who's the prophet now." They were probably as skeptical about the supernatural as their masters, the Sadducees. In which case, they saw prophecy as a complete fraud, but Jesus provided a handy butt for their derision. Having beaten him, they blindfolded him, struck him while helpless and asked him, "Prophesy! Who is it that struck you?"

Then when Jesus refused to play their game, remaining silent before their humiliation, he was handed over from Herod's guards to the Roman soldiers, and finally to Pontius Pilate, the governor himself. The climax of the torture has been captured in countless paintings of *Ecce Homo*—Jesus standing before his tormentors, suffering but silent, the crown of thorns pressed down on his head, the purple robe draped around his shoulders, the reed scepter thrust into his hands, hailed with the mock acclamations—and then the final parody of the trilingual inscription above his head on the cross: "Jesus of Nazareth, King of the Jews."

Pilate's mockery, needless to say, was the most refined and supercilious of all. He mocks Jesus for his foolish claims to be the Messiah, and he mocks the Jews for their pathetically absurd hope that any messiah, now or in the future, could ever free them from the legions of Imperial Rome. Face to face with the power of Caesar, the Nazarene pretender had no battalions. With a sneer, Pilate could mock both Jesus and the Jews with the same inscription—and kill two birds with the same stone. Kings without power are nothing more than pretenders, exiles or has-beens, just as messiahs who fail are obviously bogus. So what could be more absurd than the claims of a would-be messiah executed through the ultimate punishment and ignominy Rome could impose? What could make all the pretensions look more ridiculous now, so from the passersby to the rent-a-mob, to the conniving clergy, to the governor himself, they ridiculed, they scorned and they mocked. Powerlessness exposes all pretensions.

How long did it take for events to trigger the switch that made the disciples see the glory in the disaster? What were the events that turned this ghastly parody around, so that it became the fulfillment of Isaiah's prediction of the suffering servant who was to come? The resurrection was the decider of course, but why did it take longer for some of the disciples such as Thomas? What is certain is that as Jesus went forward to bear the sin of the world, he first bore its cruel derision. Jesus is the world's supreme fool bearer.

HOLY FOOLS

For all its profundity and pathos, the role of the fool bearer would not seem to help us much with communication, and its main significance has always been for discipleship. To follow Jesus is to pay the cost of discipleship, and then to die to ourselves, to our own interests, our own agendas and reputations. It is to pick up our crosses and count the cost of losing all that contradicts his will and his way—including our reputations before the world, and our standing with the people and in the communities that we once held dear. It is to live before one audience, the audience of One, and therefore to die to all other conflicting opinions and assessments. There is no room here for such contemporary ideas as the looking-glass self, and no consideration here for trivial contemporary obsessions such as one's legacy.

It is telling that what is probably the first known depiction of the crucifixion in Christian worship in the early centuries is graffiti-style mockery. It was found in Rome on the Palatine Hill in 1857, but goes back at least to the third century, if not earlier. It shows a crude caricature of a man with an ass's head nailed to a cross, with the words beneath, "Alaxamenos worships his God." More encouragingly, the next room of the house has a riposte that has been added: "Alaxamenos fidelis" (Alaxamenos is faithful). In short, to be a follower of Jesus is to be willing to be a fool for Christ and to join the long tradition of "holy fools" who have graced the story of the church from the beginning. St. Francis, God's *jongleur* or tumbler, stands as the best-known holy fool of all, but Ireland, Russia and many other countries have added their own distinguished exemplars of "faithful folly."

There is, however, a hint of a way forward in the way of the second fool. In praising the "holy fool," John Chrysostom, the golden-tongued preacher of Antioch and Constantinople, described him as he who gets slapped down, but is none the worse for the slapping. The reason is that in the Christian view of life, there is always a vital tension between what is immediate and what is ultimate. The immediate, which is formed by our present circumstances and our short-term prospects, may sometimes be horrific. We may be suffering a job loss, a health crisis, a public scandal, the death of a child or a close friend, or a Job-like combination of disasters. But however bad the immediate, the ultimate is always hopeful, and in the tension between the immediate and the ultimate lies the possibility of the resilience of faith.

The first time I encountered how faith made this resilience possible, my heart was silenced by its profundity. I was visiting Krakow, Poland, where I met a survivor of Auschwitz-Birkenau who had converted to the Christian faith in the death camp. Voltaire once said that heaven had given us two things to balance the many miseries of human life—hope and sleep. But the great French skeptic had forgotten humor. What had impressed the man I met was the witness of a fellow prison inmate whose Christian hope was expressed in humor, even there where nothing seemed to have meaning, let alone a funny side.

Viktor Frankl, who also survived Auschwitz, described humor as "another of the soul's weapons in the fight for self-preservation."[15] Yet it was not gallows humor that attracted the convert to the Christian faith. Nor was it a form of putdown to gain at least some moral revenge on the brutal guards (as in the superiority theory of humor put forward by Plato, Aristotle and Hobbes). According to this view, we laugh at the butt of our jokes as a way of asserting superiority over them. Nor was it escapist humor (as in the relief theory of Freud and others). According to this view, laughter is a form of release that lets off steam emotionally. No, the humor was hopeful, and it turned on the grotesque mismatch between the bleakness of their immediate prospects and the brightness of their ultimate prospects (as in the incongruity theory of Immanuel Kant, Søren Kierkegaard, Reinhold Niebuhr and Peter Berger).

To be sure, the humor was always within the ever-present sight of the execution block and the gas chambers, and it never lasted more than a few fleeting seconds. Not for one moment was Auschwitz itself ever something to laugh about. But like a flash of lightning or a momentary parting of the clouds, humor lit up a truth that was larger than anything that could happen to the poor prisoners, a truth that even Auschwitz could not censor. The seemingly ironclad world had been punctured for a second, and it could be punctured again once and for all. The ultimate could be seen to trump the immediate, so that the grim horror that was in front of them was not the last word. Heaven relativized even Hitler, Himmler and Herr Höss, the brutal superintendent of the camp—and all that in the flash of a prisoner's joke.

The writer of the letter to the Hebrews expresses this same resilience when describing the cross. He writes of Jesus that "for the joy that was set before Him" (and we might add the word *ultimately*) he "endured the cross, despising the shame" (and here we might add the word *immediately*). Some versions translate "despising the shame" as "making light of its disgrace" (NEB), a word used of clowns or jesters, and they then refer the reader again to 1 Corinthians 1, where the cross is described as God's way of subverting sin.

THE FOOL MAKER

This point leads us right to the third type of fool in the Bible—the fool maker. The fool maker is the person who (once again) is not a fool at all, but who is prepared to be seen and treated as a fool, so that from the position of derided folly, he or she may be able to bounce back and play the jester, addressing truth to power, pricking the balloons of the high and mighty, and telling the emperor that he has no clothes. This, says Paul, is what God did on the cross. If Jesus was the supreme fool bearer, God is the supreme fool maker. He simultaneously shamed and subverted the vaunted wisdom, strength and superiority of the world through the cross—shaming and subverting the world's wisdom through folly, the world's strength through weakness and the world's superiority through coming in disguise as a nonentity.

The cross, Martin Luther wrote, was the devil's mousetrap. The devil smelled cheese, and wham, felt steel. Thus we see a little baby lying defenseless in a crib at Bethlehem, and a tortured man hanging utterly derelict on a Roman cross outside Jerusalem. But those who believe that is all there is to it have taken only a surface glance at what is happening, and they have misread what is really going on in the incarnation and the cross. Look more closely, ask who the baby is and why the tortured man is dying, and you see that everything that is happening is far more than it appears to be. And as you pause and ponder, the self-chosen powerlessness can suddenly be seen as a higher power, the evident absurdity morphs into an illuminating mystery, and the nose-stopping offensiveness of all the blood and brutality turns into a heart-melting embrace. So powerless that he could not save himself, Jesus was dying to save others and embrace the whole world.

Everything that climaxed in that sultry Passover week was spring-loaded with a deeper, history-shaking truth, although under a disguise so strange that it bewildered even the closest and most ardent followers of Jesus—and the devil himself fell for the smell of the cheese. Just so did God shame the world's folly, subvert the world's pride and put death to death through the death of his Son. And the sober truth is surely that this was the way, the only way that it had to be done. There was no other way. God is always able to respond to sin and defiance with power. From the Garden of Eden and the Tower of Babel on, God had countered all the pride and evil of human imagination and set boundaries to contain all defiance against him and the order of his creation. Power, however, usually overcomes by destroying what defies it.

Thus, as Reinhold Niebuhr insisted, there is a limit to what even the power of God can do as power alone, for "such power does not reach the heart of the rebel."[16] Power can fence us in, but only sacrificial love can find us out. Power can win when we are ranged against it, but it cannot win us. Such is the hard, tenacious, willful, festering core of sin at the heart of each one of us that only the equally deliberate, tenacious love disguised in the absurd powerlessness, shame, pain, loneliness and desolation of the cross— all for us—could reach us and subvert us. *There was no other way. It takes the full folly and weakness of the cross to find us out and win us back.*

ALL WELL IN THE END

Christian fool-making, rather than dissimulation, is surely what Erasmus was doing in *The Praise of Folly*. Dame Folly capers onto the stage in her cap and bells, and soon readers all over Europe were laughing uproariously at the audacity and delicious wit with which Erasmus skewers his targets. Indeed, the book plowed the ground in which the seeds of the Reformation were soon to sprout so fruitfully and fatefully, far beyond what even Erasmus had in mind. But what matters too is the final perspective. What does it say of the whole Renaissance world if it is so crazy that the only wise person left is the fool? And who is the fool? Dame Folly is the wisdom of God in disguise once again. What God did in the incarnation and the cross in order to shame and subvert humanity at large, he had to do writ small to subvert the vanity fair of the Renaissance world. Erasmus's title perfectly captures St. Paul's understanding of what God did in the cross.

Needless to say, not everyone understood Erasmus's point. On the one hand, some people failed to understand his fool-making style and interpreted him woodenly. One stolid reviewer, a fellow cleric, wrote that now that Erasmus had written his brilliant book *The Praise of Folly*, he should consider writing a second book, *The Praise of Wisdom*. Poor man. Earnest, wooden and literalistic, he had missed the point. Erasmus *had* written *The Praise of Wisdom*, but he had written it upside down and inside out in order to be more persuasive to those who were resistant to being challenged.

On the other hand, there have always been others who praise Erasmus's skill, and stop there with a literary accolade, failing to see the significance of the fact that such fool making grows naturally out of the Christian faith. The point is not just that Erasmus was a great writer with a brilliant mind and a keen sense of wit and irony—all of which is abundantly true. The real point is that his style of creative persuasion is deeply natural to the Christian faith and absolutely necessary in defending the Christian faith both then and now.

Humor points to faith, in that both humor and faith spring up in response to the reality of the paradox and the incongruities at the heart of human experience. But while humor responds well to the lower levels of these incongruities, only faith can respond well to the higher ones. Humor in that sense points beyond itself toward faith. In Niebuhr's words, "Humor is, in fact, a prelude to faith; and laughter is the beginning of prayer."[17]

Almost all the world's greatest philosophers and poets have faced up to the paradox and incongruities that confront us when we consider ourselves and our humanity. From Psalm 8 to Shakespeare's great soliloquy in *Hamlet*, many of the world's most beautiful and profound reflections have focused on the paradox of man and woman. As part of humanity, we humans are so small and so great, so strong and so weak. We rise so high and we sink so low. We are body and we are spirit. We are mortal and we are immortal. We have a grandeur and we have a pathos. Sometimes our little lives seem like a momentary fleck on the heaving ocean, yet we are all always the center of our own universe while we live, and together as humanity we are the most powerful and influential creatures in the whole animal kingdom. We can see things as they are; we also know the way things ought to be, and sometimes the difference makes us laugh and sometimes it makes us cry. What other beings in the universe are like us in these ways? What explains this paradox and these incongruities, and even more, how can we hope to reconcile them in a way that makes life meaningful?

Unquestionably, the current vogue in thinking is to duck the incongruity by stressing only one side—in the case of the new atheists, reducing reality to what can be handled by reason and science, and denying everything else that does not fit this reductionism. Not surprisingly, Dawkins and his naturalistic cohorts have put such a stress on the naturalness and smallness of humanity that they now routinely deny aspects of our humanity that were once considered part of human greatness—human dignity and freedom being the latest to be assigned to the dustbin as "illusions."

Neither humor nor faith duck the challenge of both elements of the paradox, but in taking the incongruous seriously they each respond in a different way and at different level. Humor works at a lower level. Its genius lies in its capacity to open up a vantage point from which the world looks different, so that we laugh and do not need to take it as seriously as otherwise we might have to. To laugh at an old woman or a handicapped child tripped in the street would be heartless and indicate a deficiency of humanity. But many people would be highly amused to see a pompous politician slipping on a banana skin on the way up to receive an empty and undeserved accolade. The first case would only remind us of the everyday suffering in our world, whereas the second would encourage us to see through the foibles and pretensions of human power, and take it less seriously. The contrast between the politician's dignity and the indignity he suffers makes us laugh, and the laughter is liberating.

Niebuhr has reminded us that there is both judgment and mercy in such humor. We are laughing *at* someone or something, which reveals the element of judgment. ("He's such a pompous idiot that he's overdue for a comeuppance.") But there is also mercy in the laughter, in that we are judging it, but still taking it somewhat lightheartedly. ("Hey, we're all vain at times, so we shouldn't take it that seriously.") But Niebuhr goes on to observe that, as the incidents of wrong mount from a matter of error to matters of evil, and from common or garden evil to malignant evil, the note of judgment remains, but the note of mercy has to fall away. So humor becomes rarer and less appropriate. Real evil is not something to be taken lightly. To joke about evil may start well, but it always ends by turning meaning into absurdity and life itself into a bitter joke, as readers of the novels of Kurt Vonnegut or the watchers of Monty Python's *Life of Brian* know well.

But if frivolity falls away as we mount to see the higher levels of incongruity, and especially when they touch on evil and suffering, that is when faith then comes into its own. For nothing else can reconcile the irreconcilables. But the faith that does so still remains like humor in three ways—it is an expression of the freedom of the human spirit, it faces both sides of the incongruities squarely and it reconciles them by its creative subversion.

Many people miss the highly distinctive feature of the Jewish and Christian faiths that make such faith possible. At one extreme, the worldview of the Bible stands in contrast to the one-dimensional character of secularism. Secularists only have a single dimension to their understanding of reality—this world plus nothing. In Max Weber's famous description they are "tone deaf" to realities that are unseen; in Albert Einstein's view, they are people who "cannot hear the music of the spheres"; and in Peter Berger's apt picture, they live in "a world without windows." C. S. Lewis described the person who is enclosed in "a tiny windowless universe which he mistakes for the only possible universe."[18] Having only this world, they have no counter-reality from which to judge it, no Archimedean point of leverage from which to hope to reform it, and no heaven to relativize Hitler or any other horror. All too often such secular humanism is humorless. When it takes the ultimate incongruities of human life seriously, it can only address the darker side and it becomes angry, bitter and forlorn.

At the other extreme, the worldview of the Bible stands in contrast to the Eastern worldviews with their problem of infinite regression. Eastern worldviews put their stress on the fact that ultimate reality is always "beyond" all human categories, such as true and false, right and wrong, and this and that—it is always "not this" and "not that" (*neti neti*). But where then do you stop? Like endless Chinese boxes within Chinese boxes, or a maddening echo in the brain that sets off ever-ringing echoes that never stop, there is no solid place left on which to stand, and even the world that we think we know is reduced to illusion (*maya*). Hence the famous puzzle posed by China's Master Chuang in the fourth century B.C., "If when I am asleep I am a man dreaming I am a butterfly, how do I know when I am awake that I am not a butterfly dreaming I am a man?"

In strong contrast to secularism, the Christian view is both this-worldly and other-worldly. It has a healthy appreciation of this world, but sees it always within an equally strong appreciation of another world that throws this present world into a different light, redeeming its worst features and confirming forever its highlights. And in strong contrast to the Eastern views, the Christian view has a solid appreciation of the created reality that we know and that we may trust—even though there is another world that is needed to make this world what it should be.

Christian foolmaking grows directly from this double-edged feature of the biblical worldview, which alone does justice to the inherent discrepancies in life. The truth is not just that we defend God by using the fool-making approach, but that when we use the fool-making approach we mirror the divine fool-maker himself. The cross of Jesus is the world's supreme example of anguish, suffering and injustice, but it has nothing to do with tragedy as we experience it in Aeschylus, Sophocles, Euripides and Shakespeare—tragic drama that ends with dead bodies all over the stage, and pity and fear as the salutary emotions that lead the audience to "metaphysical consolation," as Nietzsche put it.[19]

On the contrary. We must say it with awe, with reverence and with deep gratitude, but say it we must. Faith is never flippant and rarely frivolous, and it is as foolish to laugh all the time as it is to be serious all the time, but the truth still stands: *The dynamics of the cross of Jesus are closer to those of comedy than tragedy.*

Both tragedy and comedy turn on the deep contradiction and discrepancies between the world as it is and the world as we humans wish that it would be—in other words, on present aspects of the world that are incongruous or ludicrous, and that defy the best pretensions of humanity. But whereas tragedy only reminds us of the iron bars of the prison of reality from which not one of us can ever escape, comedy shows a way to break out. In comedy, the pratfall and the setback are not the end, and in the Christian faith even death, the ultimate setback, is not the end. *Because of the cross and the resurrection there is always a way out.* Which means of course that when the contradictions are subverted and reality is turned right way up, the outcome can be gratitude, joy and hope, rather than pity and fear. Needless to say, the dynamic of the resurrection and a God who cannot be buried for long is the dynamic of a child's jack-in-the-box writ large in golden cosmic letters.

That is why, in their different ways, several of the greatest Christian thinkers such as Kierkegaard, Chesterton, Niebuhr and Berger have all argued that the gospel provides the most hopeful and humorous view of life in world history. In Kierkegaard's view, "The comic apprehension evokes the contradiction or makes it manifest by having in mind the way out, which is why the contradiction is painless. The tragic apprehension sees the contradiction and despairs of a way out."[20]

Niebuhr observed that the intimate relation between humor and faith grew from the fact that "both deal with the incongruities of our existence," and that both are "expressions of the freedom of the human spirit." But whereas laughter only deals with the incongruities at the immediate level, "Faith is the only possible response to the ultimate incongruities of existence which threaten the very meaning of our life."[21]

Berger's view is captured succinctly in the very title of his book: *Redeeming Laughter.* Both humor and faith deal with the incongruities that are at the heart of life by helping to transcend them, but humor is merely "transcendence in a lower key," whereas faith is "transcendence in a higher key."[22] His conclusion? "Sometimes we must laugh in order to perceive." Or "Comedy is more profound than tragedy."[23]

One day it will finally be seen, as Julian of Norwich famously asserted, that all is indeed well. But only when all life's upside-downs have been righted, the back to front restored, the crooked straightened, and the abnormal-normal returned to its true normality. In short, all will be well when the world's last folly has been given its comeuppance, and even the most "foolish" designs of the divine fool-maker have been vindicated for all to see as the wisdom they really are. Only then will humankind begin to understand and appreciate the surprises and delights that God has had in store all along. But in the meantime the way of the divine fool-maker gives us the motive, the basis and the dynamic for our persuasion.

5

ANATOMY
OF UNBELIEF

Beware intellectuals!" Paul Johnson's stunning summary of a study of Western intellectuals runs counter to what many people think, or at least once used to think.[1] If truth is not the Holy Grail for intellectuals, what is? Truth surely is the reason why intellectuals think passionately, read voraciously, pursue research tirelessly and argue about anything and everything interminably. Almost at the dawn of the Western intellectual tradition, Plato described philosophers in the *Republic* as those with "no taste for falsehood; that is, they are completely unwilling to admit what's false but hate it, while cherishing the truth."[2] Similarly, Aristotle wrote in his *Ethics* that the person who loves truth for the very sake of truth when nothing is at stake will still be the more truthful when someday everything is at stake.

But that was then. To be sure, there have always been people who were skeptical about anyone who knew more than they did. How could they ever find out whether the other person was trustworthy? But now we have many people for whom mistrust is the badge they wear proudly to show their schooling in postmodern suspicion, so that "mistrust intellectuals" and "question authority" go hand in hand. After all, Nietzsche and his postmodern disciples have surely won for the moment. Truth is dead, and everything is relative at best and at worst a matter of the will to power. Nothing is what it appears to be. If truth was once the stated goal of intellectuals, it is now easy to read between their scholarly lines and see the petty egos and the dirty ambitions behind the lofty aspirations for truth. Truth is finally undecidable, as the postmodern philosophers express it. At best, truth is simply the compliment you pay to sentences that you happen to agree with.

However you explain the record, what are undeniable are the facts about the story of intellectuals, and the embarrassing evidence long precedes postmodernism. Many of the celebrated makers of the modern world have been shown up for their devious handling of truth in some aspect of their thinking or their lives—including Rousseau, Shelley, Marx, Ibsen, Tolstoy, Hemingway, Brecht, Bertrand Russell, Sartre, Margaret Mead and others. Yet these are the men and women of ideas who have risen up to overthrow the guardians of traditional Western society, and who on the basis of the brilliance of their minds are now trusted to diagnose our ills, prescribe our remedies and direct the future for our children and for the world.

For all the proud Enlightenment boasts such as Kant's *Aude sapere* (Dare to know), contemporary accounts of Western intellectuals leave the myth of the dispassionate truth seeker in tatters. The real situation is frequently the opposite. Many thinkers are truth twisters. For every thinker who desires to conform his thinking to reality, there are others whose desire is clearly to conform reality to their thinking. The cleverer the mind, the slipperier the heart, and the more sophisticated the education, the subtler the rationalization. Erudition lends conviction to self-deception. Johnson's evidence is startling and his conclusion sober:

> The belief seems to be spreading that intellectuals are no wiser as mentors, and no worthier as exemplars, than the witch doctors or priests of old. I share that skepticism. A dozen people picked at random on the street are at heart as likely to offer sensible views on moral and political matters as a cross-section of the intelligentsia. But I would go further. One of the principal lessons of our tragic century, which has seen so many millions of innocent lives sacrificed to improve the lot of humanity, is—beware intellectuals.[3]

Anyone not convinced by this bald summary should read the authors for themselves and examine the evidence. But what is truly stunning is that, with some intellectuals, there is no need to pursue any inquiry because they make no bones about what they are doing. They candidly admit that truth is not their guiding consideration at all. One of the most frank is Aldous Huxley, author of *Brave New World*.

Huxley's later book of essays, *Ends and Means*, is "an inquiry into the nature of ideals," and in the course of it he is candid about his own beliefs. "All that we are," he repeats twice, "is the result of what we have thought," so it is important for us to think well, to be clear about how we think, and to choose the best worldview. "It is impossible to live without a metaphysic. The choice that is given us is not between some kind of metaphysic and no metaphysic; it is always between a good metaphysic and a bad metaphysic."[4] And how are we to decide? By observing the one that is closest to reality, and may be considered true.

Yet "no philosophy is completely disinterested," Huxley argues. "The pure love of truth is always mingled to some extent with the need, consciously or unconsciously by even the noblest and most intelligent philosophers, to justify a given form of personal or social behavior, to rationalize the traditional prejudices of a given class or community."[5] Everyone, he claims, thinks for both "intellectual reasons" (based on truth) and "voluntary reasons" (based on desires and the will).

Huxley was a deeply thoughtful and sensitive man who was unafraid to take positions that bucked the fashionable trends of his day and even of his own famous family. He criticized the dangers of false systems of meaning, such as nationalism, national socialism, communism, a false view of science, and argued that a philosophy of meaninglessness can be useful if it liberates people from such false views. Then, with considerable realism he also goes on to criticize those who go to the other extreme and claim to be able to live without any meaning at all. Those, such as the Marquis de Sade, who are consistent proponents of meaninglessness, are dangerous, while most people—fortunately for them—are not consistent. They can only live without meaning for a short time and in selective areas, and only then because they assume unacknowledged sources of meaning in other parts of their lives.

Huxley finishes with a sharp description of the problems created by this approach. On the one hand, by overriding considerations of truth and giving so much attention to personal needs, it creates a fateful divorce between truth and whatever is considered goodness. On the other, it becomes impossible in practice to live without meaning. "The mind is so constituted that a philosophy of meaninglessness is accepted only at the level of the passions and is persisted in only by those whose heredity and upbringing make it possible for them to live as though the world were at least partially meaningful."[6]

One might think that after this trenchant diagnosis of the radical dualism in human thinking, Huxley would urge us to take truth seriously and lean against any way in which we may be tempted to rationalize our needs—as Plato and Aristotle would have recommended. Instead, bizarrely, he goes on to take the very approach he was attacking. He freely admits that he "took it for granted" that the world had no meaning, but he did not discover it, he decided it. "I had motives for not wanting the world to have meaning; consequently assumed that it had none, and was able without any difficulty to find satisfying reasons for this assumption."[7] His philosophy of meaninglessness was far from disinterested. And the reason? "We objected to morality because it interfered with our sexual freedom."[8]

This admission is extraordinary. To be sure, Huxley and his fellow members of the Garsington Circle near Oxford were not like the Marquis de Sade, who used the philosophy of meaninglessness to justify cruelty, rape and murder. But Huxley's logic is no different. He too reached his view of the world for nonintellectual reasons: "It is our will that decides how and upon what subjects we shall use our intelligence." After all, he continues in this public confessional, "The philosopher who finds no meaning in the world is not concerned exclusively with a problem in metaphysics. He is also concerned to prove that *there is no valid reason why he personally should not do as he wants*, or why his friends should seize political power and govern in a way they find most advantageous to themselves."[9]

The eminent contemporary philosopher Thomas Nagel is equally candid. He admits that his deepest objection to Christian faith stems not from philosophy but fear.

> I am talking about something much deeper—namely the fear of religion itself. I speak from experience, being strongly subject to this fear myself: I want atheism to be true and am made uneasy by the fact that some of the most intelligent and well-informed people I know are religious believers. It isn't just that I don't believe in God and, naturally, hope that I'm right in my belief. It's that I hope there is no God! I don't want there to be a God; I don't want the universe to be like that.[10]

At least there is no pretense in such confessions. As Pascal wrote long ago, "Men despise religion. They hate it and are afraid it may be true."[11] In Huxley's case there is no clearer confession of what Ludwig Feuerbach called "projection," Friedrich Nietzsche called the "will to power," Sigmund Freud called "rationalization," Jean-Paul Sartre called "bad faith," and the sociologists of knowledge call "ideology"—a set of intellectual ideas that serve as social weapons for his and his friends' interests. Unwittingly, this scion of the Enlightenment pleads guilty on every count, but rather than viewing it as a confession, Huxley trumpets his position proudly as a manifesto. "For myself, no doubt, as for most of my contemporaries, *the philosophy of meaninglessness was essentially an instrument of liberation.*"[12]

TRUTH OR NOTHING

Few writers are as brazen as Aldous Huxley at this point. But he is not alone in his truth twisting. Alfred C. Kinsey's groundbreaking *Sexual Behavior in the Human Male* turned out to be based on flagrantly flawed and fraudulent data. Feminist revolutionary Betty Friedan, author of *The Feminine Mystique*, misrepresented herself shamelessly. Far from the stifled suburban housewife as she depicts herself, she was a communist activist and propagandist with a full-time maid. Celebrated deconstructionist and Yale professor Paul de Man was discovered to be a former Nazi collaborator with an appalling record of lying and deception, whose biographer described him as a swindler, bigamist and chronic deceiver whose ideas grew out of lifelong habits of secrecy.[13] Mary McCarthy described de Man as having "an intelligence that's outdistanced his morals." All these intellectuals sound like the philosopher Nietzsche describes in *Beyond Good and Evil*: "a wily spokesman for his own prejudices which he baptizes 'truths.'"[14]

Needless to say, that is only one side of the story, and two facts offset it strongly. First, it is unquestionably true that for every thinker who has been exposed as a truth twister, there are other great thinkers who are truth seekers with courage and at great personal cost. Max Weber was such a person. Arguably the greatest of all social scientists, Weber passionately pursued the ideal "truth or nothing"—similar to Emily Dickinson's "My country is Truth" and Albert Camus's "prefer truth to everything." One day late in life, when a friend asked Weber why he pressed on with his research despite the pessimism of his conclusions and despite an earlier breakdown, he replied fiercely: "I want to see how much I can stand."[15]

Few thinkers have matched Weber's courage and dedication to truth. But people of faith are among those who do—for instance, Rabbi Menachem Mendl (the "Kotzker"), who had one word on his banner, *Emeth* (Truth), or Søren Kierkegaard, whose answer to the question "What do I want?" in the last year of his life was "Quite simply: I want honesty."[16] Or Lord Acton, whose unflinching commitment to truth led him to attack his own beloved Catholic Church when he was convinced the Church was wrong. "A false religion fears the progress of all truth; a true religion seeks and recognizes truth wherever it can be found."[17]

Second, it is also unquestionable that many vital areas of human life assume and require a robust view of truth, and without it they would collapse. Business, for example, requires trust, which in turn requires truth, which is only the beginning of the reason why lies, deception and corruption are so damaging to the business world. The same is true of the entire enterprise of science, whether we are talking of trust in an ordered universe or trust in the assured results of scientific experiment through peer review. And quite obviously it is truth that is foundational to journalism, and without it, the whole world of newspapers and television slumps into a glorified gossip machine and rumor mill.

Philosopher Ziyad Marar puts it simply, "If I am to give you credit, I need to find you credible, while avoiding the risk of seeming credulous in giving credence to your discreditable account. From religious *credos* to street cred, from professional credentials to political credibility, we trade in a currency that differs from all other animals."[18] We are in fact *homo credens*, the animal that believes, and believes—we may add—that trusting crucially requires truth if it is to be warranted, and not to be seen as either groundless or foolish.

ANATOMY OF UNBELIEF

Where does this discussion leave us, and what does it mean for Christian advocacy? Do we truly seek to conform our thinking to reality, or do we also seek to conform reality to our thinking? Is this clash between truth seekers and truth twisters merely a problem for intellectuals and those who enjoy the life of the mind? Or are all humans double-faced, "dissonance in human form," as Nietzsche expressed it?[19] What does Kant's view of the "crooked timber" of our humanity mean for our thinking and understanding? And what is it that W. H. Auden glimpses when he writes that "the desires of the heart are as crooked as corkscrews"?[20] Is this merely a colorful metaphor, or is there more there that we should take seriously?

The Bible's answer takes us to the very heart of its diagnosis of unbelief, for in the biblical view *the central core of the anatomy of unbelief stems from its willful abuse of truth*. In our treatment of truth we, and all human beings, are at the same time both truth seekers and truth twisters, and in a deep, mercurial, tenacious and fateful way. Sometimes we seek to conform our thinking to reality, and just as often we try to conform reality to our thinking. As Sir Thomas More's protagonist Hythloday argued in his *Utopia*, and the seventeenth-century Jansenist theologian Pierre Nicole argued later, human beings "not being willing to render their actions to conform to the Law of God, have endeavored to render the Laws of God to conform to their actions."[21] From Genesis and the story of the fall onward, a host of passages convey this understanding, but one of the deepest is in the first chapter of St. Paul's letter to the Romans. Bursting with gratitude and pride at the glory and power of the gospel and its way of righting wrong in the world, the apostle turns to consider human disobedience and its consequences. Among the many claims he makes in a famous passage on sin and cultural degeneration, he asserts that those who disobey God "suppress the truth in unrighteousness" (Rom 1:18).

The Bible uses many strong terms to describe unbelief, including *hardening, twisting, blindness, deafness, unnaturalness, lies, deception, folly, rebellion* and *madness*, but none repays reflection more than Paul's phrase in Romans. At the heart of sin and disobedience, Paul says, is a flagrantly deliberate and continuing act of violence to truth. Sin and disobedience lay hold of truth, grasp it roughly, and will not let it be what it naturally is or say what it naturally says. In this way, the deliberate dynamic of unbelief is to suppress truth, stifle truth and hold truth hostage. What may be known about God, Paul says, is quite evident still, but it is adamantly denied by the determined act of will that is sin and unbelief.

The phrase *grasp the nettle* is too weak to picture what Paul is talking about, but it does begin to capture how the sheer force of a grip can be enough to counter the normal thrust of the nettle's sting. The experience of a hijacking comes far closer. When a terrorist hijacks a plane and holds the passengers hostage, he can put a gun to the head of the pilot and force him to fly wherever the terrorist wants, anywhere other than its intended destination. Just so, says Paul, unbelief looks at the undeniable truth of God's universe and at the unbeliever's own nature made in the image of God, but then denies their true force, suppresses their real meaning and turns their proper destination into a different one. The prophet Micah had charged that Israel's false leaders "twist everything that is straight" (Mic 3:9 NASB), but Paul goes deeper in analyzing that the heart of unbelief centers on its active abuse of truth.

It would be a mistake to hurry past this phrase or dismiss it as only a dramatic metaphor, for Paul's point grounds and underscores a variety of themes that run throughout the entire Scriptures when describing sin. Four prominent emphases recur most frequently, and together they form a multi-layered view of the dark willfulness of sin, disobedience and unbelief.

First, *unbelief abuses truth through a deliberate act of suppression.* Unbelief seizes truth, grasps it roughly, silences its voice and twists it away from God's intended purpose. By itself, truth speaks naturally and clearly, but its voice is censored, blocked and silenced, so that it is no longer allowed to speak as it does naturally:

> They say to God, "Leave us alone; we do not want to know Your ways." (Job
>   21:14 NLV)

> You who hate correction
> and turn your back when I am speaking? (Ps 50:17 NEB)

> They have denied the LORD,
> saying, "He does not exist." (Jer 5:12 NEB)

> For crime after crime of Edom
>   I will grant them no reprieve,
> because, sword in hand, they hunted their kinsman down,
>   stifling their natural affections. (Amos 1:11 NEB)

Second, *unbelief abuses truth through a deliberate act of exploitation.* Unbelief not only suppresses the real truth and twists it away from God's true ends, but wrests it toward its own ends and its own agenda.

The men who now live in Jerusalem have said, "Keep your distance from the LORD; the land has been made over to us as our property." (Ezek 11:15 NEB)

But you trusted to your beauty and prostituted your fame. (Ezek 16:15 NEB)

O Tyre, you said,
  "I am perfect in beauty," . . .
    they hung shield and helmet around you,
    and it was they who gave you your glory. (Ezek 27:4, 10 NEB)

Your beauty made you arrogant,
you misused your wisdom to increase your dignity. (Ezek 28:17 NEB)

Listen to this, leaders of Jacob,
    rulers of Israel,
you who make justice hateful
and wrest it from its straight course. (Mic 3:9 NEB)

Third, *unbelief goes further still and abuses truth through a deliberate act of inversion.* Unbelief not only suppresses truth and exploits it for its own ends, but seizes it and turns it completely upside down, inside out and the wrong way around, and then holds it there for its own purposes. Above all, through inversion we as creatures put ourselves in the place of our Creator, and we believe our own lie rather than God's truth. We make ourselves gods instead of God, so that proper self-love becomes prideful self-centering love. As Niebuhr states bluntly, "In an ultimate sense the self never knows anything against itself."[22] In terms of truth, we are always self-right. In terms of goodness, we are always self-righteous. And in terms of God, we are always our own gods.

In John Milton's "Paradise Lost," Satan is unequivocally clear: "Better to reign in hell than serve in heaven" or "Evil, be thou my good." Sartre expressed this dynamic famously when he said, "To be man means to reach toward being God." And before him, Nietzsche declared in the same spirit, "If there were gods, how could I endure not to be a god?"[23] Carl Gustav Jung recognized that this was the heart of Nietzsche's assertion of the Superman. It is "the thing in man that takes the place of God."[24] After the triumph of the Russian revolution, Lenin even had "God-defying" towers designed to demonstrate his Babel-like and Promethean pretentions, though most of them were never built. As these examples show, sin is essentially and willfully narcissistic, and it includes both a truth claim ("God is dead") and a task ("I am now out to be God in my life").

Sin, then, is the claim to the right to myself, and all our worldviews as unbelievers are in part a shrine to ourselves. This can be seen most clearly when atheism declines naturally into its religious phase, as it so often does (as in Auguste Comte's "religion of humanity," Alain de Botton's "religion for humanity" or Sam Harris's atheistic "spirituality"). We humans then become both idolater and idol, though we mask the folly from ourselves. The absurdity betrays itself, however, in various odd developments that take place. G. K. Chesterton, for instance, pointed out that the same people who scornfully dismiss the doctrine of three persons in one God as irrational, think nothing of worshiping seven billion persons in one God.[25]

Such statements are only the modern corroboration of the biblical view of sin, and the reason why John Calvin spoke of our human hearts as an idol-making factory. St. Paul made the same point centuries earlier. Unbelievers reject God and, in an act of absurd inversion, worship the creature rather than the Creator. They swap the splendor of the immortal and infinite God for breakable images of things that are puny and mortal like ourselves, and they exchange the natural, God-given view of sexuality for unnatural forms. Earlier still, the Hebrew prophets focused on this same inversion, and excoriated the skeptics and the enemies of God for the ludicrous absurdity of what they were doing in worshiping idols.

> Shall the axe set itself up against the hewer,
> or the saw claim mastery over the sawyer,
> as if a stick were to brandish him who wields it,
> or the staff of wood is to wield one who is not wood? (Is 10:15 NEB)

> How you turn things upside down,
>   as if the potter ranked no higher than the clay!
> Shall the thing made say of its maker, "He did not make me"?
> Shall the pot say of the potter, "He has no skill"? (Is 29:16 NEB)

> In your arrogance you say, "I am a god; I sit throned like a god on the high

seas." Though you are a man and no god, you try to think the thoughts of a god. (Ezek 28:2 NEB)

Fourth, *unbelief abuses truth through a deliberate act of deception that ends in its own self-deception.* Unbelief seizes God's truth, twists it away from God's purposes and toward its own, and is therefore forced to deny the full reality of the truth it knows. But in the futile act of trying to deny the undeniable, it both deceives others and deceives itself, and so becomes self-deceived. Unbelief therefore manufactures not only idols but illusions. The philosopher Marar writes, "As our hearts can't stop pumping blood, so our minds can't stop pumping illusions."[26] In that sense, all unbelieving worldviews are not only a shrine to those who hold them but a shelter from God and his truth.

The logic behind this drive to deception and self-deception is simple. If sin is the claim to "the right to myself," it includes the claim to "the right to my view of things." And since we are each finite, "my view of things" is necessarily restricted and simply cannot see the full picture. We therefore turn a blind eye to all other ways of seeing things that do not fit ours, and especially to God's view of things. As theologian N. T. Wright points out, trees behave as trees, rocks as rocks and the seas as the seas, but "Only humans, it seems, have the capacity to live as something other than what they are."[27] There is therefore a close link between the prideful love of self, its aversion to the full truth and its creation of illusions. Kierkegaard wrote, "But spiritually understood, man in his natural condition is sick, he is in error, in an illusion, and therefore desires most of all to be deceived, so that he may be permitted not only to remain in error but to find himself thoroughly comfortable in his self-deceit."[28]

St. Augustine and his later disciples, such as Pierre Nicole, developed the same point. A key part of deception and self-deception is the fact that evil must imitate good, unbelief must copy truth, and vice must mimic virtue. Thus whereas properly ordered love relates everything to God in trust, gratitude and humility, improperly ordered self-love relates everything to itself in prideful self-love. Such pride works constantly on behalf of its own body and its own mind in two ways. First, it serves the self-love of its body through the pursuit of pleasures; and second, it serves the self-love of its mind through the pursuit of approval and honor.

Needless to say, the latter is fateful as the source of our human hypocrisy. If we can act so as to produce the *appearance and effects* of proper love in spite of *motives* that are quite contrary and come from improper self-love, we can appear to be honorable and generous before our fellow humans. Just so did the Pharisees love to pray on street corners in the sight of all, and just so many big givers have loved to have their benefactions trumpeted to all when there is little real love behind their generosity. Just so, as we shall see later, does sin's imitation of good deeds provide a stalking horse for hypocrisy. We may despise blatant self-love when we see it in others, and we certainly do not want others to see it in us. So we mask our own motives to produce the consequences that will win us the approval and admiration of others. In Nicole's words, this is a "Traffick of Self-love," but one in which we "find satisfaction in this lovely Idea of ourselves."[29]

The indissoluble link between prideful self-love, aversion to truth, self-deception and hypocrisy is one of the great themes of the Bible—for example, the drumbeat repetition that "the way of a fool is right in his own eyes" (Prov 12:15). Sinful minds therefore claim both self-rightness in terms of truth and self-righteousness in terms of goodness. This theme is prominent in St. Augustine's *Confessions*, and comes directly from his own radical self-scrutiny in light of the teaching of the Bible. "Falsehood," he wrote, "is nothing but the existence of something which has no being."[30] But if this is so, "He who utters falsehoods utters what is his alone," for nothing is more private than a newly minted lie.[31] There is therefore a lie at the heart of each person's unbelief, and Augustine speaks of it as "the huge fable which I loved instead of you, my God, the long drawn lie which our minds were always itching to hear."[32] Augustine brings all the themes together in one extraordinary passage in book 10 of *Confessions*:

> Man's love of truth is such that when he loves something which is not the truth, he pretends to himself that what he loves is the truth, and because he hates to be proved wrong, he will not allow himself to be convinced that he is deceiving himself. So he hates the real truth for what he takes to his heart in its place.[33]

Some people scoff at this passage as the jaundiced thinking of a Calvinist before Calvin. But there has never been so much evidence for the omnipresence of deceit, and there has never been an age like ours that offers so many inducements to deception. For a start, this is the era of the "looking-glass self" and of "impression management," an age that is bursting with multiple reinforcements of our capacity for deception. These range from the lack of face-to-face reality in the new social media to the proliferation of modern enhancements, such as cosmetics, Viagra, Botox and plastic surgery, to the improved science of selling, propaganda and manipulation. But even these are beside the point, for modern thinking has only deepened our understanding of how human and how common deception is and always has been. As Pascal wrote centuries ago, "Human society is founded on mutual deceit."[34]

Consider the whole treatment of the unconscious, mixed motives, rationalizations, white lies, "cognitive dissonance," alter egos and "shadow personalities." Consider the place of "active forgetfulness" and deliberate "inhibition" in Nietzsche and postmodern thinking, and the former's view of humanity as "incarnated forgetfulness."[35] Think of the enduring appeal of books such as Robert Louis Stevenson's *The Strange Case of Dr. Jekyll and Mr. Hyde* and Oscar Wilde's *Picture of Dorian Gray*. Or consider D. H. Lawrence's reflections on our human capacity for self-deception. Human knowledge, he argued, is broadly of two kinds—the things humans tell themselves and the things they find out. The trouble is that the things humans tell themselves are nearly always pleasant, but they are lies. Why?

> Man is a thought-adventurer. He has thought his way down the far ages . . . which brings us to the real dilemma of man in his adventure with consciousness. He is a liar. Man is a liar unto himself. And once he has told himself a lie, round and round he goes after that lie, as if it was a bit of phosphorous on his nose-end. The pillar of cloud and the pillar of fire wait for him to have done. They stand silently aside, waiting for him to rub the *ignis fatuus* off the end of his nose. But man, the longer he follows a lie, becomes all the surer he sees the light. . . . Ahead goes the pillar of cloud by day, the pillar of fire by night, through the wilderness of time. Till man tells himself a lie, another lie. Then the lie goes before him like the carrot before the ass.[36]

In Marar's survey of the modern understanding of deception, he summarizes the situation simply: "Our minds are equipped with a convincing knack for cooking the facts, whether future, present or past."[37] Can there, then, be any quarrel with the diagnosis of the Bible, which has long seen deception and self-deception as an inescapable part of human living and a core feature of unbelief? Deceit and the folly of trusting deceit are core themes in the prophets. For example, Jeremiah:

> The heart is more deceitful than all else
> And is desperately sick;
> Who can understand it? (Jer 17:9)

Realism about deception and self-deception is a hallmark of the Christian mind. Reinhold Niebuhr was fearless in applying it to thinking about foreign relations, but how much more is it relevant to apologetics. Niebuhr argued that the folly of the modern mind is to make the precision of scientific thinking the model for all human thinking, and so to forget the bias, self-interest and moral defect at the heart of all thinking—sometimes even in thinking about science. According to his analysis, which makes St. Paul's diagnosis central, human thinking has caught itself in a triple bind. First, all human thinking is sinful. As finite, fallen and sinful creatures, our thinking can never be other than self-interested to some degree. Second, all human thinking is idolatrous. As humans made in the image of God, we still have a spiritual and rational power that can inflate even our worst and most self-interested thinking beyond its natural range. And third, all human thinking is hypocritical. Rather than acknowledging the bias and self-interest in our thinking, we are able to hide our dishonesty by aligning our ideas with higher ideals and more general interests—so that we can appear nobler and more generous than we really are.[38]

So the moral defect perpetuates itself down through history, but we refuse to admit that our problem is much more than ignorance. It turns on the impossibility of genuinely disinterested thinking because of the demonic twisting of sin. Sin insinuates itself into all human thinking, so that even the loftiest and most high-minded thinking of both individuals and nations displays certain common features. There is, Niebuhr writes, an "implicit idolatry," a "constitutional self-righteousness," a "lurking dishonesty," a "stupidity of sin" and a "spiritual source of corruption" in history that leads to a "vain imagination" and finally to "spiritual impotence."[39] This is the reason why human ideals are never able to fulfill the soaring visions of which they dream. It is also the reason why these recurring features stain all our thinking and sow the weeds of the ironies and unintended consequences that grow alongside our better ideas. Behind the crooked timber of our humanity are our crooked minds, and that crooked timber now warps even the brightest and best visions that flow from it.

If all this is so, can there be any question that our Christian advocacy must never be a matter of trundling out tried and trusty one-size-fits-all arguments and surefire proofs? Pascal described the challenge well. "We think playing upon man is like playing upon an ordinary organ. It is indeed an organ, but strange, shifting and changeable. Those who know only how to play an ordinary organ would never be in tune on this one. You have to know where the keys are."[40]

TENSION THAT WILL NOT GO AWAY

Bring these four strands of unbelief together—suppression, exploitation, inversion and self-deception. Then bring back the other metaphors that each view unbelief from one angle or another—hardening, blindness, deafness, unnaturalness, rebellion, lies, deception, folly and madness. You will find yourself looking into the heart of human darkness as the Bible understands it: the spirit and the will of human rebellion against God, of which unbelief is merely one expression. The point is not that we all exhibit all these features of sin equally and fully, but that we all do to some degree and in different ways.

We should therefore never view unbelief as flatly theoretical, loftily neutral or merely as a worldview that people just happen to have. However suave and cool its attitudes, and however rational its arguments may sometimes appear to be, unbelief is different in its heart. Deep down, the unbelieving heart is active, willful, deliberate, egotistic, devious, scheming and unrelenting in its open refusal, its deliberate rebellion and its total resistance to God and the full truth of his reality—and it can never be countered by purely intellectual arguments that ignore the power of the dark secret of this heart. Again, *the heart of apologetics is the apologetics of the heart.*

One way of summarizing the effect of the four features of unbelief is to focus on the inescapable tension and dynamic conflict inherent in unbelief. At the core of unbelief is ceaseless, unremitting and inescapable tension and conflict. *Unbelievers suppress the truth in unrighteousness, but it is still always the truth, so they can never completely get away from it.* An unbeliever's view of the world without God may contain many deep truths and have all sorts of genuine merits. But that view of the world can never be completely true, because the unbeliever will not accept God, without whom it will always be finally false at some points. Yet at the same time, the unbelievers' views of the world are never completely false, because they can never get away completely from God and his truth. Unbelief is therefore always and inherently in tension, and it can never escape this conflict. Whatever view of the world unbelief espouses, it is always partly true but twisted, and it is always twisted, though never other than still partly true.

Many implications for Christian thinking flow from this tension and conflict: it explains why our arguments can and must always appeal to reason, for the Lord of truth created his human creatures with the capacity to reason, and reason is the God's instrument to be used in the service of truth. For humans made in the image of God, reasoning is as natural as breathing, walking or smiling. Yet we always need to be ready to go beyond purely rational arguments, for the human will is in play, so our arguments are never dealing with purely neutral or disinterested minds.

It explains why humans construct worldviews and why there are so many—they are philosophical and social fictions, or *worlds within the world that provide a world of meaning apart from God and against God.* Since none are finally true, none are finally adequate, so the search for a more adequate explanation multiplies the inadequate options.

It explains why false religion is so false and bad religion so bad—religion becomes the supreme fiction and alibi that sanctions all other evasions of God.

It explains why there are both Promethean and Procrustean elements in the greatest human thinking. (On the one hand, "I am and who but I." And on the other hand, "If the truth doesn't fit life, it can always be stretched or cut down to my desired size.")

It explains the realism underlying the philosophy of Christian realism—there is and will always be a fatal moral defect in all human thinking. This means that no human thinking is ever truly disinterested and at some point it always goes wrong, and at its extremes it will become foolish and even dark and mad. Also, there will always be the phenomenon of "unintended consequences," because the element of the unforeseen in the best human knowledge will always upset the best of human foresight. Conversely, it explains why no one is ever completely wrong—there is always a mixture of truth in even the falsest and most dangerous of worldviews.

It explains why non-Christians can be "better people" than Christians, and why there are always redeeming features in the worst of people— whether they know God or not, and whatever they say about God, they are still made in the image of God and capable of humanity.

And of course it explains why all human desires, longings and aspirations point beyond themselves and toward God. The full range and depth of our desires are simply not fully covered by our unbelieving faiths and philosophies; and therefore they are not fully satisfied by what our unbelieving minds insist is true. Only Jesus and his fuller, final truth can fulfill the desire for the "something more" that cries out in all genuine human desires, longings and aspirations.

This is not the time or place to pursue the implications of all these different ideas. What matters here is a simple reason why the tension and conflict are crucial for Christian persuasion. They explain why we have a point of contact with every single human we could ever meet. If everyone in the world accepted God's truth as it is, there would be no need to persuade anyone. They would all be living fully in God's world. Equally, if everyone could live consistently in the world they each claim is true, we would have no chance of persuading them. They would be in another world altogether. But because of the inherent tension between the truth and the falseness in all unbelief, there is always a difference between what unbelievers assert they are and who they really are, and a difference between the world they say they are in and the world they are actually in—God's.

St. Paul's phrase "suppressing the truth in unrighteousness" captures the tension from the perspective of human sin, and therefore expresses it more negatively. St. John, on the other hand, expresses the same point from the perspective of God's grace and his note is more positive: "All that came to be was alive with his life, and that life was the light of men. The light shines on in the dark and the darkness has never mastered it" (Jn 1:4-5 REB).

Between Two Poles

We can take the understanding of this fundamental tension even further. If the logic of God's truth pulls in one direction and the logic of unbelief pulls in the opposite direction, unbelief will never face the full logic of either. Both destinations would be unthinkable, though for entirely different reasons, as both would mean the end of unbelief. The logic of God's truth would lead to God, and the logic of unbelief would lead to disaster. Unbelief therefore lives in tension between the two worlds. As Francis Schaeffer pointed out (and his whole apologetics turned on this point), "The more logical a non-Christian is to his own presuppositions, the further he is from the real world; and the nearer he is to the real world, the more illogical he is to his presuppositions."[41]

There are therefore two poles in the unbelieving mind and heart, which I call the "dilemma pole" and the "diversion pole." The dilemma pole expresses the logic of the fact that the more consistent people are to their own view of reality, *the less close they are to God's reality and the more likely they are to feel their dilemma.* The diversion pole expresses the fact that the less consistent people are to their own view of reality, *the closer they are to God's reality, so the more they must find a diversion.* Neither pole is necessarily closer to God, because unbelief as unbelief will not bow to God either way, but the people at either pole are relating to God and to their own claims to truth in entirely different ways.

Expressed like that, it is obvious that most people would prefer to be closer to the inconsistency but comfort of the diversion pole, rather than to the courage and consistency but discomfort of the dilemma pole. In other words, most would prefer to live *as if* God were there, with all the benefits that makes possible, even though they deny God in both theory and practice. The reverse is harder to carry off, and for that reason it is also rarer. Nietzsche's madman in *The Gay Science* is the epitome of someone who recognizes what it means to reject God consistently and face the consequences. To the self-appointed "anti-Christ" and the one who did his philosophy "with a hammer," the idea that God is dead was no yawning matter.

> The insane man jumped into their midst, and transfixed them with his glances.
> "Where is God gone?" he called out. "I mean to tell you. *We have killed him,*

you and I! We are all his murderers! But how have we done it? How were we able to drink up the sea? Who gave us the sponge to wipe away the whole horizon? What did we do when we loosened this earth from its sun?

"Whither does it now move? Whither do we move? Away from all suns? Do we not dash on unceasingly? Backwards, sideways, forwards, in all directions? Is there still an above and below? Do we not stray, as through infinite nothingness? Does not empty space breathe upon us? Has it not become colder? Does not night come on continually, darker and darker? Shall we not have to light lanterns in the morning? Do we not hear the noise of the grave-diggers who are burying God? Do we not smell the divine putrefaction?—For even Gods putrefy! God is dead! God remains dead! And we have killed him! How shall we console ourselves, the most murderous of all murderers? The holiest and the mightiest that the world has hitherto possessed, has bled to death under our knife,—who will wipe the blood from us? With what water could we cleanse ourselves? What lustrums, what sacred games shall we have to devise? Is not the magnitude of this deed too great for us? Shall we not ourselves have to become Gods, merely to seem worthy of it? There never was a greater event,—and on account of it, all who are born after us belong to a higher history than any history hitherto!"[42]

Nietzsche saw himself as a "born riddle-reader," standing watch on the mountains "posted 'twixt today and tomorrow," who could see what most people could not see yet. There was always a gap between the lightning and the thunder, though the storm was on its way. But while ordinary people could not be expected to have seen the arrival of this great event, he reserved his most withering scorn for thinkers who saw what he saw, but were unmoved and went on as before. They may have believed that God had "died" in European society, but it made no difference to them. Life would go on as it had. Such people, Nietzsche wrote, thinking of English writers such as George Eliot, were "odious windbags of progressive optimism." If God is dead, everything that once depended on God would in the end go too. Did even science-based naturalism, he wondered, come from "a fear and an evasion of pessimism? A refined means of self-defense against—the *truth*?"[43]

Nietzsche's clash with George Eliot and the middle-class Victorian optimists shows the clear difference between the dilemma pole and the diversion pole. Nietzsche was more consistent to the logic of atheism but less comfortable, whereas the English atheists were far less consistent but more comfortable. That difference has appeared again and again—for instance, in the celebrated clash in France between Jean-Paul Sartre and Albert Camus. Sartre was the more consistent to atheism and also more cold, whereas Camus was inconsistent but warm. Camus himself declared that, in spite of his pessimistic philosophy, "I am an ineradicable optimist," and one friend said of him, "Camus continues to think despair, even to write it, but he lives hope."[44]

More recently the same tension can be seen in John Gray's stinging attacks on secular humanism, as in *Straw Dogs*. As a nonhumanist atheist, he lambasts humanists for their unwarranted borrowing of concepts such as freedom and human dignity. If the Jewish and Christian faiths are false, then freedom would dissolve before determinism and the notion of human dignity made "in the image of God" would go too. It is broadly true too that certain decades are closer to one pole or the other—the countercultural 1960s being more willing to press ideas to their conclusion, whereas the 1970's "Me decade" was more content to enjoy life without thinking too deeply or consistently.

Needless to say, because the dilemma pole is less comfortable, if more courageous and consistent, there will always be fewer people close to it. There will always be many more living close to the diversion pole. But at least the dilemma pole is easier to understand, and it also runs parallel to well-known biblical themes. Above all, the dilemma pole exemplifies some of the Bible's characteristic teaching on sin and judgment.

One such theme is that *we become what we worship*. The chronicler in Kings observed that late-monarchy Israel "followed vanity and became vain" (2 Kings 17:15). The psalmist wrote similarly of idol worshipers, "Their makers grow to be like them, / and so do all who trust in them" (Ps 115:8; 135:18 NEB). Jeremiah described his generation as "pursuing empty phantoms and themselves becoming empty" (Jer 2:5 NEB), and Hosea leveled the charge that "Ephraim became as loathsome as the thing he loved" (Hos 9:11 NEB).

Another such theme is that *we reap what we sow*. Judgment in Scripture is anything but arbitrary or capricious, as if God were to zap people who disobey him like a long-distance drone strike. Most often, judgment is a matter of God leaving an individual or a society to the logic of their own settled choices. Most famously of all, Hosea declared Israel "sows the wind, and reaps the whirlwind" (Hos 8:7 NEB). Before him, Jeremiah had pronounced,

> Your own ways, your own deeds
> have brought all this upon you;
> this is your punishment,
> and all this comes of your rebellion. (Jer 4:18 NEB)

Obadiah underscored the same lesson:

> For soon the day of the LORD will come on all the nations:
>   you shall be treated as you have treated others,
>   and your deeds will recoil on your own head. (Obad 1:15 NEB)

And as we saw, St. Paul's triad of willful exchanges in Romans 1 was followed by the corresponding triad of consequences introduced by the fateful words "God gave them over."

WEAPONS OF MASS DISTRACTION

Unquestionably, it is the diversion pole that needs clarification for apologetics in our day. Proponents of consistent unbelief who are close to the dilemma pole are easy to find and to quote because their cries in the darkness are heart-rending. The Swedish playwright August Strindberg, for example, made no bones about what he saw as the crisis of humanity. We live, he believed, in a world of inconsistent and contradictory character, unintended consequences, unknown aftermaths, flux, flux and still more flux. Like Nietzsche, he had made war on God and held the Christian faith in contempt, but he was forced to admit, "I have looked for God and found the devil." The highest human achievement is only "the concealment of our vileness."[45]

But if such cries are dramatic and quotable, they are also rare, for few people are so honest. The diversion pole, by contrast, is more crowded and is also less understood. It not only describes the majority of people in any generation, it applies more than ever to certain features of our world today. The core principle of diversion, you remember, is that the less consistent people are to their own view of reality, the closer they are to God's reality. So, because they still will not bow to God, the more they must find a diversion— some form of busy, entertaining distraction behind which they can hide. The shrine to the self requires a shelter from God and his truth, for otherwise the pathetic fiction of the self's assertion would be apparent.

The idea of diversion is powerful in the Bible, but the depth of the modern understanding owes everything to Pascal and his brilliant exposition in *Pensées*. "I have often said," Pascal wrote, "that the sole cause of man's unhappiness is that he does not know how to stay quietly in his own room."[46] Why? Because we all have to surround ourselves with diversion to take our minds off ultimate reality, including the fact that we all will die. Once, after spending the evening at the house of a very wealthy woman, the painter Francis Bacon came away incensed because she had plastic flowers rather than real flowers. "The whole point about flowers," he exclaimed angrily, "is that they die."[47] As Pascal put it, "If man were happy, the less he were diverted the happier he would be."[48] But that is not how we are. "Being unable to cure death, wretchedness and misery, men have decided, in order to be happy, not to think about such things."[49]

In Pascal's time, the opportunity for a life full of diversion was the privilege of the rich and powerful. "That, in fact, is the main joy of being a king, because people are continually trying to divert him. . . . A king is surrounded by people whose only thought is to divert him and stop him thinking about himself, because king though he is, he becomes unhappy as soon as he thinks about himself."[50] Thus the hunt is more important than the capture, and the search than the discovery. "Men cannot be too much occupied and distracted, and that is why, when they have been given so many things to do, if they have some time off they are advised to spend it on diversion and sport, and always to keep themselves fully occupied."[51]

What was once the preserve of the rich and powerful is now in the hands of almost everyone in advanced modern society. The whole high-tech iWorld is so full of diversions and busy, entertaining distractions of all kinds that they have been called our "weapons of mass distraction."[52] Who today needs to think beyond the here and now when we are surrounded and equipped by so many diverting devices?

My point is not to tilt at windmills and mount a quixotic attack on one of the idols of our age, but to appreciate the biblical understanding of diversion. After all, high-tech diversions are only the beginning of the many distractions in human life that tear us away from the focused attention that an examined life requires. Even the best of pursuits can become the worst of diversions. But whatever the source of the diversion, diversion is the most common reason for what Socrates called the "unexamined life" and Martin Heidegger called "strategies for inauthenticity." It is also the explanation for why so many people are so unreasonable in their rejection of faith. As Pascal put it,

> On this point, therefore, we condemn those who live without thought for the ultimate end of life, who let themselves be guided by their own inclinations and their own pleasures without reflection and without concern, and, as if they could annihilate eternity by turning away their thought from it, think only of making themselves happy for the moment.[53]

Again, there are several biblical themes that converge powerfully with Pascal's notion of diversion. First, *diversion is futile before God and his truth, whatever its source.* There are many types of diversion in the Scriptures, ranging from manmade lies to comfortable lifestyles to false prophesies, false religion and idolatry. But they are all ultimately futile, religion included. The prophet Isaiah attacks those foolish enough to believe they can build a barrier of lies and hide from reality.

> You say, "We have made a treaty with Death
> > and signed a pact with Sheol:
> so that, when the raging flood sweeps by, it shall not touch us;
> > for we have taken refuge in lies
> > > and sheltered behind falsehood." (Is 28:15 NEB)

For Amos, the diversion was in the vast careless of the lifestyle of the rich.

> Shame on you who live at ease in Zion,
> and you, untroubled on the hill of Samaria. . . .
> You who thrust the evil day aside
> and make haste to establish violence.
> You who loll on beds inlaid with ivory
> > and sprawl over your couches. (Amos 6:1, 3-4 NEB)

Of course, the ultimate diversion is false prophecy and false religion. The prophet Jeremiah warns against the treachery of his own colleagues:

> Do not listen to what the prophets say,
> > who buoy you up with false hopes;

the vision they report springs from their own imagination,
>   it is not from the mouth of the LORD. (Jer 23:16 NEB)

When this warning was ignored, the prophet's lament underscores the lesson they had missed.

The visions that your prophets saw for you
>   were false and painted shams;
they did not bring home to you your guilt
>   and so reverse your fortunes.
The visions that they saw were delusions,
>   false and fraudulent. (Lam 2:14 NEB)

When God steps forward to judge, neither empty religion nor a false reliance on idols will keep anyone safe.

Second, *diversion may be satisfactory in the short term, but in the long term it is disastrous.* This theme recurs again and again in Isaiah. Diversions, the prophet says, are like an illusion. They work well until, all of a sudden, they do not work at all.

Like a starving man who dreams
>   and thinks that he is eating,
but wakes up to find himself empty,
or a thirsty man who dreams
>   and thinks that he is drinking,
but wakes up to find himself thirsty and dry,
>   so shall the horde of all the nations be
>   that war against Mt Zion. (Is 29:8 NEB)

Or again,

Because you have rejected this warning
and trust in devious and dishonest practices,
>   resting on them for support,
therefore you shall find this iniquity will be
>   like a crack running down
>   a high wall, which bulges
and suddenly, all in an instant, comes crashing down. (Is 30:12-13 NEB)

Or yet again,

All trust in empty words, all tell lies,
conceive mischief and give birth to trouble.
They hatch snakes' eggs, they weave cobwebs;
    eat their eggs and you will die,
    for rotten eggs hatch only rottenness. (Is 59:4-5 NEB)

"All his life long," Jeremiah inveighed against Israel's neighbors in terms that would apply to the complacent Western world today:

Moab has lain undisturbed
like wine settled on its lees,
not emptied from vessel to vessel;
    he has not gone into exile.
Therefore the taste of him is unaltered,
    and the flavour stays unchanged.
Therefore the days are coming, says the LORD.
When I will send men to tilt the jars; they shall tilt them
and empty his vessels and smash his jars. (Jer 48:11-12 NEB)

The most graphic picture of the empty futility of diversion was given by Ezekiel.

They have misled my people by saying that all is well when all is not well. It is as if they were building a wall and used whitewash for the daubing. Tell those daubers that it will fall. . . . When the building falls, men will ask, "Where is the plaster you should have used?" So these are the words of the LORD God: In my rage I will unleash a stormy wind . . . until all is destroyed. I will demolish the building which you have daubed with whitewash and level it to the ground so that its foundations are laid bare. (Ezek 13:10-14 NEB)

GOOD BREAKFAST, BAD SUPPER

We live today in the grand age of diversion, and the reasons why are obvious. With our economic prosperity, our high-tech devices and the cornucopia of entertainment pressing for our attention, we can surround ourselves with diversion from the cradle to grave. We do not focus our attention on anything for long. We do not ask what "the good life" is and what it requires. Happiness is a small circle, and it is no surprise that the last thing on most people's minds at any moment is the question of the meaning of life, the coming of death and the priorities that are needed to choose wisely. What Socrates called the "unexamined life" that is "not worth living" now seems to be the life more people have slipped into than ever before.

Most people, in other words, are happily diverted, but not conscious of it. They live life caught in "cotton wool," as Virginia Woolf used to express it.[54] What is more striking are the people who are diverting themselves and know full well what they are doing. Diversion, for them, is a deliberately chosen shield against what they know is the unwelcome but logical outcome of what they believe. The Scottish philosopher David Hume offers a clear example, for all his incisive brilliance. To live hopefully, he had to keep brushing aside the skeptical conclusions of his own philosophy.

> Most fortunately, it happens, that since reason is incapable of dispelling these clouds, Nature herself suffices to that purpose, and cures me of this philosophical melancholy and delirium, either by relaxing this bent of mind, or by some avocation and lively impression of my senses, which obliterates all these chimeras. I dine, I play a game of back-gammon, I converse, and am merry with my friends; and when, after three or four hours' amusement, I would return to these speculations, they appear so cold, and strained and ridiculous, that I cannot find in my heart to enter into them farther.[55]

Many intellectuals have shown a patronizing view of the need for beliefs that ordinary people have—for example, Henrik Ibsen's famous line in his play *Wild Duck*, "Take away the life-lie from the average man and you take away his happiness."[56] But far more interesting is their own admission of their need to live *as if* the world had meaning. There is no meaning, they admit, but in fact we need to live *as if* there is meaning even when we know there is not.

This useful fiction was given a boost by William James's philosophy of pragmatism and the notion that there is no objective truth, but something is real because it produces real effects. As James rephrased Immanuel Kant, we can act *as if* there were a God. God is therefore real not because he is truly there but because belief in him influences our actions in this world. As his younger brother, the novelist Henry James, argued, we can live with the "shared fictions" and "necessary lies" of "as if" beliefs in God, and the results can be as beneficial as if God were truly alive. Only with such shared fictions that are the residue of faith can people live together well.

Doubtless, it is our close friends and families who are the ones most aware of our diversions. One friend described the great war-time photographer Robert Capa like this:

> Only in the morning as he staggers out of bed does Capa show that the tragedy and sorrow through which he has passed have left their marks on him. His face is gray, his eyes are dull and haunted by the dark dreams of the night; here at last is the man whose camera has peered at so much death and so much evil, here is a man despairing and in pain, regretful, not stylish, undebonair. Then Capa drinks down a strong bubbling draught, shakes himself, experimentally tries on his afternoon smile, discovers that it works, knows once more that he has the strength to climb the glittering hill of the day, dresses, sets out, nonchalant, carefully lighthearted to . . . all the places where this homeless man can be at home and where his friends can help him forget the bitter, lonely, friendless hours of the night behind him and the night ahead.[57]

Novelist E. M. Forster was frank and admitted the *as if* quality at the heart of his own diversion. "The people I respect most behave as if they were immortal and as if society were eternal. Both assumptions are false: both of them must be accepted as true if we are to go on eating and working and living, and are to keep open a few breathing holes for the human spirit."[58] Philosopher C. E. M. Joad came to faith during the dark days of the Second World War, but earlier he too had argued in a war pamphlet for the same *as if* position without fully facing its inconsistency. "Though I may have my doubts as to the immortality, I have none as to the importance, of individuals. Souls are souls even if their life here is transitory, and though they may not be immortal, it is none the less the business of government to treat them as if they were."[59]

"Hope is a good breakfast, but a bad supper," the philosopher Francis Bacon remarked. The heart's strategy of diversion clearly allows many people to mask the poor quality of their evening meal and to maintain their hope beyond its real term. All this, however, is merely the penetrating biblical understanding of the anatomy of unbelief. Far from simply accidental, a matter of person's place in their family tree, or a passing mental choice in their journey through life, unbelief turns on an act of will and a habit of mind shaped by choice. But we now turn from diagnosis to the question of remedy, or how we are to speak persuasively to those who do not and will not believe.

6

TURNING
THE TABLES

"O HANG THE COMMON WORLD!" The large, somewhat sullen undergraduate couldn't take it any longer. He slammed his fist on the table and rudely interrupted the professor's speech.

"Let's give it a bad name first and then hang it," the professor went on, not realizing the mood had suddenly changed. "A puppy with hydrophobia would probably struggle for life while we killed it; but if we were kind we should kill it. So an omniscient god would put us out of our pain. He would strike us dead."

"Why doesn't he strike us dead?" the student asked.

"He is dead himself," the philosopher said.[1]

So unfolds G. K. Chesterton's dramatic story of Innocent Smith and the professor of philosophy at Cambridge University in *Manalive*—a brilliant example of one style of apologetics that we need more of today. It is a sad if understandable fact that the extraordinary popularity of C. S. Lewis in the English-speaking world of apologetics has led to the eclipse of other great Christian advocates who deserve equal attention. And surely among the foremost would be Blaise Pascal, Søren Kierkegaard and G. K. Chesterton. Lewis himself would have been the first to admit where he relied on them, but we also need to appreciate where they each have strengths that complement Lewis's own great arguments.

Dr. Emerson Eames in Chesterton's story is the distinguished professor of philosophy and warden of (the fictional) Brakespeare College, Cambridge, and the world's leading authority on pessimistic philosophers such as Schopenhauer. He had finished a busy day of undergraduate affairs and was relaxing in his rooms, and as always was open to his friends and favorite students, one of whom was Innocent Smith.

Holding his glass of port, the warden went on talking about the philosophies of pessimism until suddenly he started. Dr. Eames was looking down the cold, small, black barrel of a cocked revolver.

"I'll help you out of your hole, old man," Smith said with a rough tenderness. "I'll put the puppy out of his pain, as you suggested."

For several hours they had been discussing philosophical pessimism and logical responses to it, until something in the student had snapped. He brandished a gun and threatened to put the professor out of his misery in the very way the professor had been talking about. Quickly, the professor made a run and leapt out of the window clumsily, landing precariously on a flying buttress below his window. From there, they continued the conversation tensely, with the student brandishing his gun, ramming home the professor's own earlier points, and the professor begging to be allowed to live.

"Let me come off this place. . . . I can't bear it."

"I rather doubt it will bear you," Smith said, referring to the delicate stonework. "But before you break your neck, or I blow out your brains . . . I want the metaphysical point cleared up. Do I understand that you want to get back to life?"

"I'd give anything to get back," the terrified professor cried.

"Give anything!" cried Smith. "Then blast your impudence, give us a song!" The startled professor obliged, singing a song of gratitude for existence. Satisfied, Smith then fired two barrels over the professor's head and let him climb to safety on the ground.

To the professor's great surprise when they were back together again, Smith then asked for his indulgence. "I must ask you to realize that I have just had an escape from death."

"*You* had an escape from death?" the professor said with irritation.

"O don't you understand, don't you understand?" Smith cried. "I had to do it, Eames. I had to prove you wrong, or die. . . . The thing I saw shining in your eyes when you dangled from that bridge was enjoyment at life and not 'the Will to Live.' What you knew when you sat on that damned gargoyle was that the world, when all is said and done, is a wonderful and beautiful place; I know it, because I knew it at the same minute."[2]

Like his jesting Innocent Smith, Chesterton was out to drive his generation to see the consequences of the philosophical positions they were holding—philosophies that were neither true nor in the best interests of their own proponents. In Chesterton's own words, he was trying to "hold a pistol to the head of Modern Man. But I shall not use it to kill him. Only to bring him to life."[3] Few of us could ever match GKC's unique blend of wit, playfulness and deep seriousness, but even from this brief extract from his story, the logic of his argument should be clear. The world authority on philosophical pessimism had merely dabbled in pessimistic ideas. He had never followed his own arguments through to the end to see where they led to—and when he did, they showed him what he really believed and what it was he really treasured—life, and a very different view than the one he had been teaching.

Chesterton's approach is an example of the first of two broad responses to the anatomy of unbelief outlined in chapter five: the broadly negative strategy of "table turning." This strategy turns on the fact that all arguments cut both ways. It therefore proceeds by taking people seriously in terms of what they say they believe and disbelieve, and then pushing them toward the consequences of their unbelief. The strategy assumes that if the Christian faith is true, their unbelief is not finally true, and they cannot fully be true to it. At some point the falseness shows through, and at that moment they will experience extreme cognitive dissonance, so that it is no longer in their best interest to continue to persist in believing what they believed until then. When they reach this point, they are facing up to their dilemma, and they will be open to rethinking their position in a profound way.

In chapter seven, we will examine the second approach: the broadly positive strategy of "signal triggering." This strategy proceeds by making people aware of their human longings and desires, and what these passions point to. These are longings and desires that are innate and buried in their lives. In particular, the strategy draws their attention to what have been called the "signals of transcendence" that are embedded in their normal, daily experience. These are indicators that grow out of very positive experiences and, like beeping signals, puncture their present beliefs and point beyond them toward what would need to be true if these signals are to lead to a fulfilling destination. When people reach the point where such signals spur them to search, they become seekers and they look for answers that lie beyond their present beliefs.

Why are these two strategies needed, and what is the link between them? The simple answer is that they are both needed to reach people whose hearts and minds are closed. By its very nature, unbelief in any form is not open to God and his good news, so to those whose hearts are closed, the good news is simply not good news. That of course is where apologetics comes in. It is a form of pre-evangelism that precedes evangelism for those who are not open to God and the gospel. We must never distinguish apologetics and evangelism too neatly. But in broad terms, evangelism is the sharing of the good news, and it addresses the needs and desires of those who know they are in a bad situation. And broadly, apologetics is pre-evangelism in that it addresses those who do not realize they are in a bad situation, and therefore do not see the gospel as the good news that it is. As John Wesley advised his young preachers in his day (when the Bible still shaped the horizon of most people's lives), "Preach the Law until they are convicted, then preach Grace until they are converted." What is urgently needed in our far more post-Christian times is the creative persuasion that is the proper business of apologetics. Only so will people be opened to seeing how good is the good news of the gospel.

Two Pitfalls

When we come to the relationship of apologetics and evangelism in the overall task of Christian advocacy, we have to face up to two equal and opposite errors. One is the apologist's temptation, which is to emphasize apologetics at the expense of evangelism, and the other is the evangelist's temptation, which is to do the opposite and emphasize evangelism at the expense of apologetics. Against the first error, we must be clear that, while apologetics as pre-evangelism must often be used to precede evangelism, we must never divorce the two tasks. They should be joined seamlessly. The isolation of apologetics from evangelism is the curse of much modern apologetics, and why it can become a sterile and deadening intellectualism. Whenever apologetics is needed, it should precede evangelism, but while apologetics is distinct from evangelism, it must always lead directly to it. The work of apologetics is only finished when the door to the gospel has been opened and the good news of the gospel can be proclaimed.

Needless to say, many of us are better at one task than the other, and few are equally good at both. But both gifts are needed, and we should each be aware of where we are strong and where we need complementing because we are weak. Even C. S. Lewis admitted "that my own work has suffered very much from the incurable intellectualism of my approach. The simple emotional appeal ('Come to Jesus') is still often successful. But those who, like myself, lack the gift for making it, had better not attempt it."[4]

It is certainly the business of apologetics to go as far out, and as deep down, as the people we are trying to reach and the objections we are trying to answer. Apologetics therefore raises questions and opens doors that may take it a long way from the gospel, but it does so only to pave the way for the good news. The Scriptures know nothing of an apologetics that has no interest in evangelism. The very notion is worse than a waste of time; it is damaging. Apologetics may at times be brilliant, complex and scholarly, and climb to a rarified altitude at which only a few thinkers can breathe easily. It may therefore at times appear a long way from the simplicity of the gospel, but it must never be made into an end in itself, and it should never stand by itself. As the early church boasted rightly, the message of Jesus is both simple enough for a child to paddle in and deep enough for an elephant to swim in.

Against the second error, we must always remember that when hearts and minds are closed, it is wiser to start on their grounds, not ours. In other words, it is usually a mistake to begin with the good news before the hearer is ready or able to see that it is good. Neither the negative nor the positive strategies begin by defending or possibly even mentioning the gospel itself because people are closed. The reason is that the wilder, the more skeptical or the more hostile the arguments against faith, the wiser and more effective it is to argue against them *on their own grounds*. In such cases, Chesterton argued, the principle stands that either we must not argue with a man at all, or we must argue on his ground, and not our own.

To some who prize evangelism and are suspicious of apologetics, that smacks of compromise and is enough to convict and sentence apologetics as an illegitimate exercise and an impostor in the world of true faith. Surely, they argue, the gospel is what saves people, so whatever is considered the gospel should be enough to reach people, and any other approach, however fancily dressed, is redundant, even unfaithful. As they see it, the point is not to persuade unbelievers but to preach to them, and if they refuse the gospel preached to them, that only shows that their minds and hearts are hardened and they are beyond God's saving.

Faithful sounding perhaps, but that position is again too pious by half, and it has no warrant in the Scriptures. If the Bible knows nothing of an apologetics that does not lead to evangelism, it certainly knows nothing of preaching divorced from the needed work of persuasion. The two words *preach* and *persuade*, and the two ideas behind them, are indissoluble—most prominently in the tireless work of St. Paul, who was an apologist everywhere he went. He preached and he persuaded. He persuaded and he preached, and no one can drive so much as the beam of a laser between the two. Where hearts and minds are hardened, it is the task of apologetics to challenge them and help pry them open. Apologetics therefore starts where the unbeliever is and focuses on what the unbeliever believes, but only because that is what is obscuring the good news of Jesus. Only when the inadequacies of that unbelief have been exposed is the unbeliever in a place to see and hear the good news for what it is.

By Their Fruit

As we saw, St. Paul describes the heart of all unbelief as a way of "suppressing the truth." As such, unbelief cannot be other than partly true and partly false, though each unbeliever will have responded to the tension by taking it in either of two directions. Some, usually the few, will have been more consistent in rejecting God, and therefore ended further from God and his full reality. Others, usually the majority, will have been less consistent in rejecting God, and therefore ended closer to God's reality.

The former will be closer to the "dilemma pole," in that to the extent that they are consistent in rejecting God, they are further from God's reality, so sooner or later they must face their dilemma. The latter will be closer to the "diversion pole," in that to the extent that they are inconsistent in rejecting God, they are more comfortable but closer to God's reality, so they must find a diversion. But as stressed earlier, it is not that one is spiritually closer and one spiritually further from God. People at both poles are equally resistant to God. The difference is simply that their different forms of unbelief reject God and the gospel in different ways, so both of them require subversion either through the negative strategy or the positive strategy.

The broad negative strategy of table turning comes into its own when people are closed to God and his truth in one of two ways. First, there are the great majority of people who are spiritually closed in a general sense, in that they are fully satisfied with what they believe already. They would see themselves as contented atheists, Buddhists, Muslims, Wiccans or whatever, and they feel they have no need to look for anything else. In many cases they might not be opposed to the Christian faith, and their closed hearts could be better described as satisfied rather than hostile, though for quite other reasons they might be both satisfied with what they believe and hostile to the Christian faith too.

Second, there are other people who are spiritually closed in a different and more particular sense. They are closed because they have specific objections to the Christian faith, and therefore believe that these objections make faith unthinkable and not worthy of consideration. Examples would include Marxists, who dismiss religion as the "opium of the masses," Freudians, who see it as a matter of "wish fulfillment," and logical positivists, who view it as "nonsense." (The word *God*, they say, is less meaningful than the word *dog* because the former cannot be verified through the senses.) All of these in their various ways have dismissed the Christian faith by relativizing it— those who are satisfied by their having no need for it, and those who raise objections by seeing it only through the prism of their objections.

Peter Berger counsels that the best way to counter such relativists is to "relativize the relativizers," and so turn the tables on them.[5] Arguments, you remember, cut both ways. Relativism would indeed be devastating if it were true, but relativism is always inconsistent, and relativists always cheat at some point. They relativize the views of others, but not their own. ("Well, of course, you'd see it that way. You're a Westerner/middle class/older generation.") They relativize the past, but not the present. They relativize us, but not themselves. Their relativism is always an escape, but not a solid position that can be examined. ("I was born that way. We're wired differently. It's a generational thing. You wouldn't understand.")

When confronted with such relativism, many Christians make the mistake of responding in the same way as English or American tourists traveling abroad: they "speak Christian" more slowly and loudly, pronouncing the objectivity of their claims in ever more earnest, labored and emphatic ways. And when they still fail to get their point across, they mask their frustration by issuing dire warnings of the consequences of disagreeing with them. The result is mutual incomprehension and stalemate.

Chesterton and Berger show us a better way through turning the tables. When it comes to belief and unbelief, we need to remember that, *while no thoughts are unthinkable and no argument is unarguable, some thoughts can be thought but not lived.* This point is similar to the famous notion of "unintended consequences" that is obvious throughout human history but was spelled out systematically by the Princeton sociologist Robert Merton. We humans are finite, so our unbelief, like all our purposeful actions, can never take into account all the factors that we would need to consider to make truly wise decisions. This means there will always be unforeseen and unintended consequences, so that our best ideas will often miscarry, and some may prove very damaging. When we are talking of unbelief, there will always be unintended consequences. Unbelieving beliefs will never be truly adequate because unbelieving knowledge is never fully adequate and not finally true.

This insight is what helps us surmount two barriers that lie across our path at this point. The first problem stems from the fact that every worldview, even the falsest or the silliest, is comprehensive on its own terms. This means that it not only claims to explain all reality within its framework, but it also explains the falseness of all other worldviews. Thus the Hebrews attacked idolatry as the projection of empty "nothings," and Ludwig Feuerbach returned the compliment by arguing that faith in God itself was a projection based on nothing. So how then does someone decide between the worldviews and their competing claims?

Second, there is the added problem that every conceivable argument either has been or will be put forward by someone, somewhere, sometime. So once again, how is anyone to decide between them? Like a serpent eating its own tail, each worldview explains the other worldviews, and each argument knocks down other arguments, so we appear to be left with a dizzying vertigo and with skepticism. The Christian answer lies in the nature of truth as understood by the Bible. While it is natural that all beliefs appear meaningful and adequate to those who believe them, and so long as they believe them, all those that differ from God's truth will always fall short in one of two ways in the end. In the bright noonday sunlight of reality, their beliefs will prove either constricting or contradictory.

On the one hand, the beliefs of unbelief become constricting when they are experienced as internally consistent but incomplete, and thus too small to explain the full range of the unbeliever's experience of life and the world. Chesterton described this as the problem of the madman—the person who, far from having lost his reason, has lost everything *except* his reason. The mark of such madness is a combination of a logical completeness and a spiritual contraction. On the other hand, the beliefs of unbelief can chafe when, in spite of their greater comprehensiveness, they contradict aspirations that are central to the unbeliever—which in the worst cases makes them self-refuting, a problem Chesterton calls "the suicide of thought."

To relativize the relativists through table turning is to apply to relativists (and skeptics) the relativism (and skepticism) they apply to others, thus pushing them out toward the negative consequences of their own beliefs. With a good cigar and a glass of port in hand, Professor Eames had one attitude toward life and death in his comfortable college rooms, but quite another when grimly hanging onto to the buttress while staring down the barrel of a gun. When turned on him, his philosophy of life was cold comfort.

As Berger points out, the strategy rests on two assumptions. Relativism and skepticism are different: the former claiming that truth is dependent on the person, and the latter that truth is unknowable, but they each entail a hidden double standard—they are both inconsistent and incomplete. They each pour the acids of their relativism and skepticism over all sorts of issues, but jealously guard their own beliefs. The second assumption is that there is a link between consistency and clarity. The task of countering relativism, Berger writes, is to "see the relativity business to its very end."[6] Press skepticism and relativism to their consistent conclusions and the result is surprising. Far from paralyzing thought, skepticism and relativism are themselves relativized, the debunker is debunked, and what emerges is an almost pristine realization of the importance of truth.

Again and again the lesson is simple: all thoughts can be thought, but not all thoughts can be lived. So we should never stop halfway with skepticism, but insist on pressing ideas uncompromisingly to their conclusion. When hearts and minds collide with the wall, they will have reached the limits of their position and may then be open to rethinking. In this sense reality is what we run into when we are wrong, for when we are right there is no wall to run into—only the freedom to run. "There are times," Vaclav Havel wrote, "when we must sink to the bottom of our misery to understand truth, just as we must descend to the bottom of a well to see the stars in broad daylight."[7]

PROPHETIC SUBVERSION

Is this table turning simply a technique smuggled in by the back door at this advanced stage of the game? Far from it, for it grows from the heart of our understanding of the biblical anatomy of unbelief, and of what it takes to subvert unbelief. We can appreciate the importance of this strategy at several levels. First, turning the tables is God's own characteristic response to disobedience and unbelief. When humans abuse, suppress and exploit the truth, God becomes the fierce unmasker of lies, the grand iconoclast tearing down idols, and the radical debunker of myths. Three times in the seminal passage in Romans St. Paul says, "God gave them over" (Rom 1:24, 26, 28). Those who rebelled against God chose to follow the lusts of their hearts, their degrading passions and their depraved minds, so God gave them over to these very things. They had chosen, and their choices had consequences. Sin was the punishment of sin. In reaping what they had sown, they had judged themselves.

This debunking theme runs throughout Scripture. "I will make justice the measuring line and righteousness the level," God declared through Isaiah. "Then hail will sweep away the refuge of lies, and the waters will overflow the secret place" (Is 28:17). "I will tear down the wall which you have plastered over with whitewash and bring it down to the ground," the Lord said through Ezekiel, "so that its foundation is laid bare" (Ezek 13:14).

And many times God does the debunking by turning the tables directly. He gives people over to what they choose. He drives people—or simply leaves people—to the logic of their own bad choices. When Israel rejected God's kingship and wished to have a king for themselves like the surrounding nations, God's response was "Take them at their word and appoint them a king" (1 Sam 8:22 REB). Their choice was wrong, and their choice would have disastrous consequences, but the best way to make them see it was to push them to the logic of their choice. If you insist, persist in it. Or again, the Lord says,

> Israel did not obey Me.
> So I gave them over to the stubbornness of their heart,
> To walk in their own devices. (Ps 81:11-12)

Go ahead if you so choose, God says, but know what you are doing and where it is leading you.

Second, the same dynamic lies at the heart of prophetic subversion. Turning the tables was exactly the prophet Elijah's famous challenge to Israel in the ninth century. The great crowd of the people listening to the prophet were fence sitters, just as many modern people are advocates of what W. H. Auden called "Christian heresies"—they hold to beliefs that could not have come into existence except in a culture founded on the Jewish and Christian faiths.[8] If Baal and not YHWH is God, then follow Baal, Elijah cried, and offered the prophets of Baal the first opportunity to verify their god. With the king and queen opposing him, and the bulk of the people sitting uneasily on the fence between the Lord and Baal, Elijah knew that pious calls to return to God would have fallen on deaf and divided ears. He had to mount the challenge on their grounds.

For if YHWH is God, then Baal is not, and the fastest way for the people to see it was to push them toward the false faith that was bound to be falsified by reality. The disproof came first and cleared the ground for the proof, for with the false falsified, the true could be verified. "The LORD—He is God! The LORD—He is God!" was the people's conclusion with heartfelt conviction (1 Kings 18:39).

In strong contrast, one of the marks of the false prophets was that they failed to confront and subvert the lies and idols of the people. As the great lament cried,

> Your prophets have seen for you
> False and foolish *visions*;
> And they have not exposed your iniquity
> So as to restore you from captivity. (Lam 2:14)

Third, the same logic runs down the Christian centuries, though it is not unique to Christians. Georg Lukács, the Hungarian Marxist intellectual, tried to follow the same practice. "Do not stop halfway, but follow the idea uncompromisingly to its conclusion; the sparks produced by the collision of your head with the wall show that you have reached the limits."[9] But from Jesus onward, the dynamic is crystal clear in Christian proclamation. "The tree is known by its fruit," Jesus said—not by its seed (Mt 12:33). If you had tried to persuade the prodigal son to return home the day he left home, would he have listened? If you had spoken to him the day he hit the pigsty, would you have needed to persuade him? Always "see where it leads to," St. Augustine advised when dealing with false ideas.[10] Follow it out to the "absolutely ruddy end," C. S. Lewis remarked with characteristic Englishness.[11] "Push them to the logic of their presuppositions," Francis Schaeffer used to say. Too many varieties of unbelief are halfway houses. Too many unbelievers have not had the courage or the consistency to follow their thoughts all the way home.

It is time for the new atheists to face that challenge. Their boast has been that from Democritus and Lucretius onwards, they are the ones who face up to the nature of reality unflinchingly, however bleak it may prove to be. Nature, Lucretius said, was breathtakingly beautiful, though blind, soulless and purposeless. But the fact is that again and again they cheat—holding that certain things were true simply because they have to be. For example, Democritus taught that the atoms were absolutely determined, so all human actions were equally determined. But Epicurus and Lucretius were also moralists, who believed in the importance of free will and human responsibility. They therefore held that the atoms must "swerve," *though only rarely and very little*, if there was to be an opening for freedom. "If the atoms never swerve so as to originate some new movement that will snap the bands of fate, the everlasting sequence of cause and effect," Lucretius wrote, "what is the source of the free will possessed by living things throughout the earth?"[12]

In a similar way, the painter and avowed atheist Francis Bacon insisted on giving a central place to chance and mystery. Just as Lucretius believed that the random "swerve" of the atoms kept open a space for human freedom, so it was a central article of Bacon's faith that chance—such as a slip of the painter's hand, a dribble of paint or a collision of shapes—injected into his work the freedom of the unforeseen that a painter could introduce in no other way. Equally he rejected all explanations and interpretations of his work. If it was clearly understood that the paintings said nothing and meant nothing, and he himself had nothing to say, each viewer had the freedom to make his own response. In short, our brave new atheists live *as if* such things as freedom are true because they need them to be. Put more simply, they cheat.

Last, table turning lies at the very heart of the dynamic of Christian conversion. Death comes before life, law before grace, conviction before regeneration, and so the good news is the best news ever to those who know they are in a bad situation. Looking back over his earlier pagan life with gratitude, Augustine prayed, "You were always present, angry and merciful at once, strewing the pangs of bitterness over all my lawless pleasures to lead me to look for others unallied with pain. You meant me to find them nowhere but in yourself, O Lord, for . . . you smite so that you may heal."[13]

Needless to say, no one comes to believe in God because of table turning or through any purely negative arguments. What they do is *disbelieve what they believed before*, and they then become seekers who are open to the possibility of faith. True faith itself never grows from such negative arguments. It has to be based on what is positive—first, a positive conviction of the adequacy of Christian faith, second a positive conviction of the truth of the gospel, and supremely, a positive encounter with Jesus himself.

HOIST BY THEIR OWN PETARD YET AGAIN

Turning the tables is especially useful when encountering skeptics in a skeptical age like ours today. In a world congenial to skepticism, skeptics love to play the skeptic's card nonchalantly as if it were the royal flush that trumped all other cards and could not be countered. For many, it has become the skeptics' way of hanging out a "Do Not Disturb" sign. Simply raise a skeptical objection and retire from all argument.

But of course, the simplest response is to turn such skepticism back on itself. When I studied philosophy as an undergraduate in the 1960s, an Arctic chill still hung in the air that froze any serious appreciation of faith. One source had been the Vienna Circle's philosophy of logical positivism and the celebrated "verification principle" of A. J. Ayer at Oxford University. Only that which could be tested by the five senses could be verified as true, he insisted. Theology was therefore "nonsense," or as it was famously said, "The word G-O-D is less meaningful than the word d-o-g."

The trouble for Professor Ayer was that his verification principle could not verify itself—it was self-refuting. For to accept as truth only what can be tested by the senses is a principle that cannot itself be tested by the senses. So it too is nonsense by its own criteria. Ayer's approach, he later admitted, was a "blind alley." Years later I enjoyed a conversation with him on the train between London and Oxford, when we found ourselves the only people in the compartment. Although then retired and knighted as Professor Sir Alfred J. Ayer, he was candid about the failure of his principle. "I wish I had been more consistent," he said to me. "Any iconoclast who brandishes a debunker's sword should be required to demonstrate it publicly on his own cherished beliefs."

Ayer's false demand has both ancient precedents and modern counterparts. Celsus insisted that Christian teaching must pass the "Greek proof," and be assessed by the philosophical standards of the day in order to show that it was reasonable. Similarly, in our more scientific age, many people demand that all claims to truth must undergo strict verification procedures if they are to be given the hallmark of truth, despite the fact that many things they trust and value could never pass such test—history and love, for a start.

The same challenge could be equally thrown back to Feuerbach and his dismissal of faith as a projection, Marx and his scorn for faith as the flowers on the chains, Freud and his debunking of faith as wish fulfillment, and Dawkins and his often stated creed that all religious beliefs are only irrational. In each case the debunker's sword appears to have morphed into a boomerang and their dismissals have recoiled on themselves. The same is true of Nietzsche and his long baleful influence on our generation. If truth is only a matter of perspective, are his own books no more than his own perspective? If truth is only an expression of a resentment-based will to power, are we to judge his own claims by his own criteria?

LOGIC AND LIFE

The enormous power in table turning is obvious, but it raises questions too. An immediate one, which we will leave till a later chapter, is what if people are to push us as Christians to be true to what we say we believe? The answer,

I will argue, is that we should welcome it. On the one hand, the outcome of our not living true to our faith is hypocrisy. And on the other, living in truth is the biblical way of saying that we are living the way of Jesus more closely, and therefore being faithful and becoming more like him. The more practical question here is, how in fact do we push people toward the logical consequences of their unbelief?

Some simple considerations may be helpful. First, we should always remember that *the full consequences of a person's position have to be seen in life and not only in words*. It is important to take a person's worldview seriously, but it is a mistake to confuse persons' worldviews with them as people, or even their world-and-life view with them. The fact is that very few people are perfect, card-carrying examples of what they say they believe. Each person is their own version of their world-and-life view *lived in their own way*, and it is that living person we must deal with, not an idealized textbook example of a worldview. It is therefore a mistake to think that when we talk of the "logic" of someone's position, we are referring to the strictly logical, the rational, the intellectual and the verbal. To do this is to reduce apologetics to a game of chess, with the apologist cast as the Grand Master expected to have a computer mind with brilliant set moves and a calculated strategy for checkmating all comers.

Very few apologists are like that. Even if they were, we can be sure that the people we talk to are not like that. Very few people are strictly and consistently logical, so to catch their smaller inconsistencies is merely to annoy them and put them off. Jesus spoke of "the treasures of the heart," the things that are deep in the center of our lives that matter to us supremely and that we guard most tenaciously. Our challenge is to find the treasures of people's hearts, and then to find contradictions that mean everything to them at that level.

Many years ago I was asked to make a case for the Christian faith at a university in the north of England. A professor lingered behind after the lecture, eager to talk further. He said that neither he nor his wife had shown the slightest interest in faith before, and their interest in talking to me had nothing to do with my lecture. Indeed, they had been notoriously resistant to students sharing their faith with them over many years. He was in his mid-fifties and his wife was fifteen years younger.

For years, the professor said, he and his wife had practiced a very open relationship. He had slept with other women and she with other men. But then, to their surprise and delight, they had had a baby daughter. And almost immediately they both realized they did not want to bring her up with the ethics by which they had lived. "We have always had an open marriage," he said, "but the younger generation has taken the openness further, to the point of chaos. We don't want that for our daughter."

I have rarely talked to a professor who was more open, but the reason was touching. In a beautiful way, both he and his wife realized that somehow they loved their little girl even more than they loved each other, and wanting the very best for her, they were open to faith as never before. The challenge of the gospel had touched the treasure of their hearts and opened them at a level never touched before.

Life, then, and not just logic, is all-important. When the young Augustine sought out Ambrose of Milan to learn from his rhetoric, the bishop was wise enough to see that Augustine needed more than arguments to draw him to faith. He needed to live more in order to think more deeply, so Ambrose even brushed off the earnest entreaties of Augustine's mother Monica. Later, Augustine saw the wisdom of what Ambrose had done.

> My mother asked him, as a favor, to have a talk with me, so that he might refute my errors, drive the evil out of my mind, and replace it with good. He often did this when he found suitable pupils, but he refused to do it for me—a wise decision, as I afterwards realized. He told her that I was still unripe for instruction because, as she had told him, I was brimming over with the novelty of the heresy. . . . "Leave him alone," he said. "Just pray to God for him. From his own reading he will discover his mistakes."[14]

Unless we remember this point, our apologetics can sound like sophistry and logic chopping, and leave people unmoved. Sophists could answer any position and its opposite with equal conviction, and their very brilliance roused suspicion. They could make night into noon, and noon into night, right wrong and wrong right. But while minds were dazzled and left spinning, they were often unconvinced. This point matters for Christian apologists in two particular situations. One is when we make the mistake of attacking a straw man argument, and not the real position of the person we are talking to. The other is when we speak to people who are hurting. "But what does your argument prove?" Job protested to his heartless friends. "Do you intend to reprove *my* words, when the words of one in despair belong to the wind?" (Job 6:25-26).

Looking for the treasure of the heart, and therefore for the consequences of logic in life, is not an assault on logic, but on its misuse. It may be that a person's head is muddled, but more often the problem is that people's heads are not where their hearts are, and what matters for the apologist is where a person's heart is. The truth is that even logic can be put at the service of the crooked timber of our humanity. For logic alone can easily be made into a diversion, and can therefore become a shelter from God and his truth.

Unbelief can be extremely logical, but like an elephant trudging around and around in its moat in a zoo, such logic can be circular thinking that has got itself into a bad rut. Chesterton often came up against this vicious circle in people he engaged, and he used his wit and humor to get round it. "The moment his mere reason moves, it moves in the old circular rut; he will go round and round his logical circle."[15]

After C. E. M. Joad's conversion, he looked back on his years as a rationalist and a fierce critic of religion.

Certainly I engaged in controversies; admittedly I wrote a book on the subject, but the many words I wrote and said were not the expression of a mind engaged in thinking out those things afresh, but of a mind which was living on the deposit of thought that it had laid down in the past. I was stirring and re-applying, but not adding to the old material. In fact I was like a *rentier* living on the income from the capital his ancestors had accumulated, for it is as his ancestor that the middle-aged man of forty is entitled to regard the young man of twenty who formed his mind.[16]

Once again, that point cuts both ways. Forty-, fifty- and sixty-year-old Christians may also be trudging around in the same old ruts that their younger selves laid down in their college years. But the truth is that they shouldn't and they needn't, for if the Christian faith is true, it will be proved true the wider and wider the experience of life it engages. But that is not so for unbelief. George Orwell wryly dismissed H. G. Wells, the rationalist, as "too sane to understand the modern world."[17] Like Augustine on the journey that later led to faith, many people do not need more fresh arguments. They need fresh air.

Questions That Raise Questions

A second consideration is that we should always use questions to raise questions. Questions have their own subversive quality, which we will explore later, but there is a special role for questions in table turning. As stressed in the introduction, far too much Christian evangelism and apologetics is based on the assumption that almost everyone is open, interested and needy—when most people most of the time are quite simply not.

Needless to say, that condemns many of our efforts (and books, lectures, seminars and discussions) to be well-intentioned but ineffectual. As Harry Blamires complained decades ago, "they cater for those who are already believers, half-believers, or discontented unbelievers. They cater abundantly for uninstructed believers, for people on the brink of Christian self-committal, and for those who are uneasy in their atheism, their agnosticism, and their ill-defined theism."[18]

If this is so, it means that in our age most people are untroubled rather than unreached, unconcerned rather than unconvinced, and they need questions as much as answers—or questions that raise questions that require answers that prompt people to become genuine seekers. William Wilberforce faced the polite indifference of wealthy upper-class society in the late eighteenth century. His answer was to devise "launchers"—questions and approaches that punctured the invisible social barriers of the day and goaded people to think. The most famous was his antislavery tract: the small Wedgwood plate with the head of a slave in chains in the center, and around the edge the question: "Am I not a man and a brother?" Questions, Wilberforce knew, were more subversive than statements, and with the prestige of his friend Josiah Wedgwood's china, the little plate could raise a question that reverberated through aristocratic society.

The goal is to use questions to raise questions, and so to puncture whatever are the walls of indifference, and to do so in a style and language that speaks to the person we are engaging with. This means that we raise questions where people are. So if only a minority read serious books, we are raising questions in our serious books only for a minority. It also means that some media are better at raising questions than others, just as others are better at answering them. Films, plays, sketches, poems and cartoons, for example, are often better at raising questions than serious books, though the same books gain the edge when it comes to answering questions.

But whatever the style of the question and the medium in which it is raised, the point is the same: to probe the consequences of unbelief, and to challenge people to follow the logic of their ideas through to the end. Some Christians have won an insufferable reputation for always dispensing answers, even when no one has a question. Raise questions well, and we will be known for the searching questions we raise, to which the good news can be looked to for the only satisfactory answers. "I should therefore like," Pascal wrote in *Pensées*, "to *arouse* in man the desire to find truth."[19]

THEIR PROPHETS, NOT OURS

The third consideration is that, just as it is more effective to argue on the other person's ground, so it is wiser to argue from the other person's prophets, rather than our own. This is not only a matter of familiarity but authority. When St. Paul was in a synagogue, he preached from the Torah, but when he addressed the Athenian philosophers on the Areopagus, he quoted pagan poets from long before Jesus—the sixth-century B.C. Cretan poet Epimenides (in whom "we live and move and have our being") and the third-century B.C. Greek poet Aratus ("for we are indeed his offspring" [Acts 17:28 ESV]). Looking back again, St. Augustine understood the crucial role that pagan philosophers had in undermining his earlier paganism. "Traditional education," he wrote, "taught me that Jupiter punishes the wicked with his thunderbolts and yet commits adultery himself. The two roles are quite incompatible."[20] Later, after reading Cicero's *Hortensius*, he wrote, "All my empty dreams suddenly lost their charm and my heart began to throb with a bewildering passion for the wisdom of eternal truth."[21]

Reflecting on how the pagan philosophers had been so instrumental in his journey toward faith, Augustine commented, "These books served to remind me to return to my own self."[22] Many centuries later, Pascal drily counseled the same course for anyone searching for God: "Make them look for him among the philosophers, skeptics and dogmatists, who will worry the man who seeks."[23]

Chesterton expressed the same point in his own inimitable way. He had been struck by the "odd effect of the great agnostics arousing doubts deeper than their own."

I never read a line of Christian apologetics. I read as little as I can of them now. It was Huxley and Herbert Spencer and Bradlaugh who brought me back to orthodox theology. They sowed in my mind my first wild doubts of doubt. Our grandmothers were quite right when they said that Tom Paine and the free-thinkers unsettled the mind. They do. They unsettled mine horribly. The rationalist made me question whether reason was of any use whatsoever; and when I had finished Herbert Spencer I had got as far as doubting (for the first time) whether evolution had occurred at all. As I laid down the last of Colonel Ingersoll's atheistic lectures the dreadful thought broke across my mind, "Almost thou persuades me to be a Christian." I was in a desperate way.[24]

I learned this lesson when I wrote my first book *The Dust of Death*, which included a chapter reviewing and critiquing the influx of the Eastern religions in the 1960s. I included the story of Issa, the eighteenth-century Haiku poet from Japan. Through a succession of sad events, his wife and all his five children died. Grieving each time, he went to the Zen Master and received the same consolation: "Remember the world is dew." Dew is transient and ephemeral. The sun rises and the dew is gone. So too is suffering and death in this world of illusion, so the mistake is to become too engaged. Remember the world is dew. Be more detached, and transcend the engagement of mourning that prolongs the grief.

After one of his children died, Issa went home unconsoled, and wrote one of his most famous poems. Translated into English it reads,

The world is dew.
The world is dew.
And yet.
And yet.

The entire logic of Buddhism is in the first two lines, whereas the yearning of a father's heart cries out in the last two lines. Over the years since then, I have met a score of people who were on the road to the East either physically or spiritually, but were stopped in their tracks and turned around by that story in my book. The brief mention of a single one of their own prophets was worth more than hundreds of pages of Christian argument, and so it often is.

OUR KNEES OR OUR HEELS

What can we expect when we pray for people, and then probe and push them gently but firmly toward the place where they can see the unwelcome logic of their position? At first, we will not know where the tension in their worldview can be found. It is something we can assume because of the teaching of Scripture, but we may not be able to see it in advance. But assuming it provides an assured point of contact—the tension as the *meeting point*. Whatever people say about God—whether they ignore him, deny him, hate him, or scorn him—we always know two things about them: first, that they themselves are made in the image of God; and second, that they are living in the world of God's reality. So whatever they claim, we can be sure that there is both truth and falsehood in their belief, and the tension can be found somewhere.

As we talk and the conversation goes deeper, there will come a point at which the fact of the tension goes beyond providing us with a *meeting point* and becomes a potential *pressure point*. It then reveals where the treasure of the person's heart is and where their beliefs clash with the safeguarding of the treasure. Often, though not always, we become aware of the pressure point before they do—though it is always a matter of spiritual discernment, and it is rarely evident at the outset of a conversation or relationship.

Quite obviously, our Lord had instant discernment when he spoke to people. Again and again, the Gospels show us how he knew at once where peoples' hearts were. For the rich young ruler, for example, Jesus knew that his great wealth was his issue, the barrier to his refusal to pay the cost of discipleship, so he put his finger on it immediately. We do not have discernment like that, so we have to take the time to get to know people, to love them, to pray for them and to listen to their stories. Then, like the builder of a stone wall who takes a stone and tap, tap, tap, taps it gently until he hits the fault line and it splits easily, we have to find the fault line in the other person's thinking.

At some point the person will recognize the tension because it touches the treasure of the heart and it matters. The tension will then have gone from a *meeting point* to a *pressure point* to a *danger point*. This last term comes from Nietzsche, who observed how people refuse to face the logic of their philosophy squarely. Instead, they duck and weave like a boxer, and try to bounce off the ropes when backed into a corner of their own making. Nietzsche was impatient with such thinkers. He attacked Jacob

Burckhardt because he would not look nihilism in the white of the eye. He referred to the Swiss historian's lectures with "their profound thoughts, and their silently abrupt breaks and twists *as soon as they touch the danger point.*"[25]

If you have ever witnessed someone who is close to or at the danger point in their self-examination before God, it is a sobering moment. Only God knows when that moment truly and completely comes. We will not always know, and it is not our business to know, but it is surely the moment when, before God, they know that from then on they are without excuse. They have seen the truth, they know the truth, and they are responsible to the truth that they now know. All fig leaves are stripped away, and all alibis exposed. In their heart of hearts they know where they stand, and they are fully responsible for the decisive moment of truth. As Franz Kafka noted, it is only the biblical view of time that makes it possible to speak of the Day of Judgment in the way the Bible does at the end of history. The Day of Judgment is also "a summary court in perpetual session."[26]

Needless to say, the moment of truth does not mean that everyone is persuaded by the truth, for even at that point they always have the final choice: *to fall on their knees or to turn on their heels.* For those who fall on their knees, it is the moment when their unbelief is shown up as inadequate, when they face up fully to the reality that shows it up, and when they accept the logic of God's truth that points undeniably to God himself. Joad described how he hit that sober moment of truth as a philosopher: "The rationalist-optimist philosophy, by the light of which I had done my best to live, came to seem intolerably trivial and superficial . . . unable to withstand the bleaker winds of the twentieth century. I abandoned it and found myself a Christian."[27]

The opposite response is equally possible. A person can turn on their heels. Like a boxer bouncing off the ropes or a yachtsman changing tack, someone can try to evade the logic and sidestep the evident force of the truth. A feature of such maneuver is that people often go from one extreme to the other, with switched arguments and about-turns that are baffling. Jesus himself encountered this response from his critics. One moment they said that he was a libertine, and the next that he was a spoilsport. Chesterton encountered this tactic repeatedly:

One rationalist had hardly done calling Christianity a nightmare before another began to call it a fool's paradise. This puzzled me; the charges seemed inconsistent. Christianity could not at once be the black mask on a white world or the white mask on a black world. The state of the Christian could not at once be so comfortable that he was a coward to cling to it, and so uncomfortable that he was a fool to stand it.[28]

C. S. Lewis commented on the same response:

Such people put up a version of Christianity suitable for a child of six and make that the object of their attack. When you try and explain the Christian doctrine as it is really held by an instructed adult, they complain that you are making their heads turn round, and that it is all too complicated, and that if there really were a God they are sure He would have made religion simple.[29]

For those who fall on their knees, the prospects are bright. At that point the work of the apologist is finished and the very different, simpler and more positive work of the evangelist can take over. The good news is good news, and the party may soon be on for the return of the prodigal son or daughter. But for those who turn on their heels, and for those who squirt out evasions like a scuttle fish squirting ink to make its escape, our work is far from over, though the core objection is clearer. For these people the prospects are sober and the reason is plain. When a friend told Francis Bacon that he would prefer not to have an eternal soul than to live in eternal torment, the painter replied with a grim realism that people are "so attracted to their egos that they'd probably rather have the torment than simple annihilation."[30] At that point we as apologists must either retrace our steps and seek to do a better job at turning the tables, or we must try a different and more positive approach, as we will consider next.

• 7 •

Triggering
the Signals

At the outbreak of the Second World War in 1939, most people who knew the young English poet W. H. Auden would have considered him an unlikely prospect for becoming a Christian. Along with his Oxford contemporaries Stephen Spender and Cecil Day Lewis, he was one of the most influential English-speaking poets of his age, and many considered him a prophet. He was also an atheist, a left-wing socialist, a homosexual and a veteran of the Spanish Civil War, where he had volunteered on the Republican side for seven weeks. There might not have seemed much in his life that would draw him to the Christian faith. But what happened surprised even some of his closest friends.

When Auden arrived in the United States with Christopher Isherwood in January 1939, he was not religious, and he had not been since he was thirteen at Gresham's School in England. Both his grandfathers had been clergymen, but he described the religion he encountered at boarding school as "nothing but vague uplift, as flat as an old bottle of soda water." "At thirteen," he wrote, "I was confirmed. To say that shortly afterwards I lost my faith would be melodramatic and false. I simply lost interest."[1] From then on, confirmed by his time at Christ Church, Oxford, he was convinced that "people only love God when no one else will love them." Needless to say, the times in which he lived were hardly conducive to faith either. In his famous poem "September 1, 1939," which he wrote in a dive on 52nd Street in New York, Auden described the dismal 1930s as "a low dishonest decade."[2]

Two experiences, however, stood out among those that jolted Auden into rethinking. The first had been earlier in 1933, when he was a schoolmaster at the Downs School in the Malvern Hills. Sitting with three fellow teachers, he was suddenly overwhelmed by the sense that all their existence somehow had infinite value and that he loved them for themselves. But why? Years later he described this experience as a "Vision of Agape" (Love).[3]

The second and deeper experience came in New York two months after he had written the poem "September 1, 1939." He was in a cinema in Yorkville on the Upper East Side of Manhattan, which unbeknown to him was still largely a German-speaking area. Eager to follow news of the course of the war, he went to see *Sieg in Poland*, a documentary of the Nazi invasion and conquest of Poland. S. S. Storm Troopers were bayoneting women and children, and members of the audience cried out in support of their fellow-countrymen, "Kill them! Kill them!"

Auden was horrified. His philosophy of life at the time was a broad mix of liberal-socialist-democratic opinions, following his earlier intellectual odyssey through the dogmas of Sigmund Freud and Karl Marx. But one thread had always linked his successive convictions—a belief in the natural goodness of humankind. Whether the solution to the world's problems lay in politics, education or psychology, he believed that once the problems were addressed, the world would be happy because humanity was good.

Suddenly, however, as Auden watched the S. S. savagery and heard the brutal response of the audience, he knew he had been wrong. With everything in him he knew intuitively and beyond any doubt that he was encountering absolute evil and that it must be judged and condemned absolutely. There had to be a reason why Hitler was "utterly wrong." Profoundly shaken, Auden reflected on this experience. Just as in the nineteenth-century Dostoevsky's belief in the goodness of the Russian peasant had been shattered by the peasant depravity he encountered in Siberia, so Auden's facile confidence in human goodness had collapsed like a pricked balloon.

For Auden, the experience thrust up two troubling issues—how to account for the undeniable evil he had encountered, and how to justify condemning it with an unconditional and absolute judgment. After all, for educated people like him there were no "absolutes" of any kind in his universe. (A favorite phrase of William James was "Damn the absolute!" and in *The*

Portrait of the Artist as a Young Man, James Joyce's Stephen Daedalus repeats his mantra, "the Absolute is dead.")[4] To judge anything absolutely was naive and unthinkable, the sort of thing done only by the great unwashed. Following Nietzsche, all self-respecting philosophers had abandoned absolute judgments for relativism. And long before the day of political correctness, psychologists had thrown over absolutes in favor of nonjudgmental tolerance and acceptance.

Auden raised his concerns with his friends. "The English intellectuals who now cry to Heaven against the evil incarnated in Hitler have no Heaven to cry to," he told one friend. It was clear to him that liberalism had a fatal flaw. "The whole trend of liberal thought," he wrote the next year, "has been to undermine faith in the absolute. . . . It has tried to make reason the judge. . . . But since life is a changing process . . . the attempt to find a humanistic basis of keeping a promise works logically with the conclusion, 'I can break it whenever I feel convenient.'"[5] He spoke similarly in an interview in the *Observer*, "Unless one is prepared to take a relativist view that all morals are a matter of personal taste, one could hardly avoid asking the question: 'If, as I am convinced, the Nazis are wrong and we are right, what is it that validates our values and invalidates theirs?'"[6]

The only remedy to use when facing such evil, Auden concluded, was the renewal of "faith in the absolute." Or as he posed the challenge in a poem written soon after his visit to the Yorkville cinema: "Either we serve the unconditional / Or some Hitlerian monster will supply / An iron convention to do evil by."[7]

SIGNALS OF TRANSCENDENCE

Let me be clear. Auden had not become a Christian believer when he left the cinema, hit by this insight. That step came later. But the experience raised a sharp question for him because "I thought I had done with Christianity for good."[8] What had happened was that he left the cinema a seeker. He was clearly on his way toward faith, or more accurately he was on his way away to some new position, and definitely moving away from his old atheist faith that had failed him. He was a seeker after an unconditional absolute by which to judge that Hitler was absolutely wrong. Life had raised a titanic question for him, so much so that his whole life and way of thinking had been called into question by the experience. And the experience was one that demanded an answer, and so urgently that it brooked no evasion or delay. What he believed previously no longer satisfied him, and he was now searching for an answer that in the face of the titanic challenges of war, he knew had to be truly satisfactory.

Auden's experience is an example of what Peter Berger calls "signals of transcendence."[9] As Berger explains in *A Rumor of Angels*, signals of transcendence are "phenomena that are to be found within the domain of our 'natural' reality but that appear to point beyond that reality."[10] Such experiences beep like a signal, impelling us to transcend our present awareness and think more deeply, widely and seriously. The signal's message is a double one: it acts as a contradiction and a desire. It acts as a contradiction in that it punctures the adequacy of what we once believed. And it arouses in us a desire or longing for a new answer that is surer, richer and more adequate than whatever it was we believed before—which has patently failed.

In short, a signal of transcendence points beyond one belief and points toward another belief—or at the very least, it points toward what might be true or would have to be true if the signal's pointing is to have any satisfactory ending.

Alberto Giacometti, the Swiss sculptor and close friend of Pablo Picasso, used to describe such experiences as a "hole torn in life." In his case, he was shocked to his core by the death of a close friend when he was nineteen, and the questions raised obsessed him for more than a quarter of a century and shaped him as the artist of the fragile and the impermanent.[11] The outcome of Giacometti's search was very different from Auden's, but the "signal" or the "hole torn in life" was similar.

Others have used a plethora of words to describe such experiences, including *clues, hints, spurs, jolts, triggers, homing signals, points of bafflement, scene shifters, epiphanies, transcendent impulses* and *metaphysical hunger*. But they all attempt to capture experiences that make people realize that there must be "something more" in life than they had ever imagined, experiences that beckon them to the very door of "worlds not realized," as Wordsworth described them.[12] Sometimes such experiences are gentle. They leave only an aching longing for whatever that "something more" might be. At other times, they are stronger and more disruptive, and act as catalysts that prompt people to abandon what they once believed and set out at once as seekers for a better and more satisfying answer.

No one should confuse a signal of transcendence with any discovery that may or not be the eventual outcome of the experience. The signal is only a signal, a signpost and not the place to which it points. The signal is therefore only a pointer and not a proof, and there are always at least two gaps between the signal and the discovery. First, there is a logical gap. The signal is not itself the discovery, and people with the same experience of a signal may move toward very different destinations. We may debate and disagree with them as to whether they have followed the signal attentively and interpreted it well, but the point is that the signal itself does not conclusively determine the destination.

C. S. Lewis pointed out that culture at large and such signals of transcendence in particular are especially helpful in prompting cultured people to think and search, because they compel them to see that "reality is very odd, and that the ultimate truth, whatever it may be, *must* have the characteristics of strangeness." At the same time, he warned that there was a danger in idolizing such experiences in themselves and therefore of failing to go beyond them. Those who make that mistake have stopped too soon. They have reached only "the suburbs of Jerusalem" and the "outskirts of heaven," but have yet to reach the city itself.[13] Too much gazing at the moon may make someone a lunatic, he said, but it is an equal mistake to forget that the beauty of the moon is only "sunlight at second hand," so we would be wise to press on to see the sun itself.[14]

Arthur Koestler was one who heard such a signal but never followed through. Indeed, many years after his experience he and his wife committed suicide in a pact together. Yet he was quite clear about the time when he was young and first experienced such an epiphany.

> I was lying on my back under a blue sky on a hill slope in Buda. . . . The paradox
> of infinity suddenly pierced my brain as if I had been stung by a wasp. . . . The
> idea that infinity would remain an unsolved riddle was unbearable. The thirst
> for the absolute is a stigma which marks those unable to find satisfaction in
> the relative world of the here and now. . . . The infinite as a target was replaced
> by Utopias of one kind or another.[15]

Second, there is a time gap between the signal and the discovery. For some, the gap between the signal and the discovery, the question and answer, may be so short as to be unnoticeable. In such cases, the signal instantaneously points people to an answer that they see and grasp gratefully. For others, the gap may mean years and even decades of agonized seeking, sifting and sorting, before they make the discovery. But whether fast or slow, the journey toward meaning is one that the signal triggers.

Whatever we call such experiences—the Bible speaks of "eternity in our hearts" and the poet William Wordsworth wrote of "intimations of immortality"—what matters for apologists is to be able to understand the basis of the experiences and why we can expect them and count on them, and then encourage people to listen to such signals in their own lives—and to follow them wherever they lead, whatever it is they say they believe or disbelieve before they hear the signal.

THE TRUTH IS STILL THE TRUTH

Desire and longing play a key part in many philosophies of life down the centuries—most notably the Hindu, the Buddhist, the Greek, the Jewish and Christian, the Greek one shaping so much of Western thinking from Plato and the Neoplatonists to the Troubadours and the Romantics. Whereas Stoics and Buddhists had an essentially negative view of desire that should always be transcended, Plato and his followers claimed that all humans experience longings and desires because we are incomplete, and we are incomplete because we have essentially been "cut in half" and we long for our "other half." As the matching half of a whole that is in constant search for the other half that matches us, we are each moved and moved forward by our desires and our longings.

In the classical Greek and Roman perspective, there were four central passions (which were the counterpart of the four cardinal virtues): desire, fear, joy and grief. As Robert Wilken explains, "Desire is the yearning to possess something we do not have, and fear is the aversion to something we do not want. To these two passions were added joy, the possession of what we desire, and grief, having to undergo what we fear."[16]

The Jewish and Christian account of desire is quite different from that of the Buddhist and Stoic philosophies. There is no call to transcend or extinguish desire itself, but desire is seen as either positive or negative depending on its goal. Is it directed toward God or toward the self? And over against Plato, in the biblical account the problem is not that we have been "cut in half" but that we have been "cut off." Through our disobedience to God, we have been alienated from God and his presence. So we now live "east of Eden." We are away from the home we were given to live in. We are all prodigals now, and we are all in a far country. Yet however far away we go, there is always a longing for home that will not go away. We have been cut off, so there is always a homesickness that no other home can satisfy, a desire that no other satisfaction can fulfill, a yearning that can be assuaged nowhere else, and a restlessness that finds no rest in any other stopping place. St. Augustine's famous opening prayer to God in *Confessions* is the most celebrated expression of this view: "You have made us for Yourself, and our hearts are restless until they find their rest in You."[17]

There are therefore two sources of the desires that lie behind signals of transcendence. One is the fall, which has cut us off from God, yet has left us with a longing for what we have lost that we can never shake off. East of Eden there is always and inescapably "something missing." The other source is history, as certain generations reject or lose what earlier generations could take for granted, yet they never quite get over the sense of loss that is never stilled. (Philosopher Iris Murdoch: "But is there something where God used to be?")[18] After attending a strangely flat memorial service in 1991 for a friend who was an atheist, philosopher Jürgen Habermas wrote a famous essay, "An Awareness of What Is Missing." As many people have said to me over the years, there must be "something more." There always seems to be "something missing." Without it, life in the advanced modern world raises the nagging thought that we have too much to live with and too little to live for.

What this means for apologetics is that the universal presence of *desire* and *longing* in human thinking is the opposite side of the coin of the universal presence of *unintended consequences* in human thinking. One comes from the positive passions of desire and joy—the yearning for what we no longer have but long to possess again, and the other from the negative passions of fear and grief—the aversion to what we do not want to face, and the grief at where we have gone wrong. Importantly, these passions are not physical drives, such as hunger and thirst, but passions of the mind and heart.

The first two are positive in their thrust, and come from the suppressed truths that the unbeliever's faith cannot allow for. The second two are negative, and come from the equally suppressed truths of where the unbeliever's faith will lead to. But whatever their source, they are all powerful motivating forces, and they grow directly from the anatomy of unbelief that the apostle Paul describes in Romans as "suppressing the truth in unrighteousness" (Rom 1:18). Unless we bow to God's truth, we never have the full truth, and we are always tugging and pulling (but failing) to stretch the truth we have to cover the full reality we encounter.

In talking to unbelievers, we know they are always trying to stretch the false element in their disbelieving worldview (the "unrighteousness"), so our best apologetic approach is the negative strategy of "turning the tables" or "relativizing the relativizers" (the subject of chap. 6). We can challenge unbelievers to be true to what they believe, knowing that in the end they cannot be, because what they claim is truth is not God's full truth, so it will not stretch enough to cover reality. At some point they will then experience some form of the passions of fear and grief, triggered by their aversion to what they do not want to face—namely, that they have gone wrong and their views are ultimately false and not true.

Conversely, when we talk to unbelievers who are more open to the element of truth, we know that the truth is still there in what they believe, even though that truth would actually lead them away from what they believe, so the best apologetic approach is to "point them to the signals of transcendence" in their experience (the focus of this chapter). At some point they will then experience some form of the passions of desire and joy, triggered by their yearning to possess what they know they have lost, but long to regain.

If the Christian faith is true, fully and finally true, then all faiths that deny it are to that extent less than God's truth, which alone is the full truth. In which case, the thinking of those who press the element of falseness in their unbelief, whatever the genuine merits that remain in their thinking, will in the end always land them in unintended consequences. Press them to the logic of their assumptions and their faith will prove neither true nor adequate. Equally, the experience of those who listen to the real truth in what they believe, even when it runs counter or goes beyond the rest of their beliefs, will be in touch with desires and longings that point them beyond what they believe and toward the full truth.

The foundational assumption is always the same. Whatever anyone claims is the truth over against God's view of truth, the real truth is still the truth, always the truth, and it points toward its Creator. We are therefore homesick for truth, and through the signals of transcendence the whole of creation is inviting us to think of its Creator—and ours. Inevitably and inescapably, then, all who will not hear the signals, and all who hear them but refuse to follow them, condemn themselves to be restless. This is already the chronic state of unbelievers in the fallen world, but the problem is made worse under the conditions of the advanced modern world, and especially in the world of consumerism and its disordered desires. For a consumer society thrives by stoking unquenchable desires into unsustainable cravings and fanning them with an inflated rage for rights. The restlessness it creates by providing false satisfactions and deadening true desires simultaneously fuels the economy and destroys happiness.

It goes without saying that, because of the twin gaps of logic and time mentioned earlier, signals of transcendence always remain pointers and not proofs, and they have to be followed up. Also, they are always clearest to those who hear them, rather than to bystanders and those who hear about them later. What Saul of Tarsus saw and heard on the road to Damascus was far more than a signal. It was a soaring vision that knocked him to the ground, turned him around in his tracks, and led him groping toward Jesus. Yet for all its dramatic force, Saul's traveling companions heard something, but saw nothing, and there is no evidence that they were affected as Paul was. In the same way, other people may hear of a signal of transcendence and understand its logic from the outside, but the thrust of the signal will only have its full force for those who share enough of the life experience of the one who hears the signal. Take Auden's passion for the "unconditional absolute." It might resonate powerfully with a human rights activist fired with outrage against the vileness of sex trafficking or bonded slavery, but to a Wall Street Master of the Universe, it could as easily be dismissed as the product of an overheated conscience that is hardly a natural feature of his world.

SURPRISED BY JOY

A well-known example of a signal of transcendence today is C. S. Lewis's account of his being "surprised by joy" through persistent experiences that triggered his journey from atheism to Christian faith. "All joy wills eternity—wills deep, deep eternity!" Nietzsche's Zarathustra exclaimed in his midnight song. It was precisely such an experience of joy, recurring over many years, that forced the atheist C. S. Lewis to become a seeker and a lapsed atheist, and thrust him out on his long quest for meaning and faith.

In his biography, Lewis wrote of his search for the source of the joy: in a sense, "the central story of my life is about nothing else." At its heart, his life was about "an unsatisfied desire which is itself more desirable than any other satisfaction."[19] *Joy*, as he used the word, is sharply distinguished from both happiness, which is dependent on circumstances, and pleasure, which is always related to the senses. Joy transcends circumstances and senses. As Nietzsche said, it wills eternity. Or as C. S. Lewis described it, "I doubt whether anyone who has ever tasted it would ever, if both were in his power, exchange it for all the pleasures in the world."[20]

One of the times when Lewis tasted it occurred when he stood beside a flowering currant bush. Suddenly and without warning he remembered a time at his old family home in Belfast when his older brother, Warnie, brought a toy garden into the nursery. He was overwhelmed by a sensation of blissful joy.

> It was a sensation, of course, of desire; but desire for what? Not, certainly, for a biscuit tin filled with moss, nor even (though that came into it) for my own past—and before I knew what I desired, the desire itself was gone, the whole glimpse withdrawn, the world turned commonplace again, or only stirred by a longing for the longing that had just ceased. It had only taken a moment of time; and in a certain sense everything else that had ever happened to me was insignificant in comparison.[21]

Desire, longing, memory, sensation—Lewis's description of being surprised by joy are hauntingly evocative. But the promptings are not nostalgic, a mere yearning for the past. Nor did they stop and rest on any earthly object. They reach forward and higher and always out of reach—"they are always the scent of a flower we have not found, the echo of a tune we have not heard, news from a country we have not yet visited."[22]

As Lewis described it, the longing for joy is at first a rapier-piercing desire for an "unnamable something" triggered by sensations such as the sound of a bell, the smell of a fire or the sound of birds. But slowly all who understand what he is talking about realize that the grail lies beyond all human objects. No mountain we can climb, no flower we can find, no horizon we can ever set out for will ever fulfill our search for joy. If someone follows this quest, says Lewis, "he must come out at last into the clear knowledge that the human soul was made to enjoy some object that is never fully given—nay, cannot even be imagined as given—in our present mode of subjective and spatio-temporal existence."[23]

Does such joy point conclusively to God as the source of joy? Or is all such talk sheer romanticism, on the order of the poet's "heard melodies are sweet, but those unheard are sweeter"? Well trained in Oxford philosophy, C. S. Lewis was too good a thinker to leap too far ahead of his experience. Joy raised questions. By itself it supplied no answers. It creates seekers, not believers, and the answer would have to be searched for. It was quite possible, Lewis knew, that reality would never satisfy this unsatisfied desire that was more desirable than any satisfaction.

At the same time, Lewis also pointed out, unless these intimations are capable of fulfillment, our capacity for them is very odd. Physical hunger does not prove that someone will get bread—after all,

> he may die of starvation on a raft in the Atlantic. But surely a man's hunger does prove that he comes of a race that repairs its body by eating and inhabits a world where eatable substances exist. . . . A man may love a woman and not win her; but it would be very odd if the phenomenon called "falling in love" occurred in a sexless world.[24]

C. S. Lewis became a seeker because of joy, though his full journey to faith took many years. Auden became a seeker too because of his passion for justice and the impossibility of his condemning evil when he knew he had to, but it was not too long before he came to Christian faith. There were major differences in their subsequent quests, but for both of them it was the thrust of the signals and their questions that tore them out of complacency, forced them to query their previous beliefs, launched them across the divide between the indifferent and the concerned, and turned them into seekers.

THE POWER OF LIFE

Berger's rich discussion of other signals of transcendence is a goldmine for the Christian advocate. It covers such typical human experiences as hope, play, humor, order and judgment.[25] His discussion is fresh and invigorating, but we should see it as a brilliant rediscovery rather than as radically new, for this was a powerful theme in the early church. In the third century, for example, Gregory of Nyssa built on the Greek notion of desire and developed it in a biblical direction. His aim was to show how desires and yearning are central to what moves people to know and love God. Such passions prompt the movement to thought and action that leads to the love of God. "We are led to God by desire, drawn to him as if pulled by a rope. . . . Every delight in God becomes kindling for a still more ardent desire."[26]

Gregory's profound teaching serves to keep us as apologists in our place yet again. Our goal is not to teach people to come to know something *about* God, but to come to know and love him, and to be known and loved by him. How absurd, then, to think that we by ourselves can do what needs to be done, and we can do it simply through words. God is his own best apologist, and it is he himself who draws people to know and love him, and through life and not simply words. All humans have these ceaseless yearnings, Gregory writes, not simply because we are incomplete but because God is infinite. God's wonder and beauty become overwhelmingly attractive because they are infinite and inexhaustible. "This is what it means to see God: never to have this desire satisfied." Our other and lesser human desires for food, sleep, sex and pleasure can each be satisfied completely as they arise. "But our yearning to see God will be satisfied only by knowing God more fully and more intimately. The more we know, the more we desire to know."[27]

The same understanding of desire blazes in St. Augustine, fanned by his own experience of passionately searching for God. The Christian life itself is "holy desire." Commenting on the Epistle of John, he writes,

> That which you desire you do not yet see; but by desiring you become capable of being filled by that which you will see when it comes. For just as in filling a leather bag . . . one stretches the skin . . . and by stretching it becomes capable of more; so God by deferring that for which we long, stretched our desire; as desire increases it stretches the mind, and by stretching, makes it more capable of being filled.[28]

Others have added further examples of signals of transcendence, and of course an easily forgotten signal of transcendence is the power of a human life itself. A great deal of our human behavior witnesses to little more than the obvious fact that we are human—all too human. We are vain. We can be irritable. Petty jealousies hit us. We love a delicious morsel of gossip. And our ever-watchful eye is directed to ourselves, our interests and our agendas. We are products of this world, and our behavior is embarrassingly easy to explain. But as Thomas Nagel says, there is also a sense in which "every individual life represents far more than itself," and there are also times, unmistakable times, when the way people live points to realities beyond them that raises questions and even saves lives.[29]

The good citizens of Le Chambon-sur-Lignon were like that in France in World War II. On the most basic and practical level of all, this little Protestant village of Huguenots rescued more than five thousand Jewish children and saved them from the terrible fate of their fellow Jews in the Nazi death camps. They made their region the safest place for Jews in the whole of German-occupied Europe. But beyond this very practical rescue, the sheer quality of their lives saved people in a different way too—and even long after the war.

Philip Hallie was such a man whom the Chambonais rescued, though he had never been there before he was rescued. A Jew himself, his lifelong passion was to study the horror of the Holocaust in order to understand it, so that it might never happen again. The outcome of his research, however, was depression, suicidal depression. One spring evening in 1974, such was the dark state of his mind that he knew he had to get away from his family, so he walked to his office and sat among the books and articles of his many years of scholarly labor—his mind obsessed with the image of a white-coated Nazi doctor cutting off the fingers and toes of a Jewish or Gypsy child with no anesthesia. His reaction was dark fury, followed by a sense of impotence, then shame and then despair. His eyes raked the bookshelves in front of him, and his hand reached for a little volume on the French Resistance that he had never noticed before.

Hallie started reading listlessly, but was pulled up short when he got to the bottom of the third page. "My cheeks started itching, and when I reached up to scratch them I found that my cheeks were covered with tears. And not just a few tears—my cheeks were awash with them."[30] He was stunned. He had not cried for years. He had grown beyond tears, yet suddenly his hardened heart had cracked open, and what had done it? "Much of my joy came from sheer surprise," he wrote, and the more he thought the more he saw the deepest reason of all was "the rarity of pure goodness." Those tears were "an expression of moral praise."[31] The heart-cracking goodness of these simple Huguenots pulled Hallie back from the edge where suicide was beckoning, and led him back to life in a way no counseling or research had managed to do. The sheer goodness of the lives of the villagers had punctured the logic of his darker thinking and pointed to a possibility that restored his faith in humanity and life. There were signals of transcendence in the witness of their behavior, and the signal went beyond the abstraction of words to engage life.

Yes, No and Not Yet

As we saw with table turning, people who experience moments of truth can always say yes to God, or no. Some of today's most sensitive atheists, such as Thomas Nagel, Ronald Dworkin and Jürgen Habermas, demonstrate this secularist predicament with poignancy. Over against the new atheists, they admit that the secularized account of scientific materialism is almost certainly false. The meaning of life must transcend life, so the search for transcendent meaning is necessary and inescapable, but the atheist veto still kicks in and stops the search there: the transcendent impulse must be resisted. For Dworkin the outcome is to rest uneasily with the oxymoron of what he calls "religious atheism."[32]

Whenever we humans are face to face with God's truth, we always have the choice to fall on our knees before God or to turn on our heels, or even to put the issue off for the moment—though as Jesus warns us, we never know how much time we have left. There is always the danger that we presume on having more time than we do, so that we hear God say, "You fool. Your soul is required of you tonight."

That point is true in terms of triggering the signals of transcendence too. People can as easily ignore or stifle the signals as follow them. Besides, compared with turning the tables, triggering the signals is rarely so dramatic, and responses to the signals often take far longer to follow. The story of Kenneth Clark illustrates this in a way that is both cautionary and encouraging.

Lord Clark was an eminent art historian and critic in mid-twentieth-century Britain. He was known for his encyclopedic wisdom, his urbane sophistication and his elegant manner. He was also the youngest-ever director of London's National Gallery and the man who saved Britain's art collections during the Second World War. Many people remember him for his highly acclaimed BBC series *Civilization*, which demonstrated his brilliance as a lecturer and television performer. He had a simple mission: "to bring art to the masses" or at least to bridge the gap between the refined taste of the few and the artistic ignorance of most of the rest of us.

Clark's friends, however, knew that his public persona was a mask that concealed his heart, as it had done ever since his student days. Few knew the real Clark underneath, and few knew his private story, which included his painful childhood memories, several mistresses and the beginning of an on-again, off-again spiritual odyssey that was strictly private. There was no religion in Clark's family background, and little among his peers in the art world and the intellectual establishment in Britain in his day. His own mother was somewhat inhibited, rarely showed her emotions and had always been afraid of going to church in case she was forced to show her emotions.

At the same time, there were factors in Clark's life that opened him to the possibility of faith. He loved nature deeply, he was passionate about art and beauty, he was concerned for the spiritual roots of civilization—and above all, he had a series of experiences that seemed to point him to something beyond what he and his friends believed. One was when he was working on a book on the Flemish Baroque painter Peter Paul Rubens in Suffolk near his own home. As he finished a passage on the artist's astonishing creativity, he realized he was shaking vehemently just from his touch with such extraordinary creative power. He never claimed to be an inspired writer himself, but from then on he knew he could recognize true inspiration in others.

Another experience he described as "a curious episode" that happened when he was staying with Bernard Berenson in Florence. "I had a religious experience," he wrote. "It took place in the Church of San Lorenzo, but it did not seem to be connected with the beauty of the harmonious architecture. I can only say that for a few minutes my whole being was irradiated by a kind of heavenly joy, far more intense than anything I had known before."[33]

Had Clark been surprised by joy as C. S. Lewis had been? Far from
fleeting, as Lewis's experiences were, Clark's impression lasted for a good
while, and the two stories diverged even more sharply from then on. Lewis
was surprised by joy and went on to become a seeker, whereas Clark deliberately brushed the experience aside.

> This state of mind lasted for several months and, wonderful though it was, it
> posed an awkward problem in terms of action. My life was far from blameless:
> I would have to reform. My family would think I was going mad, and perhaps
> after all it *was* a delusion, for I was in every way unworthy of receiving such
> a flood of grace. Gradually the effect wore off, and I made no effort to retain
> it. I think I was right. I was too deeply embedded in the world to change
> course. But that I had "felt the finger of God" I am quite sure.[34]

Was that the end of the story for Kenneth Clark? Not at all. Years later, he
admitted to a friend, "I was looking for something. So I was, and still am."
In fact, the conclusion to his journey only became known after his death in
May 1985. The elite of the European art world gathered for his funeral at St.
James Piccadilly, London, but they were stunned when an Irish priest told
how Clark had come to faith and had been received into the Catholic Church
some months before he died—an account confirmed by his wife.

The modern world is highly secular in certain parts, and nowhere more
than in the world of the educated elites. Such people are notoriously "tone
deaf" and their natural habitat is "a world without windows," as Weber and
Berger have described them. But from my experience of reading and discussing Clark's story with many political and business leaders, it is always
surprising to see how many people have had experiences just like Clark's—
though they do not know what to do with them. Sometimes they say they
don't have the words to describe the experiences. More often, like Clark,
they do not feel free to follow through on what they experienced—for fear
that they might have to change their lives, or that their friends might think
they have lost their marbles.

Thank God that at the close of Kenneth Clark's life, he grasped the hand
of God, whose finger he had earlier brushed aside. For the truth is that, like
Clark, C. S. Lewis, W. H. Auden and countless others, we all have "eternity
in our hearts" and a sure road from unbelief to the joys of faith is to pay at-

tention to the signals of transcendence that life sets off. Our privilege as Christians and apologists, by our lives as well as our words, is to help people to hear, to listen and to understand those signals, and then to help them follow to where they lead.

8

SPRING-LOADED
DYNAMICS

PETER BERGER'S "YOU ARE THE MAN" is one of the most elegant, brilliant and powerful sermons never preached—an exposition of the prophet Nathan's confrontation with King David. The reason is that it was written not as a sermon but as an excursus in what is otherwise a socio-logical argument. It comes at the end of his highly original early book *The Precarious Vision*, which explores the world of social fictions, moral alibis and Christian faith. And it stands as a biblical example of what Berger calls "alternation." This is the experience through which what we take to be reality, but is really our carefully constructed fictions and alibis, is suddenly torn away as flimsy and paper thin, mere Potemkin villages that are all show and no substance—and we are thrust into a world of different possibilities.

Reality, Berger argues, is something we usually take to be solid, self-evident and given. It is something so natural and taken for granted that it is often disclosed best in our "of course" statements—something so massively obvious that it must surely have come to us along with our mother's milk. But in fact that sense of solidity is deceptive. For a start, whatever society we live in, we all experience realities in our lives that are quite different from the paramount reality of our "7 to 11 waking world." Surrealist artists and filmmakers made much of this in the twentieth century, but we do not need to follow the flight of their more extreme fancies. An obvious and down-to-earth example is the difference between waking and sleeping, which by itself raises questions about which of the two "realities" is the real one. Hence

Master Chuang's famous question cited earlier: "If when I am asleep I am a man dreaming I am a butterfly, how do I know when I am awake that I am not a butterfly dreaming I am a man?"

Apart from the differences between waking and sleeping, or states of mind induced by drugs or alcohol, there are huge differences in the ways that different societies and different worldviews see reality. The reason is that even in our waking worlds we each bring to our experience of reality the framework or view of the world in which we understand and interpret reality. Such worldviews shape the focus we bring to bear on the world, and therefore shape our attention, and this in turn affects both what we see and (importantly) what we do not see. Thus the world will look very different to an Oxford atheist, an Australian bushman, a Hindu holy man and a Catholic construction worker in a Polish shipyard.

The same will be true of an atheist, a Christian and a Hindu, and all other worldviews. The differences make a difference. For the atheist, the natural world is real and it is all there is. By definition, there is nothing beyond the world as discoverable through science and the senses, and from that perspective it is unfair to condemn someone as "tone deaf" if they do not hear what they believe is in fact not there—though that comment changes completely if it is discovered that they have closed their ears so as not to hear what is actually there.

For the Christian the natural world is real and full of strangeness and wonder, but it is not the only reality or the higher reality, so important though science is, there are ways of knowing other than through science. So the fact that atheists do not perceive another reality does not mean that it is not there. Their deafness may be willful. Even Nietzsche called that mistake an "acoustic illusion." After all, there are many sounds that humans cannot hear, but they are still objectively real and completely audible to dogs, bats and bears.

For the Hindu, in strong contrast to the other two, the natural world is not real at all. Seen from within this Eastern worldview, we only take the natural world as real in the same way that Plato's cave dwellers thought the shadows on the wall were real. As a follower of the philosopher Shankara sees it, if we view things from the ultimate perspective of the ground of all being, what we take to be real is actually *maya*, or an illusion. Some Western philosophers, such as Arthur Schopenhauer and Friedrich Nietzsche, have agreed with this view. The latter asserted,

> Although of the two halves of life, the waking half and the dreaming half, the first appears to us as incontrovertibly preferable, more important, more worthy, more worth living, even as the only half which is really lived, I would still like, however paradoxical it may seem, to assert precisely the opposite evaluation of the dream on behalf of the secret ground of our essence whose phenomenal appearance we are.[1]

In short, when it comes to different worldviews, differences make a big difference, and not only for individuals but for whole societies.

Berger uses Arthur Koestler's illustration of a children's game he had played as a boy, which shows the effects of different worldviews. The young Arthur was given a puzzle, a paper with a tangle of very thin red and blue lines that at first sight looked more of a mess than a picture. But if you covered it with a piece of transparent red tissue paper, the red lines disappeared and the blue lines formed a picture of a clown with a dog. And if you covered it with a blue tissue paper, the blue lines disappeared and a roaring lion emerged, chasing the clown across the ring. There are crucial differences in perspective between the worldviews, and the differences make a difference. Each claims to be comprehensive on its own terms, each has its own way of explaining and explaining away the others, and the question is how do we decide between them?

What Berger calls "alternation" happens when some event or experience acts as a "culture shock" that smashes against our normal way of seeing things, and causes a breach in our given views of reality that opens up the possibility of different and alternative realities. As anthropologists use the term, a *culture shock* means that we see a culture that is different from our own with new eyes, but more than that: from then on we see our own culture with different eyes. The question then is not just "How on earth could they think that?" but "How can I still think this?" The unquestioned and taken-for-granted solidity of our own reality is no more. It is now "our" view of reality, which we "happen to have because of our upbringing," and there are clearly many other possible views. Thus a world of new possibilities has opened—we can perhaps continue believing what we always believed, but with a new uncertainty that was never there before, or we can equally now look for new and different ways of seeing reality.

If such a breach of "reality" is serious enough, it might lead to the breakdown of our original way of seeing things and even to a breakthrough to a different way of seeing things. "Alternation" may therefore be understood as the sociological equivalent of what the psychologist calls a "gestalt switch" and the philosopher of science calls a "paradigm shift"—which, you will remember, was itself based on the experience of religious conversion. Through alternation, Berger argues, someone may "jump," "leap," migrate or be converted from one worldview to another and from one understanding of reality to another.[2]

Needless to say, there are factors in the advanced modern world that reinforce and aggravate the chances of alternation. Above all, the modern experience of *pluralization*—the process through which choice, choices and change are multiplied at every level of life—is a powerful reinforcement of the possibility of alternation. At first, it means only that we become aware as never before of "all those others" and the fact that their choices are very different from ours—whether the choices are about cereals and holidays, or about far more serious things such as relationships, worldviews and ways of life. But soon the acid bites deeper, and we become aware that all our own choices could be different too, and might even be better if they were. In sum, the experience of pluralization creates in modern people either paralysis or what Berger calls a "proneness to conversion."[3] We have more choices than ever before, and we are all closer and more open to change than ever before.

This idea of different realities, social fictions and alternation is crucial to apologetics in two ways. On the one hand, this understanding of different realities and social fictions throws further light on the biblical teaching about the anatomy of unbelief. It fits perfectly with the notion of our idol-making hearts and of all the fig leaves with which we as truth-suppressing humans have tried to build our Potemkin villages and hide our nakedness ever since the Garden of Eden. In that sense there may be an endless array of human worldviews, but they all share the core fact that they deny God, and they are each a shrine to the self that raises them and a shelter from the truth of God that they would avoid. In short, they are moral, social and

philosophical fictions raised to ward off what would otherwise be the unde-
niability of God's truth.

On the other hand, these same notions also throw light on the kind of
arguments (such as turning the tables) and the kind of experiences (such as
signals of transcendence) that work to puncture such fictions and trigger
such alternation (or gestalt switch or paradigm shift) between realities.
Transfer this discussion from the framework of sociology to the framework
of theology and it becomes obvious that alternation can serve the purposes
of both repentance and conversion. These are the two experiences that act
together to form the most revolutionary alternation in human life, the ultimate turnaround, first of mind, and then of heart and life and way of life.
Seen from this angle, repentance is a truth-triggered alternation, gestalt
switch or paradigm shift that is the key to radical conversion.

You Are the Man

Consider Nathan's confrontation with King David. Thanks to Hollywood,
Berger writes, even people unfamiliar with the Bible will recognize the story
of David's adultery with Bathsheba and the murder of her husband Uriah. It
takes closer scrutiny, however, to appreciate all the ironies with which the
storyteller describes the incident. It was the spring when kings go out to war,
but "this bellicose season finds David enjoying a lazy Mediterranean siesta
on the roof of his palace in Jerusalem . . . an ideal setting for erotic reconnaissance." In modern parlance, what ensued was "no big deal" for a red-
blooded and powerful Eastern monarch. The hastily arranged murder of
Uriah was no big deal either, and neither were the somewhat crude alibis
and rationalizations that followed quickly. Before Nathan comes in to challenge David, it would appear that all the needed excuses had been presented,
and all the social fictions had been erected and were in place. King David
had achieved a level of coverup that President Nixon could only envy.

The only fly in David's ointment, Berger notes, was the troublesome character of Israel's God. He did not behave like other gods and other kings, and
David's pitiless treatment of Uriah did not escape his notice. So he sent his
prophet Nathan to confront David, but how was he to do it? If Nathan had
shamed the king with an open confrontation, he might quickly have met the
same fate as Uriah. But his choice of the storytelling strategy was surely not

to save his own skin but to confront David morally and have the best hope of turning him around.

So Nathan decides to appeal to the king as judge and lawgiver, requests a hearing for a case he wishes to put before him and then recounts the details—presumably the sort of request Nathan had made many times before, which therefore aroused no suspicion. Of course, as readers of the account centuries later, we are in on the secret. We know the purpose of the story and we know the outcome: the deep conviction and repentance with which David's confession is drenched in Psalm 51. But of course David had no idea that the case he was hearing was fictional. He believed it was real, so he entered into deciding it fully engaged—so much so that he burst out at the rich man's lack of pity, "He deserves to die!"

Did Nathan thunder his famous one-line response, or did he pause for a second and then when the silence was fully pregnant, say quietly, "You are the man!" We are not told, but we know the effect. Hitting like a pile-driver blow to the stomach, the punch line lived up to its name. It tore through the flimsy façade of David's fictions, alibis and damage control. Like a sprung trapdoor, it catapulted him from the damage-controlled world of his managed truth to the world of God's inescapable truth. With one stroke, all the fictions, alibis, evasions and rationalizations were ripped to shreds and lay in a heap on the floor. The emperor had no clothes. The great King David was merely a man, naked before God and his truth. He was an adulterer and a murderer, and no better than any of his subjects.

"Here is a case for your decision, your majesty," and David, engaged, had followed along. So David's *expectation* was slowly built up in one direction, until wham, the *effect* of the punch line suddenly whiplashed him back in the opposite direction. The original view of reality was reversed and a new one revealed. The conversion-directed power of the alternation (or gestalt switch or paradigm shift) was spring-loaded within the dynamics of Nathan's parable. It sprang like a mousetrap on the unsuspecting king. And in this case, the art of the fool maker was successful. David fell on his knees, rather than turning on his heels. He repented and was restored, though the wider consequences of what he had done dogged his family for the rest of his life.

Berger shows how the whole story turns on a double debunking. First,

David is exposed through the irony with which the story is told. "There is a profound discrepancy between David the heroic king and empire-builder—and David the Peeping Tom and seducer."[4] And even this collapses into a bedroom farce in which the king of Israel tries "to play pimp to one of his servants on behalf of the latter's own wife."[5] But then David is debunked through judgment, as the judge himself is not only judged but judges himself before his own court. Like a boomerang, the same pitilessness for which, only seconds earlier, he had condemned the rich man in the case becomes his verdict on himself.

> As God's judgment confronts David in the person of Nathan, all the layers of deception and excuse are cut through with one terrible stroke. David is not standing now before his mirror, or before that other mirror that kings have in the devotion of servants like Joab. He is standing before truth itself.[6]

WITH AN EYE TO THE AUDIENCE AND THE AIM

Aside from the stories of Jesus, Nathan's confrontation with King David is perhaps the most brilliant example of creative persuasion and subversion through surprise in the entire Bible, and it has the added merit of being successful. David sincerely repented and was fully restored—so much so that despite his adultery, murder and the squalid unfolding of his family relationships that flowed from these sins, God could still give him the supreme accolade of being "a man after My heart, who will do all My will" (Acts 13:22).

Yet often we do not consider what Nathan's strategy means for apologetics, and why it had to be used in the first place. The answer is that David's heart and mind were closed and needed to be pried open, and the story was Nathan's chosen way to do this. A simple, straightforward approach might have met a very different response. The Bible contains a wealth of wisdom that underlies this approach to Christian apologetics and communication in general, but oddly, some of the lessons from this wisdom are so simple that the only surprise is that we still tend to ignore them. They are so obvious that we do not bother to follow them.

One of these basic principles of communication in the Bible is that *a speaker should always speak to where the audience is*. In other words, we have to speak to people and to be close enough to where they are so that we know we are really getting through to them, and not shouting from a distance or speaking past them and missing them. Could anything be more obvious, even as a matter of common courtesy? Yet, absurd though it might seem, many Christian apologists do not do it in practice. We would consider it extraordinarily rude if someone sat down next to us and spoke to us without looking at us or paying any attention to us while they were talking, or talking to us like a preprogrammed phone commercial. But that is what we do when we use "1, 2, 3, 4" formulas or canned, ready-made questions as if everybody was the same as everyone else, and people could be approached in a cookie-cutter manner that overrides the unique individuals they are.

To be sure, many Christians now show a greater sensitivity to genera-tional and cultural differences than a few years ago, and most people would instinctively know that they should talk differently to a skateboarding teenager than a retired banker. But beyond such surface differences, what is often missing is discernment of the deepest and most important thing we need to know about a listener. Are they truly open to God and his truth or are they closed?

Who was the most open person in the whole Bible? We are not told, but my candidate would be the jailer at the town prison in Philippi whose story is recounted the book of Acts. Given the task of guarding Paul and Silas after their preaching had caused a near riot in the town, he suddenly found his world thrown upside down by an earthquake that shattered the prison foun-dations, opened all the prison doors and shook loose the prisoners' chains—allowing a mass escape that would have been ruinous to his job and most probably his life. About to kill himself with his own sword, he was stopped only by Paul's calm assurance that all the prisoners were present and ac-counted for. Rushing in with gratitude, though still shaking with fear, he fell down before Paul and Silas, and cried out, "Sirs, what must I do to be saved?" (Acts 16:30).

When were you last asked that question where you live? Such a direct and desperate question would be extremely rare today. No one has ever approached me, going about my business in London, Brussels, Wash-ington, New York or Shanghai and asked me that—though my parents were asked that question several times in the fear-filled atmosphere of

Nanking in the weeks before the Chinese capital fell to the communist troops in 1949. And that is surely the point. The people of Nanking were desperate, and so was the Philippian jailer who faced Paul. And seeing him that open, Paul was simple, brief and to the point: "Believe in the Lord Jesus and you will be saved, you and your household" (Acts 16:31). Period. Full stop. End of the answer.

Plainly, the jailer was open, unambiguously, even desperately open. He needed no apologist and no apologetics. Neither the rationality of faith, the historicity of the Gospels nor the evidence for the resurrection was a problem to him. His problem was the likely loss of his job and perhaps even of his life, and therefore ruin for his family. He was all too aware of his bad situation, and the good news was very obviously good as the answer to his situation. Before our formula-wielding friends might have reached their second point, or the intellectually sophisticated had thought of "the logic of the jailer's presuppositions," Paul had finished and the jailer was a convinced convert. Surely the point, however, is that Paul could be that simple and brief because the jailer was that open, and so too may we be when those whom we are talking to are open.

But needless to say, not everyone is that open. There are fewer people open like that in the West than previously, and there are many other biblical examples of how God and his spokespersons speak quite differently to different people when they are closed. It is striking too that God himself declares that such is his practice and then says why. For example, when Aaron and Miriam started to resent their older brother Moses, and then grumbled against his leadership, God stepped in quickly and appeared before them. "Has the LORD indeed spoken only through Moses," they were murmuring. "Has He not spoken through us as well?" (Num 12:2).

Responding fast, the Lord called all three siblings to come out to the tent of meeting, and defended Moses bluntly:

If there is a prophet among you,
I, the LORD, shall make Myself known to him in a vision.
I shall speak with him in a dream.
Not so with My servant Moses,
He is faithful in all my household;
With him I speak mouth to mouth,

Even openly, and not in dark sayings,
And he beholds the form of the LORD. (Num 12:6-8)

In other words, the Lord's way was to speak to ordinary people through prophets, to speak to prophets through visions and dreams, but to speak face to face with only one person—Moses—and then only because of the humility of his heart. God speaks to where his audience is, and the deepest consideration is the character and condition of their hearts.

Another equally basic principle in the Bible is that *speakers should always speak in a way that reflects their aim*. For someone who is open to God, our goal is to give them all they need of the good news, so they can welcome and embrace it. But for someone who is closed to God, the challenge is a great deal harder. Our communication must contain the subversive action that serves the end we have in mind, which we are praying and working toward— that is, the about-face of repentance. Clearly, Nathan spoke with an eye toward the king's repentance. Sent by God as a prophet to speak to the king, that was his objective. But his story played its part too. It was the perfect means for the end desired. It was spring-loaded with the subversive dynamics that served God's goal effectively.

REFRAMING

Even the best principles are abstract and lack the usefulness and down-to-earth quality of real examples. So important as they are, we should hold these two principles in mind and then go on to explore some of the varied means of biblical communication that embody them. What are some of the subversive ways in which God and his people speak in order to open hearts and minds that were closed, and so serve the goal of challenging people to repentance and conversion?

First, there is the strategy of *reframing*. As we saw earlier, the heart of sin includes the attempt to frame God. Sin is the active assertion to the right to the claim to ourselves, and therefore to the right to our own view of things. It is therefore a deliberate distortion of reality that must be actively erected and ceaselessly maintained against God and the true reality of things as they really are. This false framework is precisely the fictional façade, the Potemkin village, the bad faith alibi which provides the legitimacy for the shrine all sinners build to themselves and the shelter in which they take refuge from the truth.

In short, sin frames God falsely. Thinking of him as he isn't, sin justifies itself in rejecting him as he is—and therefore draws the false view around itself like a security blanket to provide itself with an alibi for not believing or obeying God. Again, as we saw earlier, our overall attitude must then be that *the defense never rests*. Whenever and however God is not seen for who he is, but stands in the dock falsely framed and wrongly accused, we must reframe the issue and so defend God's name and restore the truth to the distorted view of reality.

The simple fact is that time and again unbelievers disbelieve in a god that we don't believe in either, a god who isn't like God at all, and a god that we could never believe in a hundred years. If God were who many people think he is, we could not and should not and would not believe in him ourselves. But the problem lies with them and their views, not with God—though sadly, their distorted views of God are sometimes shaped by Christians themselves. (Samuel Beckett described the view of God in the churches he knew as "a very small God.")[7] Their view of God is askew, wittingly or unwittingly. Sometimes it is too small and cramped. Sometimes it is quite wrong. Sometimes it is a view they have inherited without thinking or picked up somewhere, and they believe it is what Christians believe. Sometimes it a view they cling to with a perversity that is tenacious. After all, it provides what philosopher Thomas Hobbes called their "blameless liberty," not just their excuse and their alibi but their right to their hatred and disdain for God and for their dismissal of the Christian faith and way of life.

The best known biblical example of reframing comes in Luke's account of the story of the two disciples on the road to Emmaus on the evening of the day of the resurrection. Dejected and with their hopes shattered, they were making their way home, amazed that the stranger they met knew nothing of what had happened the previous week. His question elicited a recounting of the week's news that was entirely accurate, but it ended in gloom because it completely overlooked the perspective of the Old Testament writings. Needless to say, the isolated story of the cross, without the prophets to frame it from one side and the resurrection on the other, would be heartbreaking, if heroic. Jesus, however, reframes the events in the light of who he was and who he was predicted to be, and even before the penny dropped, they knew that their hearts burned within them. The reframing changed everything and their faith was reignited (Lk 23:13-35).

The disciples, of course, were just that—disciples, who should have believed more faithfully all along. For them, the reframing salvaged their shipwrecked hopes. An even clearer example for apologists is Peter's sermon on the day of Pentecost, which is often described as "the first Christian apology" because it was directed to skeptics and scoffers and those who were not followers of Jesus. The disciples, you remember, were in the upper room of a house in Jerusalem, waiting, no doubt eagerly but anxiously, for the arrival of the gift of the Spirit that Jesus himself had promised them when he left. And suddenly it happened. There was the rushing sound of a violent wind, flames like fiery tongues blazed on every head, and most amazingly, people began speaking in languages other than their own—incredibly, in fact, in the languages of all the visitors from all over the Jewish dispersion who were then packing into Jerusalem for the great festival.

Naturally the range of responses was enormous. Awe, wonder, amazement, perplexity—What on earth did it mean? And inevitably, there were the skeptics. "Oh come on, these holy-roller, country-bumpkin Galileans, they're drunk. That's all this is. They've been drinking all night. Drowning their sorrows after the loss of their leader, no doubt. But how disgraceful that they would spill out into the town in that state" (see Acts 2:1-13).

And what do we read next? That Peter and the apostles were equally mystified and uncertain what to do? Far from it. Peter stood up, and spoke out boldly. Drunk? No, these men aren't drunk, he argued. Don't be ridiculous. It's only nine in the morning. What you are witnessing is something else. In fact, what we are experiencing is what the prophet Joel saw and declared many centuries ago (vv. 14-15).

In other words, the skeptics had framed the issue falsely, and the crowds were in danger of missing what God was saying and doing. So Peter reframes the issue: he returns to the prophet Joel, drives forward through Jewish history to set out the significance of the life and death of Jesus of Nazareth in its proper framework, and then drives home the conclusion: God is calling you to repent (vv. 38-39)!

The result of this first Christian apology was spectacular, with three thousand converts added to the church that day. But while the power of Peter's speech came directly from the Spirit of Jesus, who had just come down on the church in evident power, the logical thrust of Peter's speech grew directly from his reframing of the issue. To those skeptics who dismissed the experience because they saw it wrongly, he reframed the issue, set it in its right perspective and then drove home the inescapable conclusion.

Ah yes, a skeptic can still say, all Peter did was replace one interpretive framework with another, but how do we know the outcome is more than a grand contest of "Says who?" with Peter the winner in that particular case? Such was the overwhelming power of the Holy Spirit on the Day of Pentecost that there was no need for further argument, but today there often is. In a post-Christian era many of our friends, neighbors and colleagues will reject God for a score of reasons, but we must so live and speak that they reject God for God's sake and not because of what we have said or done that has framed God wrongly. Pursuing the question of deciding between frames would take us beyond the point in hand, but let me say briefly that Christian reframing is not merely pitting one frame against another in an endless power game. Rather, Christians would claim that anyone truly interested can examine both the adequacy and truth of the alternative frames for themselves, and invite genuine seekers to make up their own minds (see chap. 12). Not surprisingly, the two issues of adequacy and truthfulness come together in the Christian view. The gospel makes better sense of what simply *is* because the way God sees reality is the truth of what is.

RAISING QUESTIONS

A second biblical strategy for confronting closed minds and hearts is to *raise questions*. Samuel Johnson, the great eighteenth-century man of letters, once remarked that "questioning is not a mode of conversation among gentlemen." To be sure, there is a way of asking questions that can be rude, intrusive and off-putting—like a prosecuting attorney gone mad. But there are three reasons why questions are essential to the human pursuit of truth. One stems from the notion of the examined life, another from the possibility of human error, and yet another from the desirability of human growth.

Asking questions is foundational to truth and meaning, especially if we have the courage to break with conventional wisdom and the curiosity to ask about first things, last things and enduring things. Such questions are useful for anyone interested in science or philosophy, but even beyond that questions are essential for anyone thinking about life and the meaning of existence itself. Take for instance Leibniz's famous question and the profound reflections it has led to: "Why is there not nothing?" (or "Why is there something rather than nothing?").

In addition, we cannot escape the fact that our thinking at any moment may always be wrong, and we may always need to grow and mature, so we should never rest on our present thinking, and we should always be open to challenge. Christians therefore prize highly the biblical notion of corrigibility, but such correction may come in two ways—through discovering the present mistakes and inadequacies in our thinking for ourselves, or through being told where we are wrong by others.

Needless to say, both these means of correction are difficult for us when we need correction—the first because none of us is naturally inclined to think we are ever wrong, and the second because none of us likes to be told we are wrong by someone else. The second problem is minimized by many situations in life where we are brought up to know that we do not know, and to know that others know much more than we do. Schooling, for example, turns on our being socialized into the understanding that the teacher knows more than we do as students, and it breaks down completely when this tacit understanding is rejected and chaos takes over. The same is true of the doctor's office, where the white coat and the framed degrees on the wall are the silent witness to the mystique of the doctor who, for all our amateur research on the Internet, is still conventionally understood to know more about medicine than we do.

Clearly, there is no such expectation when we come to apologetics and arguments about faith. In fact the opposite is the case. Everyone is naturally convinced that their own faith is adequate and true, and almost as naturally convinced that what others believe simply cannot be true, whether they are honest or rude enough to say so. That is even more the case with the mind and heart that is firmly closed—but this is precisely where questions come in. The person who will not listen to anyone from the outside who raises anything against his or her faith is still always open to the power of questioning.

Statements can be subversive, especially if the information they carry is explosive. But in most cases, questions carry a subversive power that statements cannot match, because a statement always has the quality of "take it or leave it." Some information is asserted, and it may well be interesting, but only to those who are interested—to those, in other words, who have an interest or stake in the information. "Look, it's begun to rain" will be heard differently by someone planning a picnic and someone else whose work will keep them indoors all day. Many ways of sharing our faith are similarly irrelevant to people because they have not become aware that they have an interest and a stake in the issue.

Questions, by contrast, are powerful for two reasons. First, they are *indirect*, and second, they are *involving*. A good question will never betray where it is leading to, and it is an invitation to the listener to pick it up and discover the answer for him- or herself. This constructive use of questions is often traced back to the great Greek gadfly Socrates, whose probing questions stung his generation into thinking, and exposed the illogic and complacency of their unthinking.

We should never forget, however, that God himself was a gadfly long before Socrates. What were God's first words to Adam and Eve after they had sinned? "Where are you?" (Gen 3:9). Did the Lord not know which tree they were hiding behind? How absurd! God's question smoked our first parents out of their hiding and challenged them to face up to what it was that they knew they had done. Similarly, how does God answer Job when Job's doubts have had the awful effect of pulling down the pillars of the moral universe on his own head? He does not give him a comforting answer or even an answer at all. Instead, God asks him more than fifty questions in a row until Job is called into question and comes to his senses on his knees:

I have declared that which I did not understand,
Things too wonderful for me, which I did not know. . . .
Therefore I retract,
And I repent in dust and ashes. (Job 42:3, 6)

Several of God's people in the Scriptures were adept in raising questions. King David, for instance, was not taken in by the parable of the woman from Tekoa who had been set up by General Joab. Her ruse was exposed under the barrage of David's questions, and she threw in the towel and admitted there was no way round the king's probing questions (2 Sam 14:19). Nathan may have tricked David into believing a fictional account, but the king was not going to be taken in again. He would retain the power by being the one who ask the questions.

But unquestionably the greatest question raiser in the Bible is Jesus himself. Again and again his astonishing actions raise questions by themselves, above all about himself and who he might be to be able do such things ("Who then is this, that He commands even the winds and the water, and they obey Him?" [Lk 8:25]; "Who is this man who even forgives sins?" [Lk 7:49]). But he also asks searching questions himself, of his disciples, of the wider crowds and of his enemies, questions that have resonated down the ages ("What does it profit a man to gain the whole world, and forfeit his soul?" [Mt 8:36]; "Who do you say that I am?" [Mk 8:29]). Jesus' question-raising style is especially marked in his response to the slippery questions asked of him. The enemies of Jesus ask him wily questions to catch him out and get him to incriminate himself, and how does Jesus answer such tricky questions? He asks even trickier ones in response until they are silenced ("After that, no one would venture to ask Him any more questions" [Mk 12:34]).

Many of us today are more adept at answering questions than asking them. Sometimes we are even known mockingly for having answers to questions that no one has asked, and for always offering the same answer—Jesus—whatever the question. Jesus is of course the full and final answer to all human questions, but not in a rote or simplistic way. It is when the human heart is most fully aware of its longings, dilemmas and sorrows that it can see the profundity and awe of the answers that Jesus offers, and that Jesus is—and alongside life experiences, questions are one of the most helpful ways to point someone to that awareness.

The third subversive style of communication in the Bible is using *story* and *parable*. If questioning gains its strength from being indirect and involving, stories have a further strength. They are indirect, involving and imaginative. Imagination is our most powerful human faculty. Wherever you are now, you can be thinking of your holiday on some romantic beach. You can think what it would be like to live in the times of Julius Caesar or Shakespeare or your favorite hero. You can imagine yourself as the fastest runner in the world or the first man on Mars. Imagination, in other words, is a quicker way to speed from now to then and from here to there than even the fastest modern communication.

We have seen the power of Nathan's parable; we will look later at the stories Jesus told; and in our own time J. R. R. Tolkien and C. S. Lewis have demonstrated the enormous power of stories, especially with books that can also be translated into films. Needless to say, from the early humans huddling around their fires, stories have been among the powerful means of human communication, and they still are. And as I said in the opening chapter, we use stories as apologists, not because we are cool and hip in our postmodern arguments, but because the people we are talking to are closed and not open.

The fourth style of subversive communication in the Bible is using *drama* and *ploys*. These contain the same three features as stories: they are indirect, involving and imaginative. In the opening chapter we looked at the prophet's wounding himself and his subversive challenge to Ahab that was acted out with such great effect. Coming from a family known across the world for its famous dark brew, my own favorite example of a dramatic ploy in the Bible is found in the life work of the prophet Jeremiah. In a highly unlikely move, the Lord tells Jeremiah to invite the Rechabites to the temple to join him for a drink of wine. The Rechabites were the teetotalers and fundamentalists of sixth-century B.C., so in today's terms, that would be the equivalent of the revered Billy Graham inviting his local Baptists to a sherry party at his home in Montreat, North Carolina.

You don't need much imagination to feel the tension that must have greeted Jeremiah's invitation. It was the Lord's prophet who invited them, and it was in a special room in the Lord's house that they were invited to, so what would the Rechabites do? More liberal members of the Jerusalem community must have smirked. Didn't Jeremiah know that it was taboo for the Rechabites to drink? But of course he knew, and it wasn't his own bright idea. It was God who had commanded him to do it. So what on earth would the Rechabites do? If the rest of us had invited them, the smart alecks must have thought, they would have turned us down flat. But it's the Lord's prophet who has invited them, and in the temple itself, and supposedly at the command of the Lord himself. We'd better stick around and see what will happen.

As the story unfolds, the Rechabites refuse politely but firmly, explaining why they don't drink—as if Jeremiah did not know.

We will not drink wine, for Jonadab, the son of Rechab, our father, commanded us saying, "You shall not drink wine, you or your sons, forever." . . .
We have obeyed the voice of Jonadab, the son of Rechab, our father, in all that
he commanded us, not to drink wine all our days, we, our wives, our sons or
our daughters. (Jer 35:6, 8)

What would Jeremiah say next? What on earth did he have in mind in
setting up this bizarre and ill-fated invitation? Then suddenly, as the air must
have crackled with tension, Jeremiah received a direct word from the Lord.
It must have been as if he swiveled around mid-sentence, and faced the
smirking bystanders. "The sons of Jonadab the son of Rechab have observed
the command of their father, which he commanded them," he said, "but this
people has not listened to Me" (Jer 35:16). The Rechabites, in other words,
have kept their ancestors' commands, even though they were not God's requirement for everyone, but the rest of you have not listened to God's commands that were his absolute requirement.

Berger describes the ploy as a tactic for redefining a situation contrary to
general expectations, and therefore effective in catching the other players
off-guard. As such, it is "brilliant micro-sociological sabotage."[8] Doubtless,
the citizens of Jerusalem slunk away rapidly that day, but the turning of the
tables was deeper and longer lasting that that. They would never be able to
see a Rechabite out in the streets or in the marketplace without being reminded that these people had called them into question. The despised fundamentalists were a living rebuke to their faithlessness.

WORDS, WORDS, WORDS

All such ways of spring-loading our persuasion are vital today, for words
themselves are at a historic low point in the advanced modern world. On
the one hand, modern words suffer from inattention. Everyone is speaking
and no one is listening. On the other hand, modern words suffer from inflation. Under the impact of the omnipresence of advertising and "adspeak,"
words are nothing more than tools to sell products and agendas, and the
highest and most sacred words can be used to give a leg up to the most trivial
of goods and the worst of causes. Words today are all so much "verbiage,"
"propaganda" and a matter of "words, words, words."

In direct and forceful contrast, we Christians must show again that we are both people of the Word and people who believe in words. Words are never *mere* words for us, for they are linked indissolubly to truth, freedom, worship and human dignity. Words matter because we worship the Word himself, and our words used on his behalf should be spring-loaded with the truth and power of his Word—especially to those who are closed.

The problems of inattention and inflation are only two of the oddities of communication in the great age of communication. But they show how great communicators as Christians are called to be and have often been, communication today is often harder and not easier. More importantly, they show that the best answer to the challenge is not through improved technology but through deeper theology. As I have stressed from the start, when people are spiritually, morally and intellectually closed to the gospel, there is nothing more powerful than communication that is shaped by the art of truth and the power and subversion of the incarnation, the cross and the Spirit of God.

9

THE ART OF ALWAYS
BEING RIGHT?

He JUST DOESN'T LET UP. Arguing with him is like running into a bulldozer or being thrown onto a wall of razor blades. He is arguing for the Christian faith, but he'd be the same if he argued for atheism, a political party or a football club. Regardless of the point at stake, he's simply got to be right and to have the last word." That damning comment came from someone breaking away in disgust from a discussion group in which a Christian student was waxing more dogmatic than either eloquent or loving.

Needless to say, many opinionated people would fall foul of such a comment. Albert Camus, however, was different. He admitted honestly that polemics were dangerous for him. He was so passionate that he found it impossible to take anything lightly. So debates made him angry and exposed the pride at the core of his being. When he wrote *The Rebel*, he recorded his resolution in his journal: "To tell the truth without ceasing to be generous."[1]

It is particularly sad when Christians lack Camus's honesty and display such an ugly attitude. After all, the two features the apostle Peter urges us to display when we give an answer for the hope that is in us are "gentleness" and "respect" (1 Pet 3:15 ESV). But we probably all know Christians who are anything but gentle and respectful, people who for one reason or another are incurable smart alecks or have a mountain-sized ego that devours the oxygen in any room they enter. Little though they realize it, the more they open their mouths, the more they discredit their cause. It is difficult to be around people who always have to be right. They are frankly a pain in the neck, and when we behave like that as Christian apologists, we betray our Lord. We not only contradict the "grace and truth" and the "grace upon grace" with which Jesus presented the gospel, but we present ourselves as a flat out contradiction of everything we ourselves are saying (Jn 1:14, 16). Jesus said that his followers were to be "fishers of men," so it is people, not arguments, that we should be winning.

As a well-trained orator, St. Augustine was honest in facing up to the temptation of using words as power. He admitted that in his pre-Christian days as a "word merchant" (*venditor verborum*), "I always used to win more arguments than was good for me. . . . The hot-headedness of a young man soon hardened into pig-headedness."[2] Erasmus recognized the same danger, and with a few striking exceptions he practiced what he saw as the pursuit of "eloquence" (*eloquentia*)—persuasion through pleasing discourse. His model was Jesus himself, whom he called "the persuasiveness of God."[3]

But all too often the urge to win and to win at all costs breaks through in Christian speech, whether in showy exhibitionist rhetoric or ruthless steamrollering. When John Henry Newman experienced trials at the hands of his fellow Catholics in both England and Rome, he protested vehemently to a friend against the abuse of truth when used as propaganda by the church:

> This country is under Propaganda, and Propaganda is too shallow to have the wish to use such as me. . . . I know myself, no one can have been more loyal to the Holy See than I am. I love the Pope personally into the bargain. But Propaganda is a quasi-military power, extraordinary, for missionary countries, rough and ready. It does not understand an intellectual movement. It likes quick results—scalps from beaten foes by the hundreds.[4]

Taking "scalps" is a bad habit associated with some styles of evangelism, and a similar objection has sometimes leveled against Christian apologetics and against those who relish debates in particular. Apologetics itself, it has been charged, is the art of always being right and therefore a matter of bad faith. Apologists are not out to understand but to win. Their arguments owe more to their psychology than their theology. Some people simply need to be right, and they are the ones, it is said, who take to apologetics. Humbler and more tolerant Christians, it is added, have no need to be right and would never seek to convert anyone.

That charge is unfair and wrong. A moment's thought would be enough to show how foolish the accusation is. If all forms of persuasion were to be suspect because they might represent a drive to being right, there would be no persuasion left, and ignorance would be the winner. Persuasion is crucial both to learning and to human growth, so this criticism would boomerang back against all forms of persuasion on behalf of any claim to truth.

In fact, there have always been great Christian speakers and debaters who, like our Lord, have exhibited both truth and grace. A striking feature of the early Christian centuries was the number of Christian leaders who were trained in rhetoric, even teachers of rhetoric, and acclaimed orators—and were great preachers too. Among the most famous in the Greek world was Gregory of Nazianzus, the Cappadocian Father who was a student of Libanius, the last of the great Greek rhetoricians. He was followed in Constantinople by John Chrysostom, the "golden tongued." St. Augustine had been a teacher of rhetoric, and what attracted him to the Christian faith in Milan was his admiration for the brilliant oratory of the bishop, Ambrose. All these leaders of the church were accomplished speakers, but known as much for their faithfulness and passion to proclaim the gospel in life and in word.

More recently, the church has been grateful for the high-spirited success of G. K. Chesterton in his famous debates with George Bernard Shaw, or for the humility and humor of Professor John Lennox of Oxford University in his recent debates with the new atheists. Yet not all Christian debaters have displayed that same blend of love, truth and grace. The trouble is that, like a boxing match, a debate is for someone to win and someone to lose, and there are far too many Christians of whom it has been said that they won the argument but lost the audience. Their logic outran their love. Sometimes they displayed wit and more often weightiness in their arguments, but they never backed it with winsomeness. If our arguments are too loose, we can appear incompetent, but if our arguments are too tight, we can equally appear unloving and lacking in respect. Far too many an audience has been left either impressed or offended by Christian apologists, but not won over.

TRUTH OR PERSUASION

This objection to public speakers is far from new, and it can be traced all the way back to the Greeks, where it raised its head early on in the groundbreaking classical discussion of the art of rhetoric. If we lived in a world without sin, our main goals in any debate and discussion with anyone would be to seek truth together, to arrive at the truth together, and therefore to achieve a deeper agreement between us. But that is not the world we live in after the fall, and such lofty aspirations will always run into a grittier reality. The truth is that many people have no interest in truth. They argue only to stake out their ground, to have the final say in any decision or simply to be the cock of the roost. Listen to any political debate, television discussion or academic seminar, and it is rarely hard to miss the clashing egos behind the dueling arguments. Self-interest and power, not truth, are the real objectives of much human debate, and they are able to flourish because of the fateful gap in our speech between its content and its form, or between truth and persuasiveness.

Socrates set out these issues in a characteristically sharp form. As Plato describes his mentor's conversation in *Phaedrus*, the great Greek gadfly raised the thorny issue of the relationship of truth and persuasion, and therefore the relationship of truth and virtue. Seen one way, the art of rhetoric is the art of winning arguments, but if important issues are to be debated and not debased, the relationship between truth and persuasion needs to be guarded with care. The Sophists of Socrates' day could argue so cleverly that they could make white seem black, and black seem white, and they had given a bad name to the honored place of rhetoric. Rhetoric then, and apologetics today, can easily lead to a style of argument winning that has no regard for truth at all.

Centuries later, Arthur Schopenhauer explored the same issue in his ironic essay *The Art of Always Being Right*. He knew the classical conversation well, and he also knew the specious arguments of his own day, so he set out all the tricks of the trade in order to inoculate his readers against such deceptions. Debate, he warned in the opening words, is "the art of disputing and disputing in such a way as to hold one's own, whether one is right or wrong."[5]

Should a speaker be concerned solely with truth, the whole truth and nothing but the truth, and therefore with the strict logic and merits of his argument? Or does effective persuasion require that the speaker use whatever tricks of the trade to succeed in winning others to his point of view, regardless of truth and logic? Put all the stress on truth and you may lose the argument and be a failure. But put the stress on persuasion at any cost and you may easily win but be seen as a fraud. Failure or fraud? The simple fact is that, because of our humanity, many of us would rather risk being seen as a fraud, though perhaps as a clever fraud, rather than be written off as a failure.

Quite obviously, speakers who are skilled in persuasion can turn the worse case into the better, truth into lies, lies into truth, good into evil and evil into good—or in Socrates' words "make small things great and great things small by the power of their words."[6] But that is not the end of the problem. As Schopenhauer warns, "It is easy to say that we must yield to truth. But we cannot assume that our opponent will do it, and therefore we cannot do it either."[7]

In short, truth is crucial to persuasion, just as persuasion is crucial to truth, but it takes more than truth to be persuasive, and in the daylight between those two facts there lies a gap through which every shape and size of demagogue, mountebank, trickster, con man, snake-oil salesman and fraud can squeeze with ease. Such sophists, and their modern heirs in the form of writers for hire, advertisers, PR consultants, and damage control experts will never find themselves out of a job. But the perennial problem they represent was what prompted Socrates' foundational question, "Do you know how you can speak and act about rhetoric *so as to please God best?*"[8]

The common safeguard for the Greeks, as well as for Romans who followed them, such as Cicero, was that the speaker should be a person of good sense, good character and good will. Or put differently, the dangerous gap between truth and virtue should be filled in by means of three principles: first, the reminder that truth and virtue are more powerful than falsehood and vice; second, the reminder that a speaker should be a person of character and virtue; and third, the reminder that the speaker should always address the public good and not only his or her own interest. Together, it was thought, these three principles would close the door against the wiles of the Sophists and all the dangers implicit in the gap between truth and persuasion.

The Christian equivalents to these classical principles are obvious, but my point in this book has been to underscore a different principle that is entirely lacking in the classical discussion and unique to Christian persuasion. Within important limits, Christians, too, know that truth can be counted on to have its own power to prevail, at least in the end—as stated, for example, in the old Irish maxim quoted by Thomas Jefferson: "Truth is great and shall prevail." And Christians, too, believe that that the integrity of character and the motive of the Christian persuader are crucial.

But Christians also emphasize themes that are missing from classical rhetoric altogether. On the one hand, we bring to all our communication a down to earth realism. Sin and unbelief, as the Scriptures show them to us, underscore that we must never be starry-eyed about human nature, starting from the witness of our own hearts and minds. For all the noblest human protestations on behalf of truth—and Schopenhauer's own motto was "Dedicate life to truth"—we know that, as sinners, none of us will ever truly seek truth in a wholly disinterested manner. As we saw in discussing the anatomy of unbelief, both we ourselves and everyone to whom we speak will always be truth twisters as well truth seekers. In Schopenhauer's words, all humans have an "innate vanity" and "so, for the sake of vanity, what is true must seem false, and what is false must seem true."[9]

On the other hand, we Christians must seek to communicate in a way that is shaped by the One who sends us, and therefore by the pattern of the incarnation, the cross and the Holy Spirit. The uniqueness of the message we share requires a corresponding uniqueness in the manner with which we share it. The style of our communication will therefore always be crucial to the substance, and it too must be shaped by the very truths that we proclaim. "As the Father has sent Me, I also send you," Jesus said in words that are much quoted (Jn 20:21). That certainly includes the simple fact that Jesus was sent, and so are we. But it also says far more: that the very manner in which Jesus was sent should shape the very manner in which we are sent and the manner in which we are to speak.

God has disclosed himself to us in a form that is a shocking surprise, and one that contradicts and confounds all our human expectations and ways of thinking. The Word became flesh and spoke in a human form as one of us, though incognito and in a disguise that fooled us and made fools of us. And, dare we say it again with silent reverence, *all this was because he had to, as there was no other way to subvert the stubbornness of our sinful disobedience and reach our hearts.* What a mystery, what an absurdity if not true, and if true what a wonder! The God of all power chose to become weak to subvert our puny power, the God of all wealth chose to become poor to subvert our meager wealth, the God of all wisdom chose to become foolish to subvert our imagined wisdom, and the God who alone is the sole decisive one chose to be a nobody to subvert us when we stupidly thought we were somebody. If such dire lengths were necessary for God himself, can we expect to speak differently? If our Lord had to do it in that costly way, it would be absurd to think we do justice to his incarnation by decking out our arguments in our best finery or speak worthily of his cross through arguments that preen with their own brilliance.

Shame on our folly when we think we know better than God! God's truth requires God's art to serve God's end. There is an art to truth, and an art that is shaped by truth. Christian truth requires its own art that alone communicates Christian truth, so any Christian explanation or defense of truth must have a life, a manner and a tone that are shaped decisively by the central truths of the gospel. Like the incarnation, our words are always most effective when they become person-to-person and face-to-face toward others. Like the cross, our message must pay the cost of identification, so that from the inside out it may have a chance of succeeding in its high and worthy aim. And like our reliance on the Holy Spirit, it should always be evident that any power and persuasiveness in our communication comes from him and not us. That, surely, is the context of St. Ignatius of Antioch's saying, "It is better to keep silence and to be, than to speak without being," or the often misquoted advice of St. Francis: "Preach the gospel constantly, and if necessary use words."

This challenge means that each of us as apologists must examine our own hearts. Have we loved enough to listen, or is it that we love to hear the sound of our own answers? Are we really arguing for Christ, or are we expressing our need always to be right? Are we really trying to show people how they can discover the solid assurance of a warranted faith, or are we really piling up evidence to try to convince ourselves? We love the privilege of being apologists, but is our real motive that we love to win arguments and be seen to be right and smart? "The defense never rests," we say, but are we defending the Lord, or are we defending our concern for ourselves and for our standing in the community?

Humility and vulnerability should always be among the clear marks of the Christian advocate. We do not know the answer to every question. We will not have a satisfying response to every objection. We should always be happy when people come to know Jesus, regardless of how we may have bungled our witness. We are mere midwives, and what matters is not us but the Spirit's gift of the fresh-born life of the new child of God. All we have done is provide the prompt for a few words or some forgotten lines in the play, and now the great playwright and his actors are in sync again, and the grand drama can go forward as the author intended.

Put the issue this way: Do we really think that we are more passionate about people knowing God than God himself is? How absurd. As we can see in the story of Jonah's reluctance to go to Nineveh, or in Peter's hesitation to contaminate himself by going to the Gentile centurion, or in the many re-markable accounts today of Muslims searching for God because they have seen Jesus in their dreams, it is obvious that God is reaching out to the world, and it is amazing that God waits for us or trusts us with any part at all. What really needs to be done, God is doing. As I said earlier, we are only Junior Counsels, and all eyes must be on the Senior Counsel. God is more true and more certain than our best defense of him. And if the Christian faith is true, as we believe for reasons that go far beyond us, God will remain God and our faith will remain true even when we are completely stumped and shown up for the untrained ignoramuses we really are.

We must also never forget the great danger of thrusting ourselves out in the place of God when defending God—and above all the temptation to think that God is no more certain than our best arguments for him. As C. S. Lewis admitted,

> I have found that nothing is more dangerous to one's own faith than the work of an apologist. No doctrine of that Faith seems to me so spectral, so unreal as one that I have just successfully defended in a public debate. For a moment, you see, it has seemed to rest on oneself: as a result, when you go away from that debate, it seems no stronger than that weak pillar. That is why we apologists take our lives in our own hands and can be saved only by falling back continually from the web of our own arguments . . . from Christian apologetics into Christ Himself.[10]

Too Educated by Half?

Challenges to our bad attitudes must never be ducked. The accusation of the need to always be right is serious one, and if substantiated would undermine our witness to the gospel. It would also stand as an insuperable obstacle to adopt the approaches recommended here because we would always be getting in the way. But there are other objections to apologetics and to apologists, and it is worth responding to some of the other reservations that people have toward the whole project of apologetics.

There is a very different but equally common suspicion about creative persuasion. It simply cannot be a proper Christian approach, some say, because it requires too much education. Sincerely or not, many Christians like to play the "fisherman's card"—we can only accept as legitimately Christian what would be understood in plain words by the first fisherman followers of Jesus, such as Peter and John. Never mind that the later writings of St. John, the former fisherman, are unsurpassed for their profundity. I would have to admit freely that I myself have egregiously flouted the fisherman's principle in this book, and in doing so have probably reinforced the impression that creative persuasion is only for educated people.

Sadly, we live in an age when books are no longer read as they were, and the classics are rarely taught as they once were—books that have stood the test of time and are therefore worthy of the attention of all times and all places. Even William Shakespeare seems to be more and more the preserve of the scholar and the cultured theater-goer today, so the mere mention of a Renaissance writer such as Erasmus is enough to suggest that creative persuasion must be academic, remote and quite beyond the reach of most Christians.

Not at all. I am a writer, but in fact I am neither a scholar nor an academic, and the simple answer to the objection is that the opposite is true. Many of us today, and I include myself, are not naturally adept at creative persuasion. *But the reason is not that we are not educated enough, but that we have too much education of the wrong sort.* Most people in the advanced modern world are extremely well educated by the standards of history and the levels of the rest of the world. But by the same token, modern education is strong on reason, logic, analysis, criticism and all the strengths of left-brain thinking, all of which are admirable qualities and essential for good thinking. But modern education is correspondingly weak on creativity, imagination, intuition, irony, metaphor and all the strengths of right-brain thinking, which are equally admirable and necessary. In other words, we have not been educated in as full a way as we should be and as many people were in the past. Nietzsche even argued that scholars have become "paper slaves" and "the level of real imagination in the higher institutions of learning has probably never been lower and weaker than at the moment."[11]

Be that as it may, what we need is not to pile up more courses and degrees in the vain hope of becoming brilliant persuaders when we are better educated, but to put ourselves back in touch with parts of our humanity that were squeezed out of us by our lopsided education when we were younger. Just think for a moment, and it would be obvious that creative persuasion is alive and well at the level of drama and humor where no one expects it to be cluttered with too much education of the highfalutin kind.

The Christian faith has always had a distinguished line of brilliant, creative persuaders, such as Blaise Pascal, Jonathan Swift, Søren Kierkegaard, G. K. Chesterton, Dorothy Sayers, J. R. R. Tolkien, C. S. Lewis and Malcolm Muggeridge. But their importance is greater than the fact that they belong to what is the minority party in Christian communication. Far more importantly, their approach lines up with a powerful strand of persuasive biblical communication, and they bring a timely contribution at a point where many of us in the church are lamentably weak today.

There is an old adage that perfectly expresses the prejudice surrounding the supposed reason for using stories and parables: "You can see from me how useful it can be / To use an image to tell the truth / To someone who is not very bright." But as we have seen, the problem is quite the opposite of such patronizing nonsense. The challenge to persuasion is not that people are not bright but that whether they are bright or not, they are not open to what we are saying. The brightest in fact are often the most closed.

ARM-TWISTING BY ANY OTHER NAME?

A third common suspicion is that creative persuasion is really nothing but a sophisticated form of arm-twisting or manipulation. "I am an artist," one man said to me, "and I really like what you are saying. It fits in with the whole creative and indirect way I see my art, but I have one nagging objection. The art of creative persuasion sounds manipulative. Aren't you forcing people to see what they don't want to see? That is surely an elegant form of manipulation by another name."

That question, which someone raised to me after a talk to professionals in the art world, is deadly serious, and unless it is answered, it hangs over creative persuasion like an unanswered accusation. No one likes to be manipulated, and no one should be manipulated. If freedom is the capacity for self-determination, nothing is more precious to human beings than freedom and the responsibility that goes with it, and to flout them is a violation of our humanity. The belief, the trust, the worship and the obedience to which God calls us is to be free and uncoerced. Manipulation is anathema.

But is the suspicion warranted? Is creative persuasion manipulative? Are we playing mind games with people and forcing them to see what they do not want to see? Or, to raise the question to the biblical precedents I have cited, was Nathan manipulating David through his famous story? And more importantly, was Jesus manipulating the people of his times through the parables he told?

Once again, the truth is that the opposite is the case. As emphasized earlier, by virtue of the fact that creative persuasion is indirect rather than direct, involving rather than take-it-or-leave-it, and imaginative rather than prosaic, each individual person must do the work for herself or himself. They must see the point for themselves, or not see it as the case may be. But people are never asked to see what they do not see themselves. There is no outside pressure at all. The appeal is to the freedom and responsibility of the hearer.

The different forms of creative persuasion all act in the same way as the play within the play in Shakespeare's *Hamlet*. Based on the witness of the ghost, young prince Hamlet suspected that his stepfather, Claudius, had murdered his father in order to marry his mother and seize the throne of Denmark. But he was not certain, so he devised a test to expose the king's innocence or guilt. He brought in a troupe of visiting actors and added some lines to the play they performed for the royal court. His aim was clear: "The play's the thing, wherein I'll catch the conscience of the king."[12]

Sure enough, as Hamlet watched carefully, his stepfather betrayed his guilt when he flinched visibly at the mention of a regicide. In other words, what Nathan's story did for King David, Hamlet's play did for Claudius. But what links the two stories is that neither king would have betrayed their guilt if they had not been guilty. If either David or Claudius had been innocent, they would have been entirely nonplussed. The conscience, not the courtier, is what convicts the king.

Lovers of detective stories will know the same tactic well. Some celebrated sleuth, such as Agatha Christie's Hercule Poirot, has narrowed the suspects down to three people, but which of them is the criminal? He then sets up a litmus test and invites all three to pass through it. The innocent ones pass through nonplussed and unscathed, whereas the guilty one betrays him- or herself as the criminal in the process. Again, there are no threats, no intimidation and no apologetic equivalent of "enhanced interrogation" techniques. On the contrary, Christie's portly Belgian and her amiable Miss Marple are anything but hardball players. The incrimination they look for in their tests is always self-incrimination.

WHOEVER HAS EARS TO HEAR

Is this not exactly what happened as people listened to the parables of Jesus? Consider the well-known parable of the workers in a vineyard that Mark recounts in his Gospel. When I was an undergraduate studying philosophy, there was a tendency for people to make patronizing references to the parables of Jesus. After all, Jesus was a "simple country teacher telling simple country stories to simple country people." Was that not so? In other words, we should expect him to tell stories and not to use the higher levels of abstract argument that (presumably we) the more sophisticated would use.

That condescension was to change fast in light of the revolutionary new understanding of the many-sided dynamics of communication and interpretation in the last generation. Far from patronizing, the newer views openly recognized that Jesus was one of the most brilliant communicators who ever lived—especially in his creative use of parables that challenged people to see things they were stubbornly disposed not to see.

Today, we know that in the era of the Internet, focused attention has become the rarest commodity in the world. Everyone is speaking, no one is listening, and the resulting familiarity breeds inattention. It is therefore difficult to break through the many levels of resistance and make fresh sense to people. In the same way, though for far deeper reasons, Jesus knew well that true listening is not so much physical, a mere matter of hearing with the ears. It is moral, a matter of also *heeding* with the heart. Everyone had the ears to hear, but not everyone had the ears to heed.

People could therefore "see and see, but not see," as Isaiah had warned and St. Paul later reiterated. They could "hear and hear, but not hear" (Is 6:9-10; Mk 4:12; Acts 28:26). So again and again Jesus says, with seeming redundancy but disarming accuracy, "Whoever has ears to hear, let him hear." He used parables to help people see what they did not want to see, but it was always through an invitation for each person to see the truth for themselves, rather than through manipulation or coercion.

The parable of the vineyard is a clear example (Lk 20:9-18). The idea of Israel as God's own special vineyard was a national motif that the prophet Isaiah had underscored, and there was also a well-known Jewish story of a proprietor whose vineyard was taken over by thieving tenants. In that version the owner took the estate away and gave it to the tenants' sons, who in their turn proved even worse than their fathers. So he gave it to his own son, who drove out the tenants and ran the vineyard himself. End of story.

Whether Jesus knew that particular story and adapted it, we do not know, though it makes sense that he did. But he certainly knew Isaiah, so he starts from the same point as the prophet and builds the story into a far more dramatic version with a tragic ending and an unexpected twist. Israel, as the prophet Isaiah had taught, was the Lord's vineyard, and the history of Israel was the story of the Lord repeatedly having to assert his lawful right to his full, sole ownership of his vineyard, and from time to time having to take it back from those who expropriated it.

Just as all roads then led to Rome, so Jesus had made clear that every day of his life was leading to Jerusalem, the place where all the prophets were stoned and killed. Now he is in the holy city and in the temple itself, the glorious but flawed symbol of the presence of God in Israel. On the one hand, the second temple was a wonder of the ancient world, resplendent with Herod's dream of restoring the greatness of David and Solomon. On the other hand, it was the power center of the hated Sadducees who had sold their soul to the devil and made a pact with imperial Rome in exchange for the right to rule their people under Rome.

And who is this Jesus who stands there ready for the showdown? He is the one whose self-understanding and public assertions had laid down the claim was that he was not just a prophet but the very Son himself, the Son who had come on behalf of his Father to reclaim the stolen vineyard. In short, Jesus is in the temple, his expropriated Father's house, and he is in the very presence of the high priests and their feared temple police who had seized it and now had to follow through and seize him too. He has arrived at the epicenter of his clash with the usurping authorities, and he throws down the gauntlet with a triple provocation. The temple will be destroyed, he announces, the priestly caste will be destroyed with it, and as an advance token of what he says is to come, Jesus grabs a whip and drives the traders and money-changers out of the temple.

Far from simply another delightful rural tale told in passing, the parable was a bold and deliberate provocation. And the two most explosive parts of the gauntlet Jesus throws down are in the conclusion.

Did the ordinary folk in the crowd understand the full thrust of the parable and its incendiary objective? Probably not. Most likely they were somewhat nonplussed. To them it was just another powerful story from the amazing teacher from Nazareth who had the extraordinary knack of telling stories that delighted some people but seemed to rub other people the wrong way. If it was the Sadducees whose nose was being put out of joint this time, so much the better. Their vicious monopoly of the temple trading was sheer extortion. They had it coming to them, especially those crooked money changers who were the scourge of the pious poor.

But no one had actually mentioned the Sadducees. Jesus certainly had not. Unlike a preacher today, he had not expounded the parable as he went along. He had just told the story. When he started, in fact, it might have appeared just as likely that Jesus was out to have a dig at the Pharisees. They often seemed to be the butt of his parables.

But no, not this time. You only had to watch the crowd to see who was getting the point—in spite of themselves. Judging from the body language in one section of the crowd—the uneasy shuffling feet, the clenched fists, the grinding teeth and the veins standing out on the foreheads—those upset were the temple aristocrats, the Sadducees themselves, with their guards alert and suspicious around them like so many Doberman Pinchers straining at the leash and waiting for the word to pounce.

Who had mentioned the Sadducees? All Jesus had done was tell a story.

And invited by the parable, the Sadducees had entered and engaged the story for themselves, followed along as it unfolded, and then judged and convicted themselves at the climax. They saw the point even if many of the crowd did not. They were the wicked tenants of the vineyard. They had run the temple as their own monopoly, and they and their children were the ones whom Jesus said would be destroyed. They had persecuted and killed earlier messengers from God. Now the Son himself had come to lay claim to what was lawfully his Father's, and they had already convened in council to plot to kill him.

Then comes the climax to Jesus' telling of the story. Rather than yet another contest in which the tenants win again, and this time as they thought for good, the Son predicts that his own death would trigger the final act. Caiaphas's strategy would not work. It would backfire. It was the customary Roman policy to diligently protect all the religious sanctuaries throughout the empire, and also to protect all the different priests from troublesome agitators. But instead of one man dying so that the Romans would not destroy the Jews as a whole, as Caiaphas plotted, both the rightful Son and then later the entire temple would be destroyed when the Lord, the rightful owner, would step in and destroy the tenants altogether. In other words, exactly as happened after the Romans destroyed Jerusalem and the temple in A.D. 70, the priestly caste of the Sadducees would be destroyed forever—Annas, Caiaphas and their whole conniving clan.

Then comes the final twist. Jesus finishes his parable by quoting Psalm 118, "The stone which the builders rejected has become the chief corner stone." The Son would indeed be killed. He was the Son, and he was announcing his death himself. He knew what they were plotting, and he was going toward his death knowingly and deliberately. But contrary to what they thought, his death would not be the end of the affair. The Son's cause would win. His Father would see to it. It was the day of the Sadducees that was done, sealed by their own intransigence and disobedience.

Is the parable manipulative? How so? Once again, the Sadducees were not forced to see what they would not and did not see for themselves. By the testimony of their own response, they showed that they understood the truth, and from then on, they and their actions were without excuse. Their response was self-incriminating, but they had been persuaded, not manipulated, convicted but not coerced.

MOMENT OF TRUTH

We noted earlier that in St. Paul's letter to the Romans, he defends the justice of God's final judgment as utterly and entirely unanswerable. When that day comes and judgment is made, he writes, "every mouth will be closed," and the word he uses literally means that all humans will be "apology-less" (Rom 3:19). At the great assize at the end of the days, when all history's books will be opened, when justice will be vindicated for the whole world and shalom will be restored to the last reaches of the cosmos, we will all stand before God defenseless. All human secrets will be laid bare, all alibis blown, and all excuses, evasions and hypocrisies exposed for the threadbare frauds that they are. At that moment, Paul says, the justice of God's judgments will be so apparent that not one of us will have a further case to plead in our own defense and no defense counsel will step forward to plead for us. We will be silent, defenseless and naked before God. We will know the truth, and we will know in what ways we have always known the truth. We will be apology-less.

Dare we ask what such a "moment of truth" means, and when it is in each of our lives that we know it? How it is that every single human being will have had such a moment that it will be quite evident to us and to everyone that we are all responsible? Do we ever know when we ourselves have known enough of God and his truth for that truth to be the grounds of such a just and unanswerable judgment? When is it that we can be said to know God's truth truly and unmistakably so that we are forever accountable? Do we become accountable through the "signals of transcendence" we have heard and responded to or not? What is it we will realize, when on the Day of Judgment, we are confronted with the evidence of "eternity written in our hearts"?

We are free to try to answer these questions, but our best answers would only be speculation. We are free to speculate, so long as we admit it is only speculation and we do not dress up our speculations as God's answer. But the fact is that we have no full answer to such questions now, and we can only trust in God's justice and mercy then. At the same time, it is always sobering when we see people reach such a solemn moment in their experience here and now. For there are moments when people are convicted by the truth that they see in all its unanswerable reality—and they actually see it for themselves and acknowledge it—but they still turn on their heels rather than fall on their knees.

It was at precisely that moment of truth that King David fell to his knees, whereas the Sadducees turned on their heels. He repented and returned to God, and they refused God and stubbornly went further away than ever. Without Jesus saying a single word directly to them, the Sadducees hardened their hearts and stalked off in high dudgeon. But in doing so they confirmed that they had seen the truth and rejected it knowingly. In their response to that moment of truth, they became their own accusers, their own judge and eventually their own executioners. There was no manipulation in their self-incrimination, but the justice of the indictment was no less plain. Their moment of truth—seen, considered and rejected beyond any doubt—stands as the silent witness against them for all time. As Pascal observed, when God addresses our human hearts, there is always enough light for those who desire to see, yet enough obscurity for those who do not wish to see. What makes the difference is the heart.

The false art of always being right is a deadly trap for Christian advocates. Conversely, it is a high privilege to use the art of persuasion to bring people to where they know in their heart of hearts that they are wrong, but that God's offer of grace is free. Little wonder that such a privilege and such an art can only be pursued with humility and with an overwhelming sense of God's grace to us too. Again the art of truth leads back to the incarnation, the cross and the Holy Spirit, and the life of faith continues as it began.

❖ 10 ❖

Beware
the Boomerang

Thou hast conquered, O pale Galilean; the world has grown grey from thy breath." The poet Algernon Swinburne based these words on the supposed last words of the Emperor Julian (*Vicisti Galilaee*—You have conquered, Galilean!). Julian died in A.D. 362, having failed in his attempt to return Rome to the pagan gods of his ancestors. "Grown grey" was Swinburne's own spin in the service of his nineteenth-century attack on the Victorian church and the Christian faith.[1] But the fact was that it was the classical world that had grown gray with its sense of futility, and it was the gospel that had burst over it like a lightning flash of hope. Indeed, the Christian faith had given the dying classical world the seeds of its own renewal and its links to our Western world.

Curiously, many Christians have a stick figure notion of "Julian the Apostate" that is almost as simplistic as Swinburne's but from the opposite viewpoint. Reigning briefly for only two years, Julian rejected Constantine's move toward the Christian faith, worked energetically to restore the pagan gods and values of classical Rome, but died in battle against the Persians and thus failed utterly in his attempt to restore paganism. The momentum toward the conversion of the Roman empire to Christ was inevitable and unstoppable. The hand of providence is clear and unmistakable. Julian was doomed to fail. The clock could not be turned back.

That, however, is the judgment of hindsight in which all history appears to be determined and therefore happens the way that it did. The fact is that

Julian "the Apostate" could easily have been Julian "the Restorer," and the difference between the first outcome and the second was, like the battle of Waterloo, a "close run thing." Had Julian lived, one reason for his potential success was that he knew his Christian opponents well, and his clever strategy against them was based on his intimate knowledge of how they behaved.

For one thing, it is highly probable that Julian's parents were Christian, that he had grown up as a Christian, and that he had been influenced by such giants of the faith as Gregory of Nazianzus. In other words, Julian's attacks on the faith were powerful because they were an insider's attacks. For another, Julian was an able philosopher-soldier who was said to be the best thinker to wear the imperial purple since Marcus Aurelius. And he had a clear plan for undermining the growing influence of the church—first, by moving to limit Christian rights and benefits; second, by creating a pagan church to rival Christian organizations; and third, by mounting his own apologetic attack on the Christian faith to complement earlier assaults, such as those of Celsus and Porphyry.

Most intriguingly of all, Julian's designs included a canny reliance on what he knew was the Achilles' heel of the Christian faith: hypocrisy—our constant Christian failure to practice what we preach. It is true that he famously acknowledged where the love and care of Christians outstripped that of his fellow pagans. ("It is disgraceful that no Jew ever has to beg and the wretched Galileans take better care of our poor, as well as their own, than we do.")[2] But he also counted on the well-known Christian capacity for division and strife that ran directly counter to Jesus' call for unity in his prayer before his arrest.

Julian even calculated that, counting on Christian hypocrisy, he could use toleration to deliberately foster Christian disunity. So when he became emperor, he called the Christian bishops together and told them to sort out their differences and live in peace—knowing that was probably the best way to intensify their differences and destroy their unity. Experience had taught him, he remarked to those around, that "no wild beasts are as dangerous to man as Christians are to each other."[3]

Earlier emperors had thrown Christians to the lions, and the faith flourished through persecution. But while the blood of the martyrs was the seed of the church, the battles of the faithful are the scandal of the faith. Better to let Christians hurt their own cause by fighting among each other like wild animals. When Christians fight with Christians, there is an important sense in which both are defeated already.

The Unanswerable Objection?

Exploiting Christian hypocrisy to damage the Christian faith? Julian's strategy was a refined and subtle version of what is more commonly an open, angry and disgusted attack on the Christian faith for its hypocrisy. Christians are hypocrites, it is said, vile hypocrites. They do not practice what they preach. They do not walk the talk. And no one likes a hypocrite. They talk such fine ideals, and they make such superior judgments. Indeed they brandish their judgments on others and force people to wear the scarlet letter of their disapproval, but once they themselves are exposed, shame is what they get and what they deserve. They are hoist by their own petard. In short, Christians are some of the worst hypocrites in the world, and that in itself is reason enough to reject the Christian faith. History proves beyond a shadow of doubt, the conclusion runs, that the Christian faith is simply hypocrisy incarnate.

Such attacks sting, and in the acrid atmosphere of outrage or mockery, hypocrisy can appear to be the unanswerable objection to faith. How can anyone defend the indefensible? Christian hypocrites violate their own faith in a flagrant contradiction of everything they claim, so who need take their claims seriously? In fact there is no need to attack hypocrisy with heavy artillery. Expose a Christian hypocrite and he will be seen to have falsified his own faith. Better still, have a whole community to be hypocrites together, and others can walk away and leave the faith to die.

Plainly, hypocrisy is a massive challenge for the Christian faith and for all of us as Christians. Jesus said to his disciples what the Lord had said to his people the Jews in the Old Testament: "You are my witnesses" (Is 43:10, 12; 44:8; Jn 3:28). In other words, before we are asked to preach, proclaim or try to persuade people of the claims of Jesus and his Father, we are asked simply to be witnesses for him—to provide an honest and factual account of what we have seen and heard objectively, and what we ourselves have experienced ("Once I was blind, but now I can see")—and to live lives that support what we say.

Hypocrisy is therefore damaging because it squarely undercuts our testimony before we may have said a single word. Our lives contradict our words. It is therefore one of the worst charges thrown against us as followers of Jesus—we are not living the way of Jesus, and other people can see it. In my view, hypocrisy is second only to the problem of evil and suffering that is the so-called rock of atheism.[4] Hypocrisy is also one of the easiest reasons for ducking the challenge of the gospel. If Christians are hypocrites, who need consider the Christian faith? Haven't we all heard remarks such as "Christians are all a bunch of hypocrites"? Or the common excuse, "I may not be that great, but at least I'm not a hypocrite"? Or the easy dismissal, "How on earth can Christians contribute anything when they are such hypocrites themselves?"

Such responses have been heard down the ages and across many cultures. They have also been underscored by thinkers with varying degrees of animosity toward the faith. "Every Stoic was a Stoic," Ralph Waldo Emerson wrote, "but in Christendom, where is the Christian?" "In truth there was only one Christian, and he died upon the cross," Nietzsche wrote. "Christianity might be a good thing," George Bernard Shaw used to say, "if anyone ever tried it." "For God's sake," C. E. M. Joad quipped, "don't touch the Church of England. It is the only thing that stands between us and Christianity."

Not surprisingly, Christians themselves have echoed the same charge, though with sorrow rather than anger. "If we would bring the Turks to Christianity," Erasmus wrote in *The Complaint of Peace*, "we must first be Christians." "Millions of Christians down the centuries," Kierkegaard protested, "have succeeded in making Christianity exactly the opposite of what it is in the New Testament." "I believe in the Holy Catholic Church," Archbishop William Temple lamented, "and I only regret it does not exist."

Hypocrisy is therefore a very serious problem for defenders of the faith. But what exactly is hypocrisy? Why is it so serious, and in what sense does it count against faith? Are Christians the only hypocrites, or perhaps only the worst? How are we to counter hypocrisy and achieve some measure of true authenticity? And what are the special dangers for apologists in countering charges of hypocrisy?

There are particular dangers for apologists, for example, when the church becomes worldly—when it has been assimilated to its surrounding culture, so that the faith and culture are confused. An extreme form of this happened after the Revolution in France, for example, when the Catholic Church and the political Right colluded in what became known as "the Sabre and the Font," and the same thing has happened more recently in the United States in a milder form with the convergence of the Republican party and the religious Right. Such moments give birth to powerful anti-Christian forces, but only after the heat and battle are over does it become clear that they are not so much opposed to the Christian faith itself as to the political and social uses to which the faith is being put.

Advocates for the faith have to be very careful how they respond at such times, for the temptation is to confuse the culture with the faith. As historian Henry Chadwick commented on apologetic responses to the militant anti-Christian movements in France:

> Defenders of Christian orthodoxy looked to their gates, lowered the portcullis, raised the drawbridge and boiled the oil. They had too little consciousness that part of the assault rose out of some of their own principles. . . . "Who among us would be a freethinker," asked Nietzsche, with his characteristic excess, "were it not for the church?"[5]

But there is another point that must be raised here too. As I am sure some people are thinking, *The very style of apologetics advocated here invites the accusation of hypocrisy*. Surely, then, there is a serious flaw in the approach I am suggesting. It lays the Christian faith open to an obvious attack. As one person said to me after I had spoken on the need to push people to see the logic of the positions that they have chosen over against God: "It's all very well to push people to be consistent to their unbelief. But as you've said, all arguments cut both ways. What happens if they push us back, and we do not and cannot live up to what we say? Will we not be shown up as failures at best and hypocrites at worst?"

The answer to that question is simple, though challenging. If unbelievers are pressed to be consistent to their beliefs and worldviews, and shown up when they cannot be (because their faiths are not finally true), Christians should welcome being pressed in the same way. The boomerang returns and hits us. *Where unbelievers cannot be consistent, we should be.* If the Christian faith is true and we are shown up for failing to live consistently to it, we must put that right. We are called to be doers of the Word and not hearers only. So if we are inconsistent to what we believe, it is we who are wrong and not the faith. We must therefore work to close the gap between our talk and our walk. The charge of hypocrisy is painful but bracing. It is positive if it spurs us to repentance and then to growth. In short, where unbelievers cannot finally be true to what they believe, because their faiths are not fully and finally true, we should be true to what we believe, and we must be. In this life we will never be perfect, but Christian growth is a matter of growing closer to our Lord and closer in our alignment with his truth and his way of life.

STEP ONE: WE ARE ALL HYPOCRITES NOW

Much more could be said about hypocrisy, but it is obvious that thinking through an answer to the charge of hypocrisy is a crucial part of apologetics. Such an answer may be set out in six steps, the first of which is to recognize the point at which the Christian faith and modern thinking agree without any equivocation: deception is endemic to humanity. We are all hypocrites now.

As we saw in chapter five, common to both the biblical worldview and the thinking of modern philosophy and psychology is the assertion that deception and self-deception are fundamental and pervasive in human experience. A striking feature of modern as well as postmodern thinking about humanity is that there is a gap between the inner self and the outer self, and between reality and appearance. Karl Marx spoke of "ideology," not just as a set of ideas but a set of ideas that served as weapons for social interests. Similarly, Nietzsche and Michel Foucault analyzed the "genealogy of morals" in terms of power, interests and agendas masquerading as virtues, Sigmund Freud described "rationalizing" as giving reasons other than the real reasons, and Albert Camus always talked of motives and "ulterior motives." And for the discipline of the sociology of knowledge, the gap between the inner and the outer, and between appearance and reality, is precisely why it is a commonplace truth that "nothing is ever what it appears to be." In short, what the Bible calls the "deceitful heart" and Plato called the "double game" are alive and strongly confirmed by modern thinking.

To be sure, it is fashionable today to prattle on about "transparency," "authenticity," "accountability" and "sincerity" as if these were easily attainable, and as if the younger generation prizes them and no one in history did earlier. But nothing is that easy and straightforward. Camus warned against the delusion of sincerity: "Above all, don't believe your friends when they ask you to be sincere with them. They merely hope you will encourage them in the good opinion they have of themselves by providing them with additional assurance they find in your promise of sincerity."[6]

Most people's notions of these ideals are naive, and none of the ideals is that simple. Complete transparency is impossible, true authenticity is harder than ever, real accountability is easier to avoid than before—if only because of the link between modern mobility and anonymity—and sincerity can be dangerous when it is allowed to take the place of truth. To anyone with their eyes and ears open, it is also obvious that the very same people who talk of these ideals also thrive on a robust diet of cynicism, the art of mistrust, the "hermeneutics of suspicion" and the need to have a keen "nose for BS."

As well they might, for as the Yale philosopher Harry Frankfurt writes, "One of the salient features of our culture is that there is so much bullshit. Everyone knows this. Each of us contributes his share. But we tend to take the situation for granted."[7] (BS, Frankfurt notes, is an apt term, combining the Old English word *bull*, or hot air, with the word for human waste, from which all nutritional content has been removed.)

We must not hurry past such contradictions in hypocrisy too quickly. For example, it has always been true that the same people who are fashionably skeptical and careless about truth are almost never skeptical or blasé about lying, especially when they themselves are lied to. Yet the plain fact is that a lie is a claim about reality that is stated with the express intention of misdirecting the truth and deceiving someone. A lie assumes a knowledge of the truth, and it has to. If a speaker does not know the truth, his false claim would not be a lie but an error.

Postmodern thinking is an exaggerated case of this contradiction. We might say that it is inherently hypocritical because it can only raise the charge of hypocrisy by an accusation that it cannot itself substantiate without objective truth. But the practical effect is more important. Postmoderns have a problem when they stand up against hypocrisy—they are impotent to remedy it. If hypocrisy in its essence is a violation of truth, which it is, postmodernism has no concept of truth with which to remedy the problem.

And if hypocrisy violates justice, which it does, postmodernism has no concept of objective justice either. If, as postmoderns say, "truth" is merely the compliment we pay to claims and ideas that we agree with, then "lies" are only the insult we level at claims and ideas that differ from our own. Seen that way, there are only relativities to counter relativities, supposed lies to counter supposed lies, and of course power to counter power.

Fyodor Dostoevsky foresaw this problem in the nineteenth century. In *The Brothers Karamazov*, Father Zossima warns, "Above all, don't lie to yourself. The man who lies to himself and listens to his own lie comes to such a pass that he cannot distinguish the truth within him or around him, and so loses all respect for himself and others."[8]

No one appreciated and explored this point more excruciatingly than Camus. In his novel *The Fall*, his protagonist Clamence expresses his fear that if lies are left unconfessed and distortions of reality are left uncorrected, they would mount exponentially from generation to generation to create a grand edifice of falsehood and unreality. Just as ongoing, careless waste leaves the earth environmentally polluted, lies and distortions of reality would gather pace until "the absolute murder of truth" created a world that was impossibly polluted morally and philosophically. As Clamence admits,

> A ridiculous fear pursued me in fact: one could not die without having con-
> fessed all one's lies. Not to God or one of his representatives: I was above all
> that as you can imagine. No, it was a matter of confessing to men, to a woman,
> for example. Otherwise, were there but one lie hidden in a life, death made it
> definitive. No one, ever again, would know the truth on this point, since the
> only one to know it was precisely the dead man sleeping on his secret. That
> absolute murder of truth made me dizzy.[9]

The modern world therefore faces a dilemma. Either we must find a way to counter hypocrisy, starting with a search for a standard by which to judge it and a solution by which to remedy it. Or we must follow the logic of our situation in which there is no God, no objective truth and a toxic pollution of truth, and respond to the lethal environment we have created with the only response possible: cynicism. We are all hypocrites now, so let it be. There is nothing we can do about deception and self-deception, and if we can't solve the problem, we should make the best of a bad situation and join the cynics' game. Life would then be only a dirty game to be played with dirty hands, and won with all the tricks of truthless power and manipulation.

STEP TWO: CLARIFY THE ISSUES

It follows from this first point that if we are all hypocrites now, and not just Christians, and if much modern and postmodern thinking is quite deficient in providing any remedy, we need to think through the issue of hypocrisy at a much greater depth for all our sakes—starting by clarifying the issues.

Here is a place where the street-level understanding is entirely correct. Hypocrisy is all about the gap between truth and lies, integrity and falsehood, and justice and injustice. At its heart are gaps that are covered by a pretense that is false and a pose that is a cover. Expressed more precisely, hypocrisy involves a triple violation. It is a violation of truth because the content of what it appears to say is untrue. It is a violation of justice because the claim it appears to show is unjust. And it is a violation of honesty because the communication through which it appears to speak is dishonest. If a lie is an attempt to deceive others without their consent, hypocrisy is a lie told in deeds rather than words.

Once when the great slaver turned abolitionist John Newton was praised for what he had achieved, he responded quickly: "Sir, the devil already told me that." In a similar situation, when the eminent Scottish preacher Robert Murray M'Cheyne was congratulated by a parishioner for his saintliness, he replied sharply, "Madame, if you could see in my heart, you would spit in my face." In each case, they refused to let others think that they were what they weren't. They resisted hypocrisy by exposing the gap that was its essence—the gap between the inner and the outer, appearance and reality.

Needless to say, such humility and candor can be taken too far, to the point where people who know they are hypocrites are reluctant to say anything affirmative at all. W. H. Auden liked to paraphrase the command of Jesus as "You shall love your crooked neighbor / With your crooked heart."[10] "Those of us who have the nerve to call ourselves Christians," W. H. Auden said in a sermon, "will do well to be extremely reticent on the subject. Indeed it is almost the definition of a Christian that he is somebody who knows he isn't one, either in faith or morals."[11]

Scholars can add further subtleties to this discussion, but the heart of the issue remains the same. Philosophers, for example, have identified the "genetic fallacy." There is an important difference between the *source* of a truth claim and the *standard* by which it should be assessed. It is therefore wrong to reject a claim just because of the character and condition of its source.

Uncomfortable though it can be, avoiding the genetic fallacy reminds us of the important notion of "truth baggage." Just as a parent throws out the bathwater and not the baby, and a woman wears a pearl around her neck and not the oyster, so a truth claim needs to be distinguished from the baggage carried by those who affirm the claim. Naturally, this point cuts both ways. Those more educated need to remember that a belief may be true even if it is believed by the "irredeemably uncouth," just as those less educated need to remember that something may be true even if one of the "elite" advocates it. The issue is always truth, and truth is not a matter of where someone is "coming from" or how oddly or shabbily they have behaved in the past before making the claim.

Sociologists point to another helpful distinction—the difference between credibility and plausibility. Credibility is a matter of whether a belief *is* or *is not* true, and therefore an issue for philosophy to discuss. Plausibility, on the other hand, is a matter of whether a belief *seems* or does *not seem* to be true, and is therefore an issue for sociology to explore, regardless of the merits of the truth claims. What *passes* for truth is all that then matters. Understood in the light of this distinction, it is obvious that hypocrisy damages plausibility but not credibility. It is certainly harder to believe what "a bunch of hypocrites" say they believe, but what hypocrites believe must be examined as either true or false, regardless of their hypocrisy. As we must say again and again, and in answer to many different kinds of objections: *If the Christian faith is true, it would still be true even if no one believed it, or if all who did were hypocrites; and if it is false, would still be false even if everyone believed it and there was no apparent hypocrisy in their behavior.* For the question of credibility, the issue is always and only truth.

STEP THREE: APPRECIATE THE SOCIAL BENEFITS OF HYPOCRISY

It may sound odd, and perhaps it is even dangerous for people who take virtue seriously and do so in an age that doesn't, to admit that hypocrisy has its benefits. Yet it does, or at least it does under the conditions of our fallen world so that vice can play a vital part in the successful running of society. Take for instance the celebrated maxims of the seventeenth-century French aristocrat and author the Duc de la Rochefoucauld. "Self-love is the greatest of all flatterers," he wrote, as if expounding the biblical anatomy of unbelief. And his view of hypocrisy was equally astute—"If we had no faults, we would not take so much pleasure in noticing those of others." But in his attempt to see life without either a rose-tinted or a jaundiced eye, he also pointed to the qualified benefit of hypocrisy: "Hypocrisy is the homage that vice pays to virtue."

Rochefoucauld's maxim was far more than a clever saying of his own. It echoes the profound teaching of St. Augustine that evil always imitates the good and vice mimics virtue, which in turn gave rise to the paradoxical idea that private vices can make for public benefits. This happens, as we saw earlier, when the *appearance* and *effects* of love are mistaken for the *cause* of love, and people are then praised for a virtuous motive that is actually a mask for a vice, and therefore hypocritical. This idea was picked up from St. Augustine by the little known Pierre Nicole, the seventeenth-century French writer and Jansenist theologian, and then developed more provocatively by Bernard Mandeville in *The Fable of the Bees*. It led to the eighteenth-century idea of "enlightened self-love" and later to Adam Smith's famous exposition of the "invisible hand" that orders the free market and even mysteriously rights its wrongs.

As underscored earlier, prideful self-love slavishly copies true self-love out of self-interest. It seeks the approval of others, but disguises itself because it knows it would be distasteful to others if it were seen openly as self-love. Self-love therefore masks its real motive and mimics true love, and in doing so creates the paradoxical effect that private vices may work for the public good. For example, a good deal of what *appears* as generous philanthropy is really the fruit of prideful self-love disguised as generosity and reaching out for the validation of public approval and social esteem—and in the process creating enormous social benefits.[12] It "gives to get" as a matter of an unspoken contract, rather than "giving because given to," which is the expression of true charity. But in the world as it is, this motive is only natural. Expressed Christianly, it would be utopian to think that any society can remove sin and make all citizens good. Better then, people say, to be realistic and recognize a system that encourages most citizens, however good or bad, to behave as good, even if they are not or they are not as good as they aspire to be seen.

In Oliver Stone's film *Wall Street*, Michael Douglas, as the trader Gordon Gekko, argues famously that "Greed, for want of a better term, is good. Greed is right. Greed works." He sets out his claim as the consequence of his Darwinian philosophy of the struggle for the survival of the fittest, but it can also be made to fit in with the Christian understanding of the social benefits of hypocrisy. In a fallen world, greed may be seen as both a vice in its motive and a virtue in its consequences. As Nicole argues, "There is virtually no deed inspired by charity for the sake of pleasing God that self-love could not perform for the sake of pleasing men."[13]

Plainly, this understanding of the social benefits of hypocrisy turns on a subtle revaluation of the vices in general and pride in particular. And like Machiavelli's advocacy of open hypocrisy as policy for the prince, this view has an obvious and strict limit. Machiavelli forgot that his system of deception would not work if everyone operated deceitfully as the prince did— as, say, in a postmodern world of truthless lies, hype and spin. And Nicole was wrong to think that a society would run just as well if everything was "driven *only* by self-love," yet society would still "see everywhere *only* the forms and the outward marks of charity."[14]

Nicole went too far, and the limit on his system is plain and unforgiving. Politics as the art of managing vice is a dangerous game to play, and many have ruined their societies in trying to play it. In Augustine's biblical view, only God can manage the subtleties of the process, and the theological term for God's management of the world is providence. By contrast, all would-be human providences will fail in the end, whether Hobbes's false providence of the "Leviathan" of the political state or Adam Smith's false providence of "the invisible hand" of the commercial market. Today's liberal democracy, with its culture of transgression, its drive to liberate anything and everything done by and between consenting adults, and its mania for management by metrics, appears bent on adding to history's examples of societies that failed to manage vice and the crooked timber of our humanity.

The plain fact is that vice will always mimic virtue to gain the approval it seeks to validate itself and its prideful self-love. But it will do so *only so long as virtue is esteemed as virtue*, and virtue is therefore fashionable and worth flattering. If the day ever comes that virtue is no longer fashionable, self-love and vice can drop their mask and be open about their interests and their agendas. The result will be a rapid descent to the state of nature when vice openly fights vice and the outcome is a Hobbesian war of all against all. In short, the process contains a moral and social tipping point when there is no need for pretense, when vice can show its real face as vice and society will reap the consequences of its own chosen decadence.

Quite apart from the subtleties of this understanding of the social benefits of hypocrisy, the same point can be stated more straightforwardly. It is realistic rather than cynical to observe that in a fallen world there are degrees of virtue in relation to what is right, and good and just. These are important in our human judgments of others, even though they may be blown to the winds by the grace of God. To "do good because we know it is good" is different from "doing good only because we know we are seen," and this in turn is different from "doing good only because we are afraid of being thought to be bad," which in turn is different again from "the complete abandonment of any pretense of caring about being good or being seen." The first type of action springs from what we call morality, the second respectability, the third hypocrisy, and the fourth sheer wickedness.

This means that, bad though it is and dangerous though its slipway may prove, there is a sense in which hypocrisy may be preferable to wickedness. *Hypocrisy still cares enough about virtue to want to pretend to be virtuous, or at least it recognizes that the society around still prizes virtue enough to make it worth flattering.* When neither of those conditions can be assumed, as in times of open Sodom-and-Gomorrah decadence, the world is in deep trouble. In that limited sense Rochefoucauld is right. "Hypocrisy is the homage that that vice pays to virtue."

There is yet another way into seeing the "benefits" of hypocrisy. If the charge of hypocrisy stems from our failure to practice what we preach, at least it turns on the fact that other people know the standards by which it can be judged hypocrisy. In other words, they know enough of what we preach for our practice to be seen as a contradiction and therefore hypocritical. We are followers of Jesus, and they know enough about Jesus to know that we are not living up to the way Jesus called us to live. That is bad enough, but there is something even worse. The situation becomes dangerously toxic when other people do not know how Christians should behave, and therefore confuse the way Christians are thinking and living with the way Christians should think and live. Our lax, corrupt or brazenly anti-Christian ways of life are taken to be the Christian way of life—and therefore easily rejected.

That in fact is a prime way through which people have rejected the gospel in history. And we must face the humbling fact that again and again the major defections from the church are the result of vehement rejections of unfaithful and corrupt expressions of the Christian faith in different periods of history. The spread of atheism in the West, for example, is rooted historically in the corruptions of Christendom—the "politics of dissimulation" mentioned earlier was the rotten fruit of the way Christians had corrupted themselves and oppressed others through the abuse of state power. (Consider the blatant logic of the Jacobin cry in the French revolution: "We must strangle the last king with the guts of the last priest.") There are striking examples of the same thing in our own day. For example, the multiple angry assaults on the "traditional family" are the rotten fruit of Christians corrupting the beauty and strength of the "covenantal family" of the Bible into the hated "hierarchical family" of the stereotypes so loved by feminists and others.

Still more needs to be said about this trend, of course, and there must be no misunderstanding. It is not an argument for hypocrisy, but only for an understanding of its effects. Hypocrisy is absolutely wrong, always and everywhere, and there are ineradicable problems with it. Once it is exposed, disillusionment is inevitable and its "benefits" evaporate. And if everyone plays the hypocrite and there is no virtue to flatter, hypocrisy becomes pointless and society collapses into general wickedness. But it still stands true that in a limited way and for a limited time, hypocrisy does offer some benefits. For one thing, what a hypocrite models (if falsely) is virtue. So long as he or she is not found out, a hypocrite models and therefore helps to re-inforce the behavior that he or she is pretending to live. For another thing, hypocrites may affect others by preaching what they do not practice themselves. And for yet another thing, even the outrage at hypocrisy when it is exposed challenges everyone to a useful self-examination. Just as a counterfeit implies the worth of what it imitates, so the instinctive anger we level at hypocrisy can trigger helpful questions. What does hypocrisy say of the importance and the place of the virtue it betrays? Where might we ourselves be equally guilty of hypocrisy? Do we who are outraged by hypocrisy have the standards of truth or justice that alone can provide the remedy for hypocrisy, or are we inconsistent too?

Step Four: Remember Where Moral Seriousness Came From

Quite apart from the reinforcements of hypocrisy in modern and postmodern thinking, much of our modern world provides a lifetime of schooling in hypocrisy. Indeed the advanced modern world is so perfectly suited to hypocrisy that what is striking is not hypocrisy but our continuing outrage at it. After all, we have moved from face-to-face communities to abstract global societies, from small towns to large cities, and from the experience of being known by most people to being mostly unknown. Through our restless mobility, we modern people are more anonymous in more situations than any generation in history. Not surprisingly, these trends have created parallel trends in the rise of public relations, image consultants, spin, hype, makeovers, plastic surgery, Botox and the like. The inner, the real and the unseen are irrelevant in today's world. All that counts is appearance, and the world of consumerism has lost no time in catering to every need, and then creating even more, in this burgeoning market of the appearance.

It was not always so. The Bible insists that God does not see as humans see, for "man looks at the outward appearance, but the LORD looks at the heart" (1 Sam 16:7). Plato raises the same point in his parable of Gyges the shepherd, who was able to make himself invisible. Nothing could be further from the modern view, for in the biblical and classical view, character is *who we are when no one sees*. Before the searching eye of God, image, spin and PR are utterly irrelevant—flimsy and no more effective then picking up a feather to ward off a blowtorch.

This tough biblical view is what gave hypocrisy its deep moral seriousness. God hates hypocrisy. He is especially outraged by religious hypocrisy, when religion itself is used as a cover. And God is never deceived. He is angry, Isaiah declared,

> Because this people draw near with their words
> And honor me with their lip service,
> But they remove their hearts far from Me. (Is 29:13)

It is this radical critique of the Jewish Scriptures that Jesus sharpened even further. He used a straightforward and descriptive word that was the Greek word for "acting or playing a part on a stage," but gave it the explosively charged moral meaning that it has had in the Western world ever since— thanks to him.

Jesus opened his withering fire on three kinds of hypocrisy. The first is the hypocrisy of pretense, when we put up the front of being better than we really are. ("So when you give to the poor, do not sound a trumpet before you, as the hypocrites do in the synagogues and the streets, so that they may be honored by men" [Mt 6:2].) The second is the hypocrisy of blame and judgmentalism, when we criticize others despite moral faults of our own. ("Why do you look at the speck that is in your brother's eye, but do not notice the log that is in your own eye?" [Mt 7:3].) And the third is the hypocrisy of inconsistency, when we lay down moral requirements for others that we do not apply to ourselves. ("But woe to you, scribes and Pharisees, hypocrites, because you shut off the kingdom of heaven from people; for you do not enter in yourselves, nor do you allow those who are entering to go in themselves" [Mt 23:13].)

Can any of us walk scot-free and claim we are innocent of all these hypocrisies? What is as clear as the noonday sun is that Jesus was far harder on hypocrites than he was on sinners, and he was especially hard on those who used religion as a mask to cover their actions and their real motives. His scathing attacks put into perspective the earlier point made about the benefit of hypocrisy. Whatever limited benefit hypocrisy may hold for society, there are clearly no alibis or excuses for individual hypocrites. God himself is not deceived. Better to know the shame of exposure that leads to confession and forgiveness than be allowed to maintain the mask that hides a reality that one day will be judged sternly.

STEP FIVE: SAY NO TO RETALIATION, AND DARE TO CONFESS

Whenever we are attacked, the oldest response in the human book is to say, "You too!" From a small child's "Tit for tat," to a lawyer's *tu quoque* defense, to the viciousness of a Corsican blood feud, the easiest answer to insult or injury is always to retaliate, especially when the accusation itself is unfair or unjust. I have stressed that all arguments cut both ways, which is an important advice for the world of rhetoric. And I have urged a form of it earlier—"relativizing the relativizers," for example. But if such a response is carried out in a spirit of retaliation, it will most certainly backfire. To accuse someone of the very charge they have leveled against us ducks their point and introduces into the conversation more heat than light.

A skillful rejoinder with humor and love is different from retaliation. More importantly, retaliation in kind was never the way of Jesus. He called us as his followers to live his way and to love our enemies, forgiving without limit, returning good to those who wrong us, and taking into ourselves the wrong they do to us—as he himself did on the cross. And of course, Jesus called us to confess our wrongs and therefore to admit our opponents' charges when they are right.

Confession is under a cloud in many circles today, partly because our modern culture is swinging undecided between the memory of the once predominant Jewish and Christian culture of guilt and the new modern culture of shame (as in the trials by the media and the social media). Some people think confession is dubious because it must surely always have been coerced—perhaps by some guilt-inducing authority pressuring someone on the couch or in the confessional, or perhaps by some politically correct court of public opinion before which those who sin against the currently fashionable sin must grovel and make amends. Others simply consider confession weak—running up a white flag when we are no longer strong enough or brazen enough to keep up the stonewalling and "plausible deniability" that are key tactics in the art of damage control and of surviving public scandals.

The truth is that, properly understood, confession is a key strength of the Christian faith and a vital part of countering hypocrisy. For a start, open, voluntary confession is part and parcel of a strong and comprehensive view of truth, and therefore of realism and responsibility. Whatever we do and have done, whether right or wrong, is a matter of record and reality. Responsibly owning up to it therefore aligns us to reality and to truth in a way that liberates. And far from being weak or an act of surrender, confession is the expression of rare moral courage, for in confessing a person demonstrates the strength of character to *go on record against himself or herself.*

Again, the result of free confession is freedom. By contrast, deception is self-serving in the short run but disastrous in the long run, as Walter Scott captured so brilliantly in his poem "Marmion": "O, what a tangled web we weave / When first we practice to deceive." Lies entangle us in a thickening web of unreality. But when we confess, we face the truth, shoulder the responsibility for what we have done, and walk forward without the complicating clutter created by lies or the fear of exposure. If we get back in line with truth and reality, there are no more shoes to fall and no more truthful witnesses to contradict us. Making a clean breast of things clears the air and opens the way forward. On the other hand, without confession, there is no freedom, only a groping along a tortuous path through a thicket of lies and distortions, which one day will hold us fast and from which there will be no escape.

Such open confession is essential in countering charges of Christian hypocrisy for three reasons. First, things have been done that are unequivocally evil or wrong. Second, these things have been carried out by Christians, and often in the very name of Christ. And third, the things done wrong have been flagrant contradictions of the teaching and example of Jesus. We or other Christians have not practiced what we preached, and what we or they have done has left a terrible stain on the Christian church and on the name of Jesus. Read for example Christopher Hitchens's compendium of readings, *The Portable Atheist*. A sorry but unmistakable feature leaps out. Atheists gain their main emotive force not by setting out the purported glories of their worldview, which in the end is in fact extremely bleak, but in attacking the evils and excesses of Christians and Christendom. Something has surely gone terribly wrong when Christians are the best atheist arguments against the Christian faith and Christendom their best argument for atheism.

Needless to say, our confession of hypocrisies has to be specific, and we each have to fill in our own sins, the wrongs of other Christians, the failures of the churches that we know or the crimes of the church down the ages that bear closely on those to whom we are talking—the darkness of anti-Semitism and of the pogroms to our Jewish friends, for example, or the excesses of the Crusades to Muslims and the errors of the Inquisition to scientists, and so on.

Pope John Paul II demonstrated this moral courage when he openly confessed the sins of the Roman Catholic Church more than one hundred times in various settings. Needless to say, even this was never enough for some of his critics, and for some of these nothing would ever have been enough—not even if he apologized for being Catholic. In other words, we do not confess for effect. Rather, confession always has its eye toward the truth, and it addresses the Lord first and foremost, as well as the victims. Bystanders are not our primary concern. It is against the Lord and our victims that we have sinned, and it is supremely to the Lord and then our victims that we confess. Bystanders come into the picture only to confirm the integrity of the forgiveness and its consequences.

Even before Pope John Paul, C. S. Lewis understood the crucial importance of confession as he argued for the Christian faith.

> If ever the book which I am not going to write is written, it must be the full confession by Christendom of Christendom's specific contribution to the sum of human cruelty. Large areas of the world will not hear us until we have publicly disowned much of our Christian past. Why should they? We have shouted the name of Christ and enacted the service of Moloch.[15]

To be sure, the pogroms, the Crusades and the Inquisition were long ago and far away, and therefore easy to confess for most of us. We were not involved. What hurts our witness today is often things that are far smaller and much closer to home. We may have demeaned our spouses and treated our children with anger, modeling a view of God that bears no resemblance to our Lord. We may have indulged in juicy gossip and degraded a rival, and contradicted any notion of loving our neighbor as ourselves. We may have lost our cool under challenge and defended the faith with a haughty disdain for the arguments of others, betraying our insecurity rather than the assurance that comes with truth. In sum, we may have been hypocrites. In which case we have not practiced what we preach. We have become the sharpest rebuttal to our own arguments and the most damning objection to our own faith. As followers of Jesus, we must not duck the enormity of a simple but shattering fact: with relatively few exceptions, such as some branches of Buddhism, almost all the most militantly secularist societies in history have been the product of Christian societies. The church is a leading spawning ground for atheists.

We have pointed to the way of Jesus, and then through our behavior we have stood squarely in the path of anyone who might like to join it. Plainly, there is a time in our arguments to confess, and confession and changed lives have to be a key part of our arguments. When it comes our responding to hypocrisy, words will never be enough.

STEP SIX: SUBMIT TO THE TOUGHEST COUNTER-HYPOCRISY PROGRAM EVER

There is a common impression today that, with the collapse of the former Christian consensus in the West, Christians are undone by hypocrisy and disconcerted by relativism. In other words, we are thought to be simpletons who are comfortable only with absolutes and with the clear categories of black and white thinking.

Far from it. As we saw in an earlier chapter, the biblical view offers not only the deepest grounding for truth under the very God of truth, it also provides the most radical understanding of relativism. The ultimate distortion of truth comes not from gender, race, class, culture or generation, but from sin. "It's a gender thing / a race thing / a class thing / a cultural thing / a generational thing. You wouldn't understand" has been given a far deeper level of relativism because of sin. It's as if Paul says, "It's a sin thing. They will not understand." Because of creation, we and all other humans are essentially, though only partly, truth seekers still. But because of the fall and our continuing active disobedience, we and all other humans are also essentially and willfully truth twisters.

That insight reenters the discussion here, but to serve a different point. Earlier, it served to throw light on our understanding of the biblical anatomy of unbelief. Here it throws light on how we can work to escape hypocrisy through the way of Jesus. If unbelievers seek to suppress the truth in order to avoid God, and in the process become truth twisters, we who by grace are now believers seek to be true to the truth in every area of our lives, and so to become truth seekers and truth livers—those who walk in the light and are committed to live in the truth.

This means that Christian growth is the opposite side of the coin of Christian persuasion. Where unbelievers fend off the truth as a deliberate action of their unbelief, we as believers should pursue and adhere to the truth as the deliberate action of our faith. After all, Jesus calls his followers to himself and to a way of life, and not first to a creed or a set of beliefs. Many

Western traditions have gone wrong there. Our challenge is not so much to believe orthodox truths, though that too is vital. It is to walk before God in his way, and so to practice the truth and "live in the light" that in some genuine though incomplete way we actually become "people of truth."

Truth is therefore essential for both countering the charge of hypocrisy and escaping the life of hypocrisy. God is the God of truth. Jesus is the way, the truth and the life. The Scriptures are the truth. The gospel is the word of truth. Conversion is a turnaround triggered by truth. Discipleship is the way of life that is living in truth. Confession is a realignment with the truth. Spiritual growth is life formation through the power of the Spirit of truth. And the Last Judgment is the final vindication and restoration of truth for humanity and for the very cosmos itself.

The Christian faith is therefore nothing if not concerned for truth, and we Christians are nothing if not called to be people of truth. As Christians we stand or fall, prosper or decline, by truth. The apostle John sets out both the negative and the positive implications of this fact in an unmistakable way. In his letter he points to the negative and to the lie we create when we do not walk the talk: "If we say that we have fellowship with Him and *yet* walk in the darkness, we lie and do not practice the truth" (1 Jn 1:6). He captures the positive in his gospel, in the celebrated words of Jesus himself. "If you continue in My word, *then* you are truly disciples of Mine; and you will know the truth, and the truth will make you free" (Jn 8:31-32).

Christians are hypocrites, people say, and all too often they are right. Like all human beings, Christians are hypocrites, and I who write this certainly am. ("If you could see into my heart, you would spit in my face.") But Jesus represents history's most powerful assault on hypocrisy, and offers the world's strongest counter and remedy. Without truth there is no freedom, and without truth there is no freedom from hypocrisy. No one has ever seriously accused Jesus of hypocrisy, no one has ever been more severe on hypocrisy than Jesus, and no one has ever offered a sterner but more gracious and effective cure to hypocrisy than Jesus.

So the charge of hypocrisy is serious, and one that we must never avoid. It boomerangs back on us with searching questions that we must not duck. But it is answerable, and there is a way forward that cannot be matched anywhere else—a way forward that is not found with us as Christians but with our Master. As with so many objections to Christian faith, when the seemingly unanswerable objection is properly understood, it serves not as a barrier but as a powerful attraction to Jesus and his way of life.

11

KISSING JUDASES

I WAS ONCE INVITED to a dinner with a Roman Catholic cardinal. He was a friend of Pope John Paul II and had been one of those who elected his successor, Pope Benedict XVI. The main topic of the evening was the state of religious freedom around the world, but the conversation ranged far wider, and it was both deep and delightful. Just as we were about to finish our coffee and end the evening, he suddenly changed the topic and asked me about the crisis roiling the worldwide Anglican Church. Not wanting to be drawn on what Francis Schaeffer used to call a "soup question" rather than a "dessert question" (one that requires asking early in a meal to do justice to its importance), I replied somewhat lightly, "The Anglican Church is flourishing in many parts of the world, especially in the Global South, but it certainly has huge problems in the West. But then, you had your Borgia popes."

Instead of brushing off the remark, as I expected, the cardinal became serious. "Yes," he said, "Alexander VI (with his record of incest, murder, bribery and corruption) was one of the worst leaders ever to have led the Christian church. But he never denied a single article of the Apostles' Creed, whereas several of the Episcopal bishops flout the teaching of the church catholic and deny the very heart of the Christian faith—and still stay on as Christian leaders. That is the shame of the Episcopal Church, and that is unprecedented in Christian history."

The cardinal was correct. Few churches in two thousand years have tolerated and even celebrated more heresy, syncretism, apostasy and paganism than the Episcopal Church. To be fair, the Episcopal Church is not alone, and many others from the Protestant mainline traditions are hard on their heels. Even as I write, a leading Episcopal bishop is quoted as welcoming people to a multifaith occasion with a syncretism that was simultaneously a blatant contradiction of Jesus, a syncretism that the prophets Elijah, Isaiah and Jeremiah would have excoriated, and a lurid example of muddle-headed thinking: "Greetings to you in the name of Yahweh the Almighty, in the name of Allah the beneficent and merciful. Greetings to you in the name of the Eternal One who gave the Buddha his great enlightenment, and in the name of the Hindu's Supreme Being that orders the cosmos."[1]

Many revisionists in the Protestant liberal churches, followed by the extremes of Catholic progressivism and emergent evangelicalism, have reached the point where their thinkers preach "a different gospel," some of their leaders are hardly recognizable as Christian, and some have joked that they recite the Apostles' Creed with their fingers crossed. And as the above quotation shows, such revisionism is rife with new forms of toxic syncretism. But the cardinal's response also highlights a wider task facing contemporary apologetics and the church at large. *Some of today's deadliest challenges to the Christian faith come from within the church itself, yet in many parts of the church Christian apologetics is weak, poorly understood and openly dismissed as an unworthy and a wrong-headed enterprise.* Without faithful and courageous apologists, men and women who are prepared to count the cost, the church is vulnerable to the challenges it faces internally as well as externally.

Can there be any question that today's "grand age of secular apologetics," which is both post-Christian and pluralistic, is no time for Christians to be voiceless and lacking in persuasion? If ever there was a time when it was vital for all Christians to be bold and winsome advocates on behalf of their faith, it is now. No one can fail to see the blizzard of challenges sweeping down on the Christian faith today and calling for a clear response. From questions about the origins of the universe (Leibniz's "Why is there not nothing?") to the challenges of scientism, to attacks on the existence of God and the person of Jesus, to the exposure of the sins and hypocrisies of the church, to recurring questions about evil and suffering raised by natural disasters, to the validity and importance of truth, to the contested place of religion in public life, to the purported irrationality and menace of religion of any kind, to the relationship of the Christian faith to other religions and the response of Christians to new technologies and alternative lifestyles— the church faces an unprecedented barrage of questions, challenges and attacks on its core message, its view of the world and its way of life.

Not surprisingly, such grave assaults from the outside have led to serious erosions on the inside too, and all this at a speed and on a scale that is without precedent in Christian history. Were the Christian faith not true, and true in the sense that it would still be true even if no one believed it and false even if everyone believed it, Christians might well be tempted to be discouraged as they look at the spreading cowardice and compromise within the church today.

At such a moment, hesitancy in speaking out faithfully on behalf of the good news of Jesus is inexcusable. There are clear, strong responses to all the issues thrown at Christians today, and the world is both owed an answer and is actually waiting for the answer that only the church can give—even if the world is slow in waking up to that realization. There is therefore no need for any Christian to fear or take alarm. At the same time, we must recognize that almost every word we say in public today requires an element of persuasion, yet for many Christians persuasion has become a lost art. Such people insist rightly on preaching, proclamation, pronouncements and even protest, and all these forms of communication are essential and have their place. But without persuasion, they are like a television commentary with the sound turned off—all moving mouths, but mute.

Such efforts may demonstrate a Christian's faithfulness and make him or her feel good that they have spoken out, but they are pointless. They do little or nothing to convince the hearers. It is time to restore Christian persuasion to its central place, to reunite evangelism, apologetics and discipleship, to recognize that Christian advocacy is a task for all Christians, to count the cost of speaking out, and to appreciate that persuasion must be directed to challenges *within* the church as well as without. St. Paul's advice to the elders of the church in Ephesus speaks to us too. We will have enemies from the inside as well as the outside, for "from among your own selves men will arise, speaking perverse things, to draw away the disciples after them" (Acts 20:30).

There was no lack of intellectual and theological controversies in the first three centuries of the church, but they mainly engaged the theologians— such as the conflicts that occasioned the rise of the historic creeds. But there is a clear-cut difference from our controversies today. The intense and protracted battles of the early Christians, such as those that gave rise to the Nicene Creed in A.D. 325 and then flowed from it for decades, were almost all internal. In the triumph of Athanasius and orthodoxy over Arianism, the church was wrestling with itself as to how best to articulate the theological meaning of the decisive revelation of God in Jesus that had formed the church and was essential to its identity.

Today's major battles are quite different, and they require apologists as well as theologians. The issues are mostly external, sometimes triggered by the attacks of critics and scoffers from the outside, but more often set off by Christian capitulation to cultural ideas and behaviors considered so progressive or fashionable that it is unthinkable for Christians not to espouse them too—such as the craven abandonment of the lordship of Jesus, the authority of the Scriptures, and three thousand years of the decisive Jewish and Christian understanding of marriage as between a man and a woman.

Battles over issues such as these are thankless, unpopular, costly and even dangerous, and it is no less hard to stand *contra mundum* today than it was for Athanasius and his steadfast fellow believers in North Africa and elsewhere. But this is no time for Christian apologists to miss their moment and to duck the unpopular issues out of a mistaken concern for the narrow priorities of "preaching the gospel" to those outside the church. The apologist's brief covers false teaching and false behavior wherever it is found, whether inside the church or outside in the wider culture. A century of brilliant Christian apologists, such as G. K. Chesterton and C. S. Lewis, who on the whole were also popular, is now followed by a time when the faithful apologist may soon be as vilified and endangered as the Hebrew prophets in the run-up to the fall of Jerusalem.

Don't Persuade, Proclaim!

Years ago, when I went to Oxford University to pursue my graduate studies, I had a series of interviews with various professors, one of whom became my tutor for a while. He was an eminent professor, whose rooms at Christ Church were said to be haunted by the ghost of Cardinal Wolsey, who had died there in 1530. An extraordinarily genial man and scholar, he was very encouraging, though one day I happened to mention the word *apologetics* in passing. The professor noticeably stiffened. "Excuse my candor," he said, "but I would never use that word again if I were you. *Apologetics* is a dirty word in Oxford."

Apologetics has traditionally held an honored if controversial place in Christian history. Almost all the greatest theologians, including St. Paul, St. Augustine, Thomas Aquinas and John Calvin, were also unashamed apologists, and Pascal, who was an apologist, though not a theologian, stands as a leading spokesman for the faith. Benjamin B. Warfield, the nineteenth-century Princeton theologian, argued that the Christian faith "stands out among all religions as distinctively 'the Apologetick religion.'"[2] Yet in the last century apologetics did indeed become a dirty word in many parts of the church, and not only in the more theologically liberal community but in the theologically conservative community too. As Benjamin Warfield lamented, "Apologetics has been treated very much like a step-child in the theological household."[3]

In conservative circles, a powerful trend has dismissed apologetics by saying in so many words, "Don't persuade, proclaim!" The bulk of the evidence for this is anecdotal and unrecorded. It can be heard in widespread throwaway remarks and in countless sermons, but it has also been voiced by several distinguished Christian leaders.

There are two major arguments behind this more conservative dismissal of apologetics. The first objection to apologetics is that it is said to deny or diminish the authority of the Word of God. This claim can be heard from leading voices in both neo-orthodox theology and evangelicalism. Karl Barth admitted that dogmatic theology is essentially apologetic. "Dogmatics too has to speak all along the line as faith opposing unbelief, and to that extent all along the line its language must be apologetic."[4] But as he fought tenaciously for truth, revelation and authority against the errors of nineteenth-century liberalism, he came down against apologetics, at least as it was understood in his day. "Good dogmatics is always the best and basically the only possible apologetics."[5]

Writing from prison under the Nazis, Dietrich Bonhoeffer expressed the same view even more trenchantly. "The attack by Christian apologetics upon the adulthood of the world I consider to be in the first place pointless, in the second ignoble, and in the third un-Christian."[6] Jacques Ellul, the great French lawyer, social scientist and Christian author, was equally blunt: "To suppose that it is still possible to have a crusade or an apologetic is to be out of your mind."[7]

The same views were, and are, prevalent in certain evangelical circles too—and notably, in some pietistic student groups in the elite universities and also among some of the best-educated leaders. For example, Martyn Lloyd-Jones, who was often described as a "prince of preachers," used to attack the apologetics of his day for its undermining of preaching and the power of the Word. "I am not sure that apologetics has not been the curse of evangelicalism for the last twenty to thirty years."[8]

It would be tempting to soften such neo-orthodox and evangelical dismissals as merely a reaction to the poor apologetics of their day, and it was certainly that, but for many the problem went beyond that too. And regardless of the motive, the long-term legacy of such attitudes created a suspicion toward apologetics that remains disastrous still. But its immediate result was to leave Christians vulnerable to the accusation that the Christian faith had no answers to intellectual objections. George Orwell scorned apologetics as "the defense of the indefensible."[9] And Anthony Flew, who later became a theist but was long the leading atheist critic of the faith, remarked famously, "Belief cannot argue with unbelief: It can only preach to it."[10]

The second conservative objection to apologetics is that it dries up spontaneity and diminishes a direct reliance on the Holy Spirit. In this case, the objection was often well-founded, and those who rejected apologetics because of it were more common in evangelical circles and among those who, to their credit, took the work of the Holy Spirit seriously. Once again most expressions of this objection were spoken informally rather than published, and the objection was usually leveled against varieties of evangelism and apologetics of a certain period. But in dismissing all formulaic apologetic approaches (as I have done too), there was no attempt to set out a better way, and the legacy of the objection has been a suspicion of all apologetics among the more spiritually minded.

Not long ago, for example, there was a common attack on apologetics that argued that "springs need no pumps," as the objection was expressed. All Christian witnessing should be spontaneous and a direct reliance on the Holy Spirit, so when Christians resort to teaching methodology and debating different styles and approaches to apologetics, they have already lost their way. Many times I have heard it said that as soon as we start to analyze the processes by which men and women are brought to faith in Christ, we are in danger of limiting the Holy Spirit. Or again, that we should be unhappy about the complications that are generated by theoretical discussion, about the divisions that are exacerbated by attempts to establish a consensus, and about the time and energy that is absorbed in all these debates. In short, the argument went, the church that has to discuss apologetics is by definition off course even before it opens its mouth in public.

To be sure, many of these dismissals of apologetics were justifiable as a criticism of what apologetics had become in the last century. It is true too that apologetics is too important to be left to apologists (including me), so it must constantly be corrected, revised and renewed according to the standards of the Scriptures. The approach argued here is one that is at least shaped intentionally by biblical truth and especially by the truths of creation, sin, the incarnation, the cross and the Holy Spirit. But if any errors and weaknesses are detected here or in any form of apologetics, they must be diagnosed and remedied by the standards of the Scriptures so that apologetics remains faithful and does not fall foul of the risk of being sidelined when it is so needed today.

Don't Defend, Dialogue!

Over against the conservative tendency, the liberal tendency to dismiss apologetics has been to say, "Don't defend, dialogue!" This attitude is most pronounced in the postmodern era, and in that form it has infected not only liberals but many younger conservatives too. As a young man said to me recently, "Apologetics is dead, the victim of its own modernist triumphalism. All we can do today, when there is no objective truth, is to dialogue with humility and with confession, hoping that our sincerity will appeal to others."

Earlier, we examined the error of allowing apologetics to be caught in the toils of the modernist/postmodernist controversy. Both philosophies have their benefits for Christian apologetics, above all the importance of truth in modernism and of stories in postmodernism. Both also have their costs, above all the dangerously inflated place of reason in modernism and the extreme conclusions about relativism and power in postmodernism. The Christian faith therefore agrees significantly and disagrees significantly with each of these philosophies. Plainly then, to capitulate to postmodernism and abandon apologetics would be both philosophically foolish and spiritually unfaithful.

But the trend toward "dialogue rather than defense" has far older and wider roots than postmodernism. It goes back to the Enlightenment and its claims about the purported triumph of reason and the consequent crises of certainty for faith—above all, rational certainty, historical certainty and cultural confidence. After the collapse of confidence in the classic theistic proofs, for example, philosopher Ronald Hepburn concluded, "If we are convinced that Hume and Kant and their successors have once and for all refuted the arguments of rational apologetics, we are faced with a choice between agnosticism (or atheism) and the discovery of an alternative method of justifying belief."[11]

The result of such a conclusion was the quest for a new stance for liberal faith. Reeling back from what was felt to be too much triumphalism and too little listening, liberals carved out a trend toward openness, listening and reciprocal receptivity—one that too easily became syncretism. Apologetics (and evangelism) was out. In 1967, the Uppsala Assembly of the World Council of Churches announced as a theme the craven notion that "the world must set the agenda for the Church." Similarly, Wilfred Cantwell Smith, a professor of comparative religion, spoke for many when he drew the general conclusion that liberals were expected to take: "'Dialogue' between members of differing traditions is fast replacing the polemics, debate, and monologue preaching of traditional missionary policy."[12]

This seismic shift was reflected internally as well as externally. From then on, theologian Peter Baelz argued in the 1974 Bampton Lectures, theology's approach should always be "exploratory rather than declamatory and a method which is cautiously reflective rather than bravely apologetic." Traditionally, it was said, the theologian's task was internal, to explore the faith of the church, in order "to be certain," whereas an apologist's task was external, in order "to be convincing" to those outside the church. But this changed decisively. Theology's role was to explore the doubts in faith, and apologetics was abandoned altogether as inappropriate. Or as Langdon Gilkey wrote more carefully, "Kerygmatic theology, the theology addressed by the 'believing' Church, must also be apologetical theology, a theology addressed to the 'doubting' world—for the Church is the world in so much of its spirit."[13]

Playing the Harlot

Christian apologetics today is in far better health than it was a few decades ago, not least at Oxford, where there is now a flourishing Centre for Christian Apologetics. In fact the robust recovery of recent apologetics gives it a spiritual and philosophical strength not seen for centuries. But as far as the world of the educated elites is concerned, the damage had been done already, and the effects of the recovery have yet to be felt as soon they may be. In the meantime, philosophers dismissed apologetics altogether. Samuel Thompson, for instance, called it a form of special pleading and an "illegitimate discipline."[14] Others were sadder and more puzzled. As a Christian, Ninian Smart lamented, "By consequence of all this, the humanist is liable to encounter a misty faith, somewhere between Thomism and the Conservative Evangelicals. If this intermediate position is impossible, it is a poor show for ecumenism and, as I believe, for the faith."[15]

Even Bertrand Russell, grand old atheist though he was, shed a crocodile tear over the collapse of traditional apologetics.

> In our day, only the fundamentalists and a few of the more learned Catholic theologians maintain the old respectable intellectual tradition. All the other religious apologists are engaged in blunting the edge of logic, appealing to the heart instead of the head, maintaining that our feelings can demonstrate the falsity of a conclusion to which our reason has been driven.[16]

Since Russell wrote those words, the situation has changed beyond recognition. A distinguished cadre of brilliant Christian philosophers, scientists, historians, sociologists and theologians has risen in the last generation with books and arguments that make the new atheists sound shallow, strident and irrational.[17] But for all the improvement, we have yet to reap the dividends of this thinking across the educated circles of the West. The barn door had been left open and the horse had bolted. Besides, and this is the concern of this chapter, such a superb articulation of the historic Christian faith came too late to arrest the Gadarene plunge of Christian revisionists into faithlessness and an alien gospel.

The Enlightenment was unquestionably the main catalyst for the emer-
gence of Protestant liberalism, but there have been two other major factors.
One was the rapid and brilliant advance of science and technology, and
their sense of time as progress, and the other was the impact of globalization and in particular the explosion of diversity in a world in which
"everyone is now everywhere."

It was the Enlightenment that created the little watchword "One can no
longer believe," and this became the liberal alibi for all who wished to break
with the past and welcome the purported triumph of reason over faith. But
the same conclusion followed the advances of technology and the explosion
of diversity. Those who put their trust in technology can never afford to be a
minute behind. So "one can no longer believe" was the cry of the chronological
snobs and the techno-idolaters as they discarded whatever was not the "latest
and greatest, and the newer and truer." And again of course, the issue of truth
does not ruffle the thoughts of the relativists. So "one can no longer believe"
when "all those others" around us believe so differently from us.

Owen Barfield and C. S. Lewis called this attitude "chronological
snobbery," and G. K. Chesterton skewered it mercilessly.

> An imbecile habit has arisen in modern controversy of saying that such and
> such a creed can be held in one age but cannot be held in another. Some
> dogma, we are told, was credible in the twelfth century, but is not credible in
> the twentieth. You might as well say that a certain philosophy can be believed
> on Mondays, but cannot be believed on Tuesdays. . . . What a man can believe
> depends upon his philosophy, not upon his clock or the century.[18]

The fallacy of chronological snobbery is in full throat today, and it represents
a major hurdle for Christian faith. The reason is that such snobs are so
blinded by scientific and technological progress as the supreme model for
human progress that they regard faith as automatically retrograde. In the
ears of such secular progressives, any call to "return" will sound reactionary.
But the greatest of the prophets have always been dismissed by their contemporaries as reactionary. And for those who understand that the church
always goes forward best by going back first, the prophet's call to "return" is
actually the first step toward real progress at a level far deeper then science
or technology. "Repent" was central to the first recorded words of Jesus as

he announced the arrival of the kingdom of God, so "repent and return" are anything but retrograde. They are a call to come back addressed to those who must face up to the fact that they have gone the wrong way and are therefore an absolute requirement for going the right way.

Needless to say, revisionists and heretics are made, not born. In my experience of knowing several of the leading ones, many are acutely aware of the broader cultural climate around them, but they are also reacting consciously to some bad experience of Christians or the church in their past, which like an unhealed wound they have never gotten over—an abusive family, for example, or a narrow-minded church, a hypocritical Christian leader, an unthinking Christian group at university and the like. Two of the leading liberal theologians at Oxford in my day spoke openly in these terms, using their past as an alibi for their present. Such wounding experiences are deeply personal, and they need to be addressed individually and intimately. But from that point on, it is possible to trace the stages through which revisionist thinking commonly passes as revisionists react to their past and move toward to a rejection of truth and orthodoxy that becomes unfaithful.

No one is motivated to compromise from the outset. Unfaithfulness is the end product and not the goal. If there is a conscious and positive goal that offsets the pain of the earlier experience, it is usually a search for relevance. The bad experience, whatever it was, was felt to be so awful that it rendered the church and orthodoxy irrelevant, so there must be a better way. All Christians are called to be "in" the world, but "not of" the world. But whereas the conservative tends to put the accent on the second term, the liberal generally puts it on the first. The laudable goal is to be in the world and relevant to it, especially if some painful experience made any previous stance untenable. Slowly, and without the counterbalance of the second term ("not of"), the slide toward revisionism begins until the revisionist is both "in" and "of" the thinking of the world.

STEP ONE: ASSUMPTION

The first step that starts the slide is the crucial one. It is taken when some aspect of modern life or thought is entertained as not only significant, and therefore worthy of acknowledging, but superior to what Christians now know or do—and therefore worth assuming as true. The classic example is

Rudolf Bultmann's famous remark that modern people cannot use electric light and radio, or call on medicine in the case of illness, and at the same time believe in the New Testament world of spirits and miracles. Without stopping to think, Bultmann and those who follow his example pass from a *description* that is proper ("The scientific worldview has tended to increase skepticism") to a *judgment* that does not follow at all ("The scientific worldview makes the New Testament world of spirits and miracles impossible").

In the confusion between the description and the judgment, a new authority is brought in unawares. The accuracy of the description is obvious, so who can disagree with the authority of the judgment? Repeat such a judgment a few times in a climate of opinion shaped by a chorus of thinkers saying, "Today it is no longer possible to believe x, y or z," and before long the judgment will sound self-evident and unquestionable. The judgment is definitely a new authority, however, and comes out of a different worldview—in this case, secularism. The judgment is no longer weighed and measured; it weighs and measures everything else. Subtly it becomes the yardstick for thinking, an assumption that is no longer challengeable.

This step has become even more natural in the advanced modern world because of our modern obsession with numbers—our so-called mania for metrics. In such a climate the pollster is king and data is all-decisive. Considerations such as truth and falsehood, right and wrong, wise and foolish must then give way to statistics, opinion surveys and pie charts. Whatever the issue and however serious the issue, whether major like the form and function of marriage or minor like the use of marijuana, trends then run from normalization ("a clear majority now believes") to legalization, with barely a passing nod to morality or tradition. Certain wings of the church can then be guaranteed to follow suit with alacrity. Indeed, after repeatedly responding in the same way, their pattern is predictable, and anyone can forecast their vote by assuming the authority they have already assumed. Before they declare their opinions in public, we can safely predict their affinity to public opinion.

Step Two: Abandonment

The next step follows logically from the first. Everything that does not fit in with the new assumption made in step one is either cut out deliberately or slowly abandoned to a limbo of neglect. What is involved in this step is not merely a matter of altering tactics but of altering truth itself—as seen from the perspective of the new worldview. St. Paul was a master of changing tactics, preaching from the Torah in a synagogue and quoting from the Cretan poet Epimenides on Mars Hill (referring to God in whom "we live and move and have our being" [Acts 17:28 ESV]), but he never changed the truth. He reduced the differences between himself and his audience almost to the vanishing point, but only so as to stress the distinctiveness of his message once his hearers had seen his point.

With the revisionists, however, the removal or modification of offending assumptions is permanent. What may begin as a matter of tactics soon escalates to a question of truth. They assume that something modern is true and proper. Therefore anything in the tradition that does not fit must go. The old views may now be philosophically impossible, unfashionable or politically incorrect, and they have to go. What results is a Procrustean move: revisionists stretch or lop off biblical revelation to fit the shape and size of the modern bed.

The "God is dead" movement and the broad "secular theology" of the 1960s provide another classic case. The "secularization theory" (that the more modern the world becomes, the less religious it also becomes) was broadly accepted at the time and had been for two hundred years. It has since collapsed, but when it was influential, it carried assumptions that made transcendence embarrassing and immanence all-important. So Bishop John Robinson in his bestselling *Honest to God* (1963) assumed that secularization was a sure and certain thing, and therefore that it was time to discard old images and replace old practices. Each one was therefore buried in its regulation shroud of caricature. God, we were told with numbing repetition, was not a "grandfather in the sky" but "the ground of being." Prayer was no longer to be a matter of "celestial shopping lists" but of "meditation."

Each generation has its own list of straw men that need dismissing, and changes that absolutely must be adopted if the church is to have a chance of surviving. Today's caricatures are more likely to be about attitudes toward truth and doctrine. Once regarded as a matter of courage and conviction, truth and beliefs are now said to brand Christians as "arrogant," "exclusive," "judgmental," "intolerant" and "hate-filled." But whatever the generation and whatever the claims, the revisionist movement is the same. Something modern is assumed, and something traditional is abandoned.

STEP THREE: ADAPTATION

The third step follows as logically from the second as the second followed from the first. Something new is assumed, something old is abandoned, and everything else is adapted. In other words, what remains of traditional beliefs and practices is altered to fit comfortably with the new assumption and the unspoken worldview that is behind it. The direction of course will be determined by the new assumption. If the premises assumed are secularist, the results will turn in a secularist direction. If they are Marxist, existentialist, psychotherapeutic, pantheist, feminist, homosexual or capitalist, the results will be as distinctive and different as these philosophies. As Pascal warned centuries ago, "If we submit everything to reason, our religion will have no mysterious and supernatural element. If we offend the principles of reason, our religion will be absurd and ridiculous."[19] "Garbage in, garbage out," as the inelegant current expression states.

As with the second step, this third step cannot be faulted either logically or theologically if considered on its own. For one thing, adaptability is a requirement of any crosscultural communication. For another, advance is a requirement of our God who is always on the move. God is the God of the new. He is not like the gods that are the cosmos deified and therefore the "same old, same old" system under a new name. Jesus himself said that new wine requires new wineskins, and the Christian faith has shown an unrivaled capacity for both advancing and adapting. But everything depends on the assumption in question, and therefore what is advanced and adapted. If any Christian has uncritically brought in some un-Christian assumption of the day, the advance will be a false promise and the adaptation will be a betrayal by definition. Jesus' comment that new wineskins are required for new wine is not a license to palm off poor wine or even vinegar under the false label of a classic vintage.

STEP FOUR: ASSIMILATION

The fourth step in revisionism is the logical culmination of the first three. Something modern is assumed (step 1). As a consequence, something traditional is abandoned (step 2), and everything else is adapted (step 3). All that then remains is for the leftover Christian assumptions to be absorbed by the modern ones—completely. At this fourth step (assimilation), revisionism capitulates to some aspect of the culture of the day while still calling itself Christian. It is absorbed by and assimilated into the culture with no distinctive Christian remainder.

The term *revisionist*, rather than liberal, is apt. Revisionists revise the faith to the point where it is essentially different and unrecognizable. The result is what St. Paul condemned as "a different gospel" and pronounced in most unpostmodern terms as "anathema" ("accursed") (Gal 1:8). Protestant liberalism is replete with examples of such capitulation. Indeed, since its rise in Germany in the eighteenth century, part of the history of Protestant liberalism is the story of the passing philosophical and cultural presuppositions of its day, for liberal theology in its extremes has generally followed the spirit of the day as surely as a dog's tail follows its nose.

Some liberals might dispute this indignantly, but they need only look at the evidence of liberal theologians' criticism of their own predecessors. What is it that they criticize? Their predecessors adhered uncritically to the philosophical and cultural presuppositions of their day and sold out the faith. The eminent Protestant historian Adolf von Harnack was undoubtedly a liberal's liberal, and how was his "liberal Protestant Jesus" dismissed? "The Christ that Harnack sees," one critic wrote famously, "is only the reflection of a Liberal Protestant face seen at the bottom of a deep well."[20] Modern theology, as another of his critics put it, "mixes history with everything and ends by being proud of the skill with which it finds its own thoughts."[21]

That is the dynamics of revisionism in a nutshell. Study today's philosophy, and tomorrow's new theology will follow as thunder follows lightning. Earlier, Barth wrote of theologians "trotting behind the times, as theologians so often do."[22] Berger noted that liberal theology has often appeared as a "sequence of mood theologies," and others have commented more bluntly still.[23] Historian James Hitchcock concluded,

> It is by now a law that religious liberals will discover and espouse various aspects of American culture just as true secularists become disenchanted and begin to look for realities which the religious progressive is trying to forget.

. . . By definition the churches will always be "behind" the world and frantically struggling to catch up.[24]

Full-blown revisionism was once the natural preserve of extreme Protestant liberalism, and its proponents still lead the field by miles. But they no longer run alone. "Emergent Evangelicals" have emerged and aged until now only nostalgia or denial allows them to still claim that they are emergent. But as their emergent sell-by date has passed, they demonstrate the effects of being weaned on the diet of their day—post-modern uncertainties, a relentless rage for relevance and a burning desire to be always seen as "innovative" and "thinking out of the box." Not surprisingly, the result in the extreme cases is an Evangelical revisionism that is a recycled Protestant liberalism with the same feeble hold on the Bible and truth, nonchalance about authority, a patronizing stance toward tradition and the church catholic, and a naive idea of their own importance as heralds of newer, fresher gospels, and an uncritical stance toward the future.

"Don't trust anyone over thirty," the 1960s radicals cried. "Don't trust anyone under three hundred," came Thomas Oden's wise reply. "Vox temporis" (the voice of the times) is no more trustworthy than "vox populi" (the voice of the people) when set against "vox dei" (the voice of God).

If people really believe that whatever is emerging, whatever is new, whatever is coming next must automatically be an improvement on the present, there is little we can do to stop them in our permissive, anything-goes era. But we can point out firmly that when they have given up the sole standard and authority by which they could assess whether anything is an advance or a regression, they condemn themselves to inevitable failure. Soon such voices will join the dusty Protestant liberal artifacts in the museums of their times. To maintain Christian identity, there must be clear Christian boundaries. In C. S. Lewis's wise words, "A 'liberal' Christianity which considers itself free to alter the Faith whenever the Faith looks perplexing or repellent *must* be completely stagnant. Progress is made only into *resisting* material."[25] What moves according to the times dies with the times. As Simone Weil and others have established beyond question, only someone in touch with the eternal can hope to be eternally relevant—and faithful too.

KISSING JUDASES

To be sure, only a few take the revisionist road to the end. But the further the revisionists go, and the more extreme they become, the more disloyal they are to Jesus and the more damaging they become to the Christian faith. Ninian Smart lamented the damage to Anglicanism long before the Episcopal Church aggravated the problem in today's form. A university colleague had said to Smart, "My wife is an atheist, but she wants to be an Anglican as well. Is there anything she can read?"

"My dear fellow," Smart replied, "We've got plenty of books showing how the trick can be done." But he then reflected sadly, "It was difficult to find books on how to be a theist."[26] The Oxford philosopher Basil Mitchell often used to remark in the same vein, "The trouble with modern theology is that there is nothing left to *dis*believe in." Indeed, it is now difficult to think of what might actually constitute a crisis of faith for the Christian revisionists. Revisionist faith has so lost its authority that it has become compatible with anything and everything, and so means nothing.

At the extreme, revisionist Christians sink beneath the waves still proclaiming their good intentions: they are only speaking for "a new kind of Christianity for a new world," sure that they know "why Christianity must change or die." But the church survives and few are fooled by their newfangled theologies. The passing brands of revisionism die in their turn, and their brave new gospels rarely sell outside their own circles because they are only saying what the skeptics believed already. "At that point," one critic remarked acidly, "the creed becomes a way of saying what the infidel next door believes too."[27] Or as Oscar Wilde quipped to a trendy cleric even earlier, "I not only follow you. I *precede* you."

Worst of all, the postmortems always reveal the same kind of spiritual and theological cancer. Revisionism represents a fatal loss of *authority* (with the spirit of the age taking over the driving seat), a sad loss of *continuity* (breaking itself off from the tradition of the wider church across the continents and down the centuries), a serious loss of *credibility* (with unbelievers who already believed what the revisionists believe and have now passed on to something else), and finally a total loss of *identity* (as the revisionist faith is no longer recognizably Christian, even to its successors).

In sum, the revisionists and their repeated apostasies are guilty of what the prophet Hosea attacked as "the spirit of harlotry," Isaiah as "playing the harlot," and Cyprian as acting as "prostitutes." The most brazen of them are streetwalkers who ply their trade with every fresh idea coming down the street. But it was Kierkegaard who used the most damning term of all. Such revisionists are "Kissing Judases." "To be sure," Walter Kaufmann added in seconding the term, "it is not literally with a kiss that Christ is betrayed in the present age: today one betrays with an interpretation."[28]

Christian advocates, then, must be ready to focus their attention on those inside the church as well as those outside—resisting modern revisionism just as St. Paul resisted ancient Gnosticism and St. Athanasius stood fast against Arianism and the world of his day. Are today's evangelists and apologists prepared to count the cost and pick up their crosses again and truly be *contra mundum*—even to the point of scorn, shame, and perhaps imprisonment and death? Let there be no misunderstanding: the greatest crisis now facing the church in the West today is the crisis of authority caused by the church's capitulation to the pressures of the sexual revolution, and in particular to the bullying agenda of the Lesbian-Gay-Bisexual-Transgender-Queer coalition. It will not do for evangelists and apologists to keep silent for fear of losing opportunities to present the gospel. As Luther made plain in his day, to fight the battle at any point other than where the battle is being fought in one's day is to lose the battle. Pastor Martin Niemoller's famous regret in failing to stand against National Socialism in his time carries an equivalent warning for evangelists and apologists today. They raised the question of authority, but I was an evangelist and an apologist and not a theologian, so I didn't stand up . . .

There is no question that the inside task is far harder and more thankless for apologists than addressing the open enemies of the church. It requires a costly courage as well as faithfulness. Outside attacks often stiffen Christian responses, whereas inside revisionism saps the strength of believers through its many confusions, betrayals and the overall discouragement of opening ourselves to accusations of self-righteousness. After all, who are we to suggest that we are right and anyone else is wrong, and to assert that we have the gospel and they do not?

Yet as always, we must remember what is at stake, and remember the courage of those who have stood before us. St. Paul minced no words in calling the proponents of a different gospel "accursed." C. S. Lewis bucked all the tenets of academic correctness in describing the modernist theologian as an "infidel in all but name."[29] Berger described the revisionist process as self-defeating and a *reductio ad absurdum*: "a recipe for the self-liquidation of the Christian community,"[30] "a bizarre manifestation of intellectual derangement or institutional suicide" and something coming from a "script for the theatre of the absurd."[31] Alasdair MacIntyre dismissed such revisionism equally scathingly. "It is now announcing to the secular world what the secular world has been announcing to it for a rather long time."[32]

In short, extreme revisionism today is nothing less than a toxic form of anti-apologetics and calls for a robust response. But we are not just defending ourselves, Christian orthodoxy, the church itself or even the Christian faith. We are standing up for the honor and the name of the One in whom we trust and whom we love. It is Jesus and his Father whom the revisionists are betraying, and so long as this is so, Christian apologists have a job on their hands. The name of God is dishonored and the defense must never rest.

12

CHARTING
THE JOURNEY

SOME YEARS AGO, I was in a hospital in the Washington, D.C., area because of a suspected brain tumor (which fortunately proved to be nothing). As I was waiting to undergo a brain scan, a nurse entered the room briskly and said, "Excuse my asking, but are you claustrophobic?"

"No," I answered.

"Good," she said. "Some people can't take the scanner. Our name for it is the 'coffin machine.'"

"Thanks very much," I replied lightly. But five minutes later I couldn't get her words out of my mind. Both that session and the next turned out to be a sort of personal life review that I had not expected. It was as if I was lying in my own coffin in the dark, and just as a drowning person sees life flash before his or her eyes, so I saw the years of my life scroll across my mind. When the two experiences were over, I was left with an overpowering sense of the wonder of the journey of life—not just the journey of my own life but the fascination of the journeys of so many others whose stories I have heard them tell or I have read.

The idea of the journey is the most nearly universal picture of our little lives on planet earth, and what it means for us is to make the most of the world and the times in which we live. "Midway on our life's journey I found myself in a dark wood." So begins Dante's famous metaphysical adventure story, *Divine Comedy*. From the Hebrew book of Exodus to Homer's *Odyssey*, Virgil's *Aeneid*, Geoffrey Chaucer's *Canterbury Tales*, Miguel de Cervantes's

Don Quixote, John Bunyan's *Pilgrim's Progress*, Mark Twain's *Huckleberry Finn*, Joseph Conrad's *Heart of Darkness*, Herman Hesse's *Siddhartha* and Jack Kerouac's *On the Road*, the theme runs on and on—and these are only the Western examples. Life is a journey, a voyage, a quest, a pilgrimage, a personal odyssey, and we are all at some unknown point between the beginning and the end.

The picture of the journey also covers our human searches within the overall journey of our lives, and nowhere more aptly than our journeys in search of the meaning of life itself. Just before his execution under the Athenian democrats, Socrates famously declared that "the unexamined life is not worth living."[1] It is one of the most quoted classical sayings outside the Bible, but it is followed less than it is quoted. And if Socrates is correct, it would mean that many people, even highly educated people, are leading lives that are not worth living. They simply have not thought enough or cared enough to think for themselves about the meaning of life. They have not examined such big questions as the nature of the universe, their own identity and purpose, a foundation for deciding about right and wrong, the prospects for humanity, which worldview makes the best sense of it all, and so on.

Does meaning matter? Philosopher Ronald Dworkin's cheap dismissal is often quoted, "Philosophers used to speculate about what they called the meaning of life. (That is now the job of mystics and comedians.)"[2] But that of course is too cynical. "Man cannot stand a meaningless life," Carl Gustav Jung claimed.[3] Anthropologist Clifford Geertz agreed. "The drive to make sense out of experience, to give it form and order, is evidently as real and pressing as the more biological needs."[4] But if meaning is so important, what accounts for the striking carelessness in pursuing it? On the one hand, some have explained it in terms of Pascal's notion of *diversion*, which we examined earlier. Unable to face the final reality of death and our own mortality, we surround ourselves with busy, entertaining distractions—our "weapons of mass distraction." On the other hand, others have explained it in terms of *bargaining*. Later, later, later, we say, as we put off the key decisions about life. We will attend to it later, always wanting to gain more experience, more knowledge or more power first, until finally there is no more "later," even for those who attempt to strike a bargain with the devil to gain more time.

ONE WAY, MANY WAYS

But fortunately there are those who do wish to lead an examined life, and our goal as apologists is to spur many more—praying that the pursuit of the examined life and the quest for meaning will lead them directly to Jesus. How then can we chart the journey for those who do wish to lead an examined life, and who do think and care? And what does the journey mean for us as apologists, who know that the human search for meaning is finally answered only in Jesus and following his way, but that there are also many other ways to attract and divert the seeker? What can we expect as we pray and engage those who are searching? Just as a trusted caddie walks a championship golf course with a professional golfer to help him know the lie of every green and the position of every sand trap and clump of trees, or a Grand Prix racing driver drives the track to discover the challenge of every straight and every corner and chicane, so as apologists we should ponder the journey toward faith and know how it progresses as well as its principles and its pitfalls along the way. Pilgrim's progress applies to seekers as well as disciples, and our task is to be skilled guides for the journey to faith.

My purpose in outlining the four stages of the search is simple: so that we may each become trustworthy guides to those we meet who are at any stage of their search. Trusting a Christian is often the critical prelude to coming to trust in God. With the Christian faith, there is an essential link between choosing and conversion, conversion and choosing. As a converting faith the Christian faith is necessarily a chosen faith, and those who trust and live the faith are the best ones to share it with others.

The view of the seeker's journey that follows is based on the record of the Scriptures, the witness of numerous personal journeys in history, and the best of many modern insights into how we know what we know, how we change our minds, and how we grow in life. In that light, I would suggest that we view a thinking person's journey toward faith as a progress with four main stages. In an earlier book, *Long Journey Home,* I have attempted to set out a description of that journey in a way that would provide guidelines for interested seekers.[5] Here, I would only summarize the same stages of the journey and add some comments that underscore the significance of each stage for us as apologists. Charting the journey toward faith is important for apologists as guides as well as for seekers who take to the road.

Let me be clear. The course of the journey outlined here is not a proposal for a new four-step apologetic method. I am not interested in any mechanical, surefire technique even at this late stage. Nor is it an attempt to construct a four-rung ladder of ascent by which the mind (and the soul) can climb toward God by their own strength in the manner of the Platonists, or a proposed natural theology to be reasoned through in the style of the Enlightenment. Over all our human efforts to find God by ourselves and to satisfy God by ourselves, God pronounces his implacable and unending no. The Christian faith always stands before humanity as revealed, and therefore addresses us as a word to be believed or disbelieved, and not something we have reasoned out from scratch. As Origen stated in answer to Celsus long ago, the gospel is not a matter of natural religion. It is not about the ascent of man but about the descent of God.

But if this description of the journey is a broadly accurate road map that thinking people take, knowing it will help us ascertain where people have reached on their journey, and how we can best encourage them forward to the destination. Let me be clear too that this is not meant as a map for everyone to follow. It is a description of a thinking person's journey toward faith, but that means it is not the only way. Jesus may be the only way to God, but there are as many ways to Jesus as there are people who come to him. Thinking people may not be the majority of those who come to faith in Jesus, and not all thinking people will come in this way. I once shared a platform with the eminent management guru Peter Drucker. Asked by a questioner how he had become a Christian, he answered with a brilliant summary flash of what had led to his conversion: "It was the best deal!"

Too much Christian advocacy is about arguments that are static and engaged at arm's length, whereas the emphasis on the search as a journey puts the accent on the seeker's movement. Everything depends on the invitation and challenge to the searcher to start moving. The English painter Francis Bacon used to say that "artists stay much closer to their childhood than other people."[6] But the truth is that most people do, though artists are more aware of it—which is why the friendly question "Tell me your story" so often draws out such a deep and personal response. In listening, we are loving a person, and in loving we are inviting him or her to be aware of the road on which they are traveling, and to show who they think they are and where they believe they have landed on their journey in life.

Needless to say, the stress on the journey and movement has its pitfalls. By slowly spelling out this description of a thinking person's journey, I run the risk of making it sound labored, pedestrian and too sharply distinct. In real life, few people think slowly, systematically and at the same measured speed from A to Z. Sometimes our thinking may be slow and steady. At other times, it can be bogged down for what seems to be ages. But we can also experience spurts and make intuitive leaps that thrust us toward insights and conclusions in the flash of a second.

C. S. Lewis was definite about the moment when he came to put his faith in a broad Christian theism, but not about the moment when he moved from theism to a directly personal faith in Jesus as Lord and God. He described it as happening somewhere en route to London's Whipsnade Zoo. "When we set out I did not believe that Jesus Christ is the Son of God, and when we reached the zoo I did."[7] A high-speed elevator can pass through a hundred floors so fast that the hundredth floor seems like the second or third. And in the same way, a seeker's thinking can move through certain stages of the search with such speed that it seems the separate stages were not important or even there. Buildings, however, are constructed steadily with all the floors built in their turn, and in order to be helpful wherever we find the seekers that we engage, we as apologists needs to understand more of the overall journey than the seekers we talk to, whether they prove to be tortoises or hares.

A TIME FOR QUESTIONS

The first stage in a thinking person's journey begins when their previous sense of the meaning of life is thrown into question, and for that reason the person becomes a seeker—searching for a better answer to the question of the meaning of life. As humans, we all need to live with a sense of meaning and belonging, and so to make sense of our lives and find security in our worlds. André Kertész, the legendary Hungarian photographer and father of photojournalism, felt his émigré status keenly and used to call Paris his "best girlfriend." Once he was told by his brother, "Loneliness is not for you. You have to *belong* somewhere."[8]

Call such a sense of meaning and belonging a faith, a philosophy of life, a world-and-life view or a religion. Many receive it without thinking from their culture and their tradition, along with their mother's milk, as it were, while others think it through for themselves in a long, agonized search and sometimes with a cataclysmic conversion. Plato called such a sense of meaning a raft on which we navigate the seas of life. Aldous Huxley called it a cave in which we shelter against the storms of the wider world. And of course, in their very different ways both the Buddha and Jesus invited their followers to live according to their way of life.

But whatever the term we use and whatever the process, what matters for each of us is the adequacy and truth of what we come to believe is the meaning of life—and therefore the source from which we derive our sense of identity, purpose, ethics and community. That is also why, like a power outage in a well-lit home, any disruption of meaning is so important. The experience of breakdown that turns life into a question mark may be intellectual or emotional or practical. It may come from the storms and stress of life, such as illness and death. It may be caused by our passage through the seasons of life, such as a midlife crisis or retirement. It may be caused by grand historical crises, such as the crisis of Marxism after the collapse of the Soviet Union. Or it may be triggered, as we saw earlier, by "holes torn in life" or by "signals of transcendence."

But what is the significance of this first stage for apologists? First, we should warmly welcome this stage as the making of a real seeker and the beginning of a genuine search. Whatever its origin, the breakdown of the previous meaning is potentially the way to a breakthrough to new meaning. So the new seeker is well ahead of most people, for the sad fact is that most people at any moment in life have not even reached this stage. They are leading unexamined lives and are satisfied with what they believe, and therefore indifferent or hostile to the gospel. They believe whatever they believe, and that is the end of it. They are not asking the questions that might lead to truth and meaning. Most likely, they have never thought deeply about what they believe, so consciously or not and with solid reasons or not, they believe in its adequacy and truth. Such people have not yet set out on the quest for meaning, and they are not seekers, so our task in speaking to them is the harder one. We have to be the ones, as we saw in earlier chapters, to raise questions and press arguments that challenge the adequacy and truth of what they believe until they too become seekers—the beginning of the true search.

But the person for whom life has become a question mark is quite different. Such people are no longer complacent or satisfied with what they used to believe. Life has raised a question that acts like a pebble in a shoe or a bur under the saddle. They need an answer, they have become seekers, and even if they are only just setting out, at least they are on the road. Our task, then, is to find out exactly where they are in the search. By inviting them to tell us their stories, and by listening with love and attention, we can understand where the treasure of their heart lies, what their burning question is, what direction they looking for the answer, and then consider how we can best help them to move forward in their search.

Second, we should be realistic about the term *seeker*. Too often the term is used loosely today, and merely refers to someone who is undecided, to those who browse idly or to people who are really indifferent to any and all beliefs. In short, the term *seeker* is often a polite word for those who are better described as "channel surfers" and "hoppers and shoppers." They are simply not serious. Our challenge with the latter is to make them serious, turning them from browsers into seekers by showing them that the consequences of their browsing are more serious than they thought. But for people who have reached stage one by themselves, there is no need to do that. True seekers are already serious. Their sense of meaning and belonging has been called into question, and they have begun to search urgently for an answer to life that is better than what they believed before.

Third, it is important to close off a Freudian objection that is commonly raised at this point. "Ah, there you go again," a critic may say. "You're proceeding exactly as I thought. You are starting with a question and a need, just as the great psychoanalyst said. But underneath all this fancy talk of journeying, what you are showing is that people come to believe because of their needs—which exposes what faith really is. Faith is simply a crutch, a projection or a matter of wish fulfillment."

But Freud and his friends have jumped in too soon. The fact is that at this stage no one believes anything. Questions and needs do not create faith. No one *believes* because of questions and needs. Rather, the effect of questions and needs is to make people *dis*believe. They no longer believe whatever it was that they believed before, because what they used to believe no longer answered their questions. Questions prompt them to become seekers, and they then set out to search for better answers. Maybe they find an answer in minutes, maybe they search for years, maybe they resort to an answer that others think is wrong, and maybe they never find any answer at all. But whether they succeed or fail, and whether their search is short or long, whatever they eventually come to believe and why they come to believe it comes at a later stage and for different reasons.

Contrary to Freudian objections, questions and needs create disbelief and not belief. The great journalist and television personality Malcolm Muggeridge was famous for his long and strenuous search through many fields of life, from education at Cambridge University to politics in the Soviet Union to religion in India. But the logic and momentum of his journey was captured perfectly in one comment: Muggeridge knew what he disbelieved long before he knew what he believed.[9]

Arthur Koestler was another for whom the negative so clearly came first.

> I had sung "God bless the Magyar," and had seen the defeat of my country. I had cheered Karolyi's Democratic Republic and had seen it collapse; I had identified myself with the Commune of the Hundred Days and had seen it swept away. I had lived in a communal settlement and sold lemonade and operated a press agency. I had been a tramp and had half starved to death. I had seen my family go the dogs. I had run off to spend countless nights in the whores and in Brothels; and had gained sufficient insight into French politics to disgust me for ever.[10]

Not surprisingly, his childhood friend Eva Striker described him as "the most unhappy of all of us," and a reporter added, "as well as the hungriest for a new faith."[11] Disbelief makes the seeker, but contrary to Freud, it takes reason to make the thinking believer. As Peter Berger notes, "Nothing opens the mind like a good fiasco," but the fiasco says nothing about what better conviction the mind should close on and why.[12] If faith without reason can be a crutch and a projection, so also can unbelief without reason.

Earlier, we saw the important gaps between a signal of transcendence and the discovery that it may lead to. In the same way here, we must clarify the relationship of questions and answers. At stage one, seekers are aware of a question to which they want an answer, but the question by itself does not determine the answer. In sum, stage one is crucial because questioning leads to searching, but this stage is about questions and not about answers. The seeker hits a gigantic question mark in life. This question is what constitutes him or her as a seeker, one who therefore sets out to search for a better answer.

A TIME FOR ANSWERS

The second stage in the quest for meaning follows naturally from the first. When life becomes a question, the search is on for an answer. For many people, this stage is so much the heart and soul of the quest for meaning that it can be inflated out of all proportion and seen as the whole of the quest— just as apologetics can sometimes be narrowed to focus on this stage alone. But unquestionably this stage is crucial, for the alternative to meaning is meaninglessness, chaos, disorder and nonsense. So what is the significance of the second stage for the apologist?

First, the second stage of the search for meaning is typically more *conceptual*. Whatever has tripped the former believer, or the believer-now-turned-seeker, and shown up some problem in their life or in their thinking, it represents something of a blow, a wound or at least an irritant. To be sure, seekers want to look for a satisfying answer to their question, but they also want to protect the point at which they now feel vulnerable. Once bitten, twice shy is their immediate concern, so they send out the mind ahead by itself to do the searching.

Like deploying a scout, an advance guard or a preparation team, a seeker often sends his or her mind ahead on a reconnaissance mission, while guarding their heart until a sure and solid answer is found. The mind's job is to survey the terrain where possible answers may be discovered, and then to size up the serious options and bring back to the heart the answer that looks like the surest and most promising. That is what makes this stage seem conceptual. As apologists who love and listen to the person at this stage, we of course engage with this discussion of ideas on its own level, knowing the vital importance of ideas. But we also know that far more than ideas are at stake. We are engaging with the seeker's ideas, but behind them is the whole person whose entire future—indeed, whose eternal destiny—will be at stake in the choices he or she makes.

Second, this stage of the search is not only conceptual but *critical*. For more than any other stage it determines the outcome of the journey and the solidity or otherwise of the eventual answer. It is one thing to say that the different faiths, philosophies of life, worldviews and religions are different. That is obvious to anyone but the mushiest of relativists. But it is quite another to see that the differences also make such a difference, and as I have underscored, they make a difference not only for individuals but for whole societies. The reason is that world-and-life views are not only like lenses through which we see life, but they are like a city within which we live life. They shape what we see and what we experience—and also what we may never be able to see and what we may never be able to experience.

C. S. Lewis is widely and justly quoted for his remark: "I believe in Christianity as I believe that the Sun has risen: not only because I see it, but because by it I see everything else."[13] It was probably his masterly rendering of John Milton's comment in *Areopagitica*, "If we look not wisely on the Sun it self, it smites us into darkness. . . . The light which we have gain'd, was giv'n us, not to be ever staring on, but by it to discover onward things more remote from our knowledge."[14] But that idea goes back far earlier to the Bible itself. The psalmist, for example, declares to God, "For with You is the fountain of life; / In Your light, we see light" (Ps 36:9). Importantly too, it is true of every single faith and also of art and literature. As the French philosopher Maurice Merleau-Ponty argued in his last essay "Eye and Mind," we do not so much *see* great art, as see *according to it*.[15]

That is true of faith far more than art. Each faith provides a lens through which we see life and a city in which we live in the world. But in doing so, each faith, being different from other faiths, focuses on some things and blurs or banishes other things to the point that they are nonexistent. Some things we see and experience, and some we do not see and experience at all. Those who choose Hinduism as their faith focus on the final reality of the universe as *Atman*, the unchanging and impersonal ground of all being, but that means they will never be able to find a foundation for the supreme worth of an individual human being—a Dalit or "untouchable," for example. In the Hindu worldview, the worth and dignity of the individual Dalit is simply not there. The faith excludes it.

Equally, those who choose to be atheists can celebrate the world of the here and now and all that is within the realm of science, but by that token they are tone deaf to transcendence and everything that lies beyond the world of science, let alone anything that comes from outside the world altogether. In the "windowless world" of the naturalist, the secularist and many other modern people, those with such an impaired vision can only see the flickering shadows on the wall of the cave and not the sunshine outside. Nor can they hear what Einstein called "the music of the spheres" that others hear. In their worldview the sunshine and the music are simply not there—for example, Charles Darwin's sad admission that he was less and less able to appreciate the music of Handel's *Messiah*. The philosophy excludes it. Or in the homey comment of G. K. Chesterton, "Most present day Anglo-American philosophers have the same conception of reality as that held by a slightly drowsy, middle-aged business man right after lunch."[16]

Put differently, what we know is always shaped by the kind of attention we bring to our knowing, just as the kind of attention we bring will always shape the reality we experience. As Iain McGilchrist illustrates from his brain research, like Gertrude Stein's rose, a mountain is a mountain is a mountain. But a mountain may also mean many different things to different people, according to the different lenses through which they see it and then experience it. To a pagan Greek, it may be the dwelling place of the gods. To a Portuguese navigator, it can be a landmark. To a South African mining engineer, it spells wealth. To a French painter, it offers a subject for the next canvas. And to a nineteenth-century English climber, it stands as a challenge to be climbed simply because "It's there."

Stage two is therefore hugely critical for the seeker, in that the answers adopted will from then on shape the world of the seeker who comes to believe them. In Augustine's terms, there is a world of difference between living in the City of Man and the City of God. The apologist must always hold these long-term outcomes in mind with both urgency and sensitivity. At one level the discussion at stage two can appear to be no more than an academic discussion about different faiths and different ideas, but at another level it is about beliefs, which when believed will shape the seeker-turned-believer in every cell and fiber of their lives and in ways that have eternal consequences.

Both the differences between the faiths and the differences they make are masked by what each faith sees as self-evident, which therefore make the views of others ridiculous, absurd or "not the way we see things." For Westerners, for example, common sense views external reality as self-evidently "real," but the Hindu view of reality as "illusion" is equally self-evident to Hindus. Among the crucial differences between the two world-views, of course, is that the Western view—more properly, the Jewish and Christian view of the world—gave birth to modern science and the Hindu view could not. The differences make a difference, and not to judge and evaluate them out of misguided attitudes to tolerance and nondiscrimination would be foolish.

This point is crucial when discussing such experiences as miracles and healings with advocates of either the Eastern religions or Western naturalism. Experience by itself will never be conclusive. It proves nothing to either of them. As C. S. Lewis pointed out, "If a man doubts whether he is dreaming or waking, no experiment can solve his doubt, since every experiment may itself be part of the dream. Experience proves this, or that, or nothing, according to the preconceptions we bring to it." The same is true for secularist skeptics. "Whatever experience we have, we shall not regard them as miraculous if we already hold a philosophy which excludes the supernatural."[17] Or again, "Nothing is wonderful except the abnormal, and nothing is abnormal until we have grasped the norm."[18] In short, coming to believe in a worldview such as the Christian faith is not a matter of changing your mind and acquiring some interesting new facts about life. It is nothing less than a matter of being given a new framework for seeing and therefore seeing everything in life in a completely new way.

Third, this second stage is essentially *comparative*. There are many answers on offer in the modern world, and there are many salespeople hawking their wares for the eager and the unsuspecting. Clearly, it would be foolish for any seeker to accept the first offer he or she comes across and look no farther. Like a young couple considering a home to buy, or a student sizing up different universities to apply to, the seeker who is wise has to compare, assess, evaluate and finally judge all the options and their consequences. The imagination is engaged as the organ of meaning. "If I were to be convinced that the world is that way," the seeker says, "what difference would it make, and would it be adequate for thinking and living?" Such comparisons, however, have their own problems, and there are many objections to the whole idea of comparisons today.

First, comparison is said to be odious because definitive choices appear exclusivist and intolerant in the postmodern era. As one student objected to me, "Making comparisons is a sneaky way to raise yourself up and try to make yourself look taller by cutting off other people's heads."

Second, comparison is said to be dangerous because it only serves to reinforce a sense of relativism. As the Oxford chaplain Ronald Knox frequently quipped, "Comparative religions make people comparatively religious."

Third, comparison is said to be misguided because it fails to see that all religions have an aspect of truth, they are all equally valid ways to God, and anyway there is a common core underlying them all, if we would only look for it.

Fourth, comparison is said to be futile because it is impossible. We only have one short life, and if anyone really wanted to explore all the faiths on offer, it would take three lifetimes and a billionaire's bank balance to do justice to the task.

It should be plain by now where we stand on the first three objections, in light of the strong Christian view of truth. But there are simple responses to the fourth that are worth noting. It is true that there are an almost countless number of faiths and philosophies of life in the room, so how are we to go about exploring and evaluating them? The answer is that despite the overwhelming variety, there are two factors that limit the range of options for the serious seeker. For one thing, each seeker has his or her specific questions, and that cuts down drastically on all the possible questions that need to be investigated. For another, there are only so many "families of faiths" in the room, and this narrows the choices even further.

One of the greatest roadblocks to taking seriously any search for answers is the prominence today of the great transgressors—those whose wealth, power and modern celebrity give them the capacity to flaunt their cynicism and nihilism in the face of serious searching and to live without any apparent need to discover meaning. The painter Francis Bacon was such a man. He had an overpowering need to overturn all convention and exceed all limits. Life for him was lived between "two voids," the nothing before we were born and the nothing after we die. Thus, when he said that "we come from nothing and we go to nothing," there were few who challenged his constantly repeated assertion of the futility of life. "In the brief interval in between, we can simply drift and try to find ourselves," he said. And then, raising his glass, and with a voice dripping with irony, he would add, "Since the whole thing is such a charade, we might as well be brilliant."[19]

Who, hearing such bravado, could be content to search for any answer that anyone else had already found? Only a wimp, afraid to think for himself, could believe an answer shared by the crowd, let alone submit to living by it. That, for the one-off Nietzschean man, was the futility of life as "a game played out for no reason."[20] "I don't believe in anything," Bacon would say, "but I'm always glad to wake up in the morning. . . . It's mad, I know, because it's optimism about nothing. I think of life as meaningless and yet it excites me."[21]

Bacon's bravado at least makes clear that few people today look to art for ultimate answers. William Butler Yeats was once among those who hoped for more. "The arts are, I believe, are about to take upon their shoulders the burdens that have fallen from the shoulders of the priests."[22] But the arts no longer have the social or philosophical importance they did a century ago. Nor do most people look for answers from science, which never tackles the deep whys of life. (Ludwig Wittgenstein: "We feel that even when *all possible* scientific questions have been answered, the problems of life remain completely untouched." Or Ortega y Gasset: "Life cannot wait until the sciences have explained the universe scientifically. We cannot put off living until we are ready.")[23]

Perhaps more surprisingly, many of the wise ones do not even look to philosophy for answers to the meaning of life. Few would be as dismissive as Eugene O'Neill who often referred to philosophers as "foolosophers."[24] But some, such as Leszek Kolakowzki, a distinguished philosopher himself, admit that after three thousand years philosophy has come up with no agreed and unchallengeable answers to the many questions it has usefully tackled. As a way of thinking clearly, philosophy has merits that are essential and undeniable, but as the sure guide to the meaning of life, it falls far short.

For mere mortals who are not cowed by the forbidding clouds of sophistication, there are the more tried and trusty paths to meaning—usually according to one or other of the great families of faith. The term *family of faiths* describes faiths that have a common family resemblance because they share the same view of what they regard as the ultimate source of reality in the universe. Seen that way, there are three major families of faiths in the world today. The first is the Eastern family of faiths, which includes Hinduism, Buddhism and the New Age movement. For this family, the ultimate source of reality is the impersonal ground of being. The second is the secularist family of faiths, including atheism, agnosticism, naturalism and materialism. For them the ultimate source of reality is chance. (Richard Dawkins: the universe is the result of a "stroke of good luck.") And the third is the Abrahamic family of faiths, including Judaism, the Christian faith and Islam. For them, the ultimate source is the personal and infinite God whom the Jews and Christians call YHWH and the Muslims *Allah*.

Richard Weaver's maxim that "ideas have consequences" is generally accepted today. Yet oddly, the short-sightedness bred by our secularist culture prevents people from acknowledging what is obvious in the history of civilizations, that "faiths have consequences" too. Indeed, the evidence for the second maxim far outweighs the evidence for the first, though of course the two are related. From the major differences between the faiths, major consequences for history and civilizations flow out in all sorts of directions. In my experience, the two issues that highlight the comparison more than any others for seekers are the issue of human dignity and worth, and the problem of evil and suffering. Run those two issues through the lenses of the three families of faith and the results are starkly different, and they highlight the choices dramatically. But those issues may not be the crucial issues for many seekers. What matters for each seeker is the particular question they have in mind and the "live options" they have come across and are looking at. Those factors will determine where their answer is likely to come from, and that is where we must help them.

For the Christian apologist, however, the general principle is still vital, "Contrast is the mother of clarity," and it is clear that the Bible is not squeamish about comparisons. In the Old Testament, God invited people to compare him with anyone or anything else, whether superpowers or other gods. Compare God with anyone and anything and you see he is incomparable ("To whom would you liken Me?" [Is 46:5]; or again, "I am the LORD, and beside me there is no other; / Besides Me there is no God" [Is 45:5]). Compared with the forces of creation, God is their Creator and Maker and therefore incomparably *Other*. And compared with all the many idol gods, which are only the forces of creation personified and projected in a thousand forms, God is always incomparable and *Only*. In the New Testament, Jesus asked his followers to state all the other views of him that people held, in order to focus their minds through comparison and challenge them to see that he was unique and incomparable ("Who do people say that I am?" [Mk 8:27]; "I am the way, and the truth, and the life; no one comes to the Father but through Me" [Jn 14:6]).

What is at stake throughout this second stage of the journey is meaning and adequacy. Does the meaning of any faith that a seeker may consider answer the seeker's questions? And does it do so in a way that switches on the light and fits like a key, so that the seeker's life is lit up and he or she has a solid foundation for living? Contrast is the mother of clarity, and meaning and adequacy are the goals to be evaluated at this stage of the search for meaning.

A TIME FOR EVIDENCES

The third stage in the quest follows as naturally from the second as the second does from the first. Once a seeker's questions attract them more to one family of faiths rather than to others, and then to one faith whose answers they think are the most adequate, the natural question then arises, but is that faith true? Yes, the faith is illuminating and its answers appear solidly adequate, but would believing it be warranted, or is the faith a fiction? This third stage involves what the philosopher calls "justification," the scientist calls "verification" or "falsification," the lawyer calls "doing due diligence," and in common parlance is simply a matter of "checking it out." No one wants to be fooled. *Caveat emptor* (Let the buyer beware) is as true for seekers as it is for shoppers.

If the focus of the previous stage was adequacy, and the imagination was the servant of the search for meaning, the focus of this stage is truth, and reason is the servant of truth. This stage carries an unusual importance today—for both seekers and apologists. Adequacy is always a crucial issue for the seeker, but so in fact is truth, though truth tends to receive less attention in the postmodern era. The only solid and final reason to believe anything is the conviction that it is true. Claims about truth should be therefore foundational for any faith that lays claim to be rational. Claims about truth should also be open for investigation to everyone who cares to examine them. This is emphatically the case with the Christian faith. With its bedrock beliefs in a God of truth, whose word is truth and whose people are called to become people of truth, truth claims are all-important for Christians. They are always open for investigation, and no honest question is off-bounds.

If that were not enough, truth is important for Christians today for another reason. Truth is the best shield and safeguard against an array of modern and postmodern objections to Christian faith. Many Christians have skipped over the question of truth, often unwittingly, and they cover its absence with all sorts of genuine but inadequate answers. They believe in God because faith "works for them" or "the family that prays together stays together" and so on. Such faith may be sincere, but it will always be vulnerable. From one side it will be open to doubt, and from the other it will be open to all the accusations of modern skepticism—that faith is only "bad faith," believed for reasons other than that it is true, and that it fears to face the challenges surrounding truth. There has to be a moment when, as Chesterton puts it, he and millions of Christians with him believe in the Christian faith because the key "fits the lock, because it is like life." "We are Christians," he continues, "not because we worship a key, but because we have passed a door; and felt a wind that is the trumpet of liberty blow over the land of the living."[25]

This third stage is where the Christian apologist must be ready with much needed explanations and caring encouragement. Some people need to understand why truth has become so controversial today. Others may need to appreciate how today's skepticism is the predictable result of yesterday's overreach in the drive for certainty without God. Still others need to be assured that the Christian view of truth will never go out of fashion for long, that skepticism never lasts and that truth is an essential for countless human enterprises, such as business, science, journalism and most of all, personal relationships. Most importantly, every seeker will need to be encouraged to investigate the claims of Jesus and the gospel for themselves, and to be convinced why the final reason to believe is that the Christian faith is true. As a key to life, it fits the lock.

A small aside is worth noting here. One of the most futile arguments in contemporary apologetics is the debate between the so-called evidentialists and presuppositionalists. But what should be clear from this description of the journey toward faith is that the answer is not either-or, but both-and and which-when. Both presuppositions and evidences are a key part of our apologetic approach, and the real question is which to focus on and when.

Think of the relationship of presuppositions and evidences like this. Before people reach stage one, they are closed to God, and their unbelief is a matter of false presuppositions, as St. Paul explained. At that stage a discussion of evidences may sometimes intrigue them, but evidences are rarely likely to make them change their minds. The unbelieving framework of their thinking will eat up all that contradicts it, so that Christian evidences will carry little force at this stage, and they will probably wash off the unbeliever's mind like water off a duck's back. As Koestler admitted about his commitment to communism after that phase of his many beliefs, he had an "automatic screening machine in his mind."[26] He classified "everything that shocked me as the 'heritage of the past' and everything I liked as the 'seeds of the future.'"[27] Dealt with in that way, no purely intellectual set of evidences could shake his faith in Marxism and the Party. It took life and history to do that, but only later.

Everything changes, however, when people reach stage one and become seekers. For those for whom life has raised a question are in the process of breaking with their old presuppositions and searching for better ones. They are now open and the framework of their previous faith no longer works to explain away all else. At stage two, presuppositions are the very nub of the issue for seekers, for what they are looking for is alternative presuppositions to answer their questions. If in their search they were to presuppose that any new faith was true, would it illuminate their world and provide solid answers to their questions? Stage three, by contrast, is all about evidences, and properly so. But when the evidences for the Christian faith—say, the evidence for the reliability of the Gospels or for the historicity of the resurrection of Jesus—come into play at this stage, they are no longer "bare facts" or "Christian facts" that could be eaten up within an unbelieving framework. They are now facts that make sense within the framework of the biblical worldview, and they are now considered with an open mind because the seeker now has an open mind. At this stage, Christian evidences serve to support a solid grounding for the seeker to investigate the adequacy and the truth of the Christian faith.

Truth is controversial today, but there must be no shying away from stage three and its insistence on the question of truth. And once again the conclusion at the end of this stage is plain. Far from an embarrassment to the Christian faith, the Bible's insistence on truth is an ace that trumps all other cards. There is no faith that takes truth more seriously than the Christian faith, and with greater consequences for its whole view of life. Christian faith therefore stands and falls unashamedly by its claims to truth.

A TIME FOR COMMITMENTS

The fourth stage is the one in which all the previous stages culminate naturally and completely in the commitment of faith that brings a seeker to what is nothing less than reality itself. Questions have created a seeker and spurred a search for answers (stage 1). In its turn the discovery of what is thought to be a meaningful and adequate answer (stage 2) has pointed toward the question of whether there were solid reasons to believe that answer. If that issue is resolved and belief in the answer can be found to be a warranted belief (stage 3), then everything comes together to make the seeker step forward as a whole person to place their trust wholeheartedly in God (stage 4).

Faith then becomes personal and experiential, not just a matter of knowing about God, but knowing God as reality. It is no longer merely conceptual as it was earlier. Spurred by its questions, the mind has searched for and found an answer, and then has become convinced of the adequacy and truth of the answer, so now the whole person shoulders his or her responsibility and makes the step of faith that is the fulfillment of the journey. As C. S. Lewis says, "truth is always *about* something, but reality is that *about* which truth is."[28] The journey toward faith is then complete—though of course this description is also hopelessly incomplete for an important reason. It is a narrative that has only described things from the seeker's side.

What are some of the things that we as apologists should bear in mind at this final stage of the journey as we invite seekers to come home to faith? First, describing things from the seeker's side is only half the story. Just as the Spirit of God is the Senior Counsel and the lead apologist, so his work in attracting, convincing and convicting seekers is the work that really matters. We take our task seriously as apologists, but we must never get our little part out of perspective or forget that a big part of our part is to pray for those we are talking to. What God himself does through his Spirit is what counts and what makes it real.

Intriguingly, this fourth stage of the journey is often when God's presence becomes plain for the first time. The wholehearted step of faith of the new believer is far more than simply his or her own step. At one moment a seeker making her commitment knows as she has never known anything before that she is more responsible for the step of faith than for any other choice in life, and that she has never been more fully herself than in taking it. But the next moment she knows too that the One she thought was the goal was all along the guide as well. She knows that she has not so much found God as that God has found her. All the time the seeker thought she was seeking, but actually she was being sought, for God can only be known with the help of God. "The hound of heaven," as the poet Francis Thompson called God, has tracked the seeker down.

To think otherwise and put too much emphasis on the human search for God is to get things back to front. As C. S. Lewis expressed it delightfully, it is to view our search as akin to "the mouse's search for the cat."[29] Indeed, he wrote, "I never had the experience of looking for God. It was the other way around. He was the hunter (or so it seemed to me) and I was the deer." But that was what forearmed him against "the subsequent fears that the whole thing was only wish fulfillment. Something one didn't wish for can hardly be that."[30]

The fact is that without God, we cannot know God. For a start, we are incapable of knowing God by ourselves, so he has to disclose himself—in revelation. But beyond that, God is a person and not an object, so if we are to know him, he must keep on showing himself to us—in relationship. Knowing God therefore begins and ends with God, and it is a gift whose name is grace. But love like that calls for love in return, and the Christian faith that it forges is not the knowledge of a spectator, let alone the prying of a voyeur. It is the knowing of a lover.

All this comes together in this final stage of the journey toward faith. A key part of the moment of commitment is when a person's seeking suddenly blossoms into knowing, knowing into trusting, and knowing and trusting into loving God and the unmistakable knowledge and experience of being loved by God. What perhaps started out only as desire has become satisfaction. What may have been purely theoretical has suddenly merged into living reality, and what was once only a matter of curiosity has been transformed into love.

This means we must never let apologetics become dry, for love should be the alpha and the omega of all our endeavors. Love is the source, and the means, as well as the goal of apologetics. If love is not the climax of the journey toward faith, Christian persuasion lacks its essential spirit and its true goal. As apologists we are never out simply to establish an idea or to prove a theory. We stand as witnesses to a Person who is love, and out of our own love for him we are introducing others to being known and loved by him, so that they can know and love him in their turn. Without love, as St. Paul has told us, apologists too are only noisy gongs and clanging cymbals.

Second, the step of faith is fully rational. Christian faith is a warranted belief, but while it is not less than rational, it is certainly more than rational because it is the commitment of a whole person. And we as people possess emotions and wills as well as minds. "Faith is nothing if it is not thought through," St. Augustine wrote in words that are the Christian equivalent of Socrates' prizing of the "examined life."[31] Thinking is a crucial part of believing, for we should only believe what is believable. "Not everyone who thinks believes, since many people think in order not to believe; *but everyone who believes, thinks, thinks in believing, and believes in thinking.*"[32]

Augustine's statement, the example of his own strenuous search and the manner in which countless thinking people have moved through these stages with care on their journey to faith in Jesus are enough to blow apart the absurd contemporary charge that the essence of Christian faith is unreason—that it is a matter of fideism, a belief without reason and against all reason. That charge is a calumny that is ludicrously wide of the mark, yet critics such as Richard Dawkins chant it again and again it like a children's ditty, as if saying makes it so. But who is the irrational one now? For what could be more irrational for a scholar than to reiterate erroneous claims long after they have been roundly contradicted by some of the most brilliant philosophical minds of our age and the record of many of the most brilliant minds of the centuries.

Properly understood, the rationality of a profoundly warranted faith serves a double purpose. It silences the charge of fideism, and it also provides the grounding for a proper trust in reason that rationalism has never found. Thinking Christians think in believing and they believe in thinking. Let the evidence of history speak for itself. It is time for the honest atheist to admit it. There are real differences between atheism and the Christian faith, but that Christian faith is irrational is not one of them.

In his classic epic poem *Inferno*, Dante remarked that reason has "short wings." Reason in that sense is like a penguin. Penguins are proud, beautiful and lovable birds, whereas, thanks to Samuel Taylor Coleridge's poem *The Ancient Mariner*, the connotations surrounding the albatross are almost all negative ("an albatross around his neck"). But the fact is that when it comes to flying, the proud and lovable penguin cannot fly at all, whereas the mighty albatross, with its eleven-and-a-half-foot wingspan, rides the winds as the unrivaled monarch of the oceans. Just so, reason is essential in life and worthy of all the highest tributes given to it, but there is something Dante recognizes and our noisy new atheists fail to understand. When it comes to knowing God and the deepest forms of knowledge in the universe, the albatross soars above the penguin. The highest flights of human imagination, experience and love must use reason to reach higher than reason can ever reach by itself.

Third, as we have seen all along, there is always the chance, even at this late stage, for a seeker to turn on his heels rather than fall on his knees. Nietzsche spoke of thinkers refusing to face up to the "danger points" in their thinking, and ducking and weaving like a boxer to escape them. G. K. Chesterton and C. S. Lewis described the sometimes hilarious and often contradictory excuses and evasions that people make when avoiding the truth. At this stage the most common way of avoidance is the refusal to decide at all. The journey then changes. It is no longer a journey toward meaning. Instead, the journey itself is made into the meaning. Better to travel hopefully, it is said, than to arrive. The search is its own reward. The search for meaning becomes the meaning of the search, and the search goes on and on without end.

There is one last pitfall at this point. Modern people are caught between two follies, and both end sadly. On the one hand there are those who have no interest in the "examined life" because they think that, with no need to search or journey, they have already arrived. On the other hand there are those who think that their passion and their way of life should be to journey without end. Meaning, if there is any such thing, is like the mechanical rabbit at the greyhound track: it can never be caught. The search for meaning is the meaning of the search. The secret of the good life is the life spent searching for the good life.

To such people, it is unthinkable ever to arrive, for what they really fear is that to choose is to close all other options and to condemn themselves to boredom. Openness is what counts, complete openness. After all, there may always be someone or something else a little farther down the road—a better job, a more satisfying relationship, a more fascinating country, a more fulfilling faith. But such unending travel with no destination is futile, and it ends like the curse of the Flying Dutchman—people find themselves on the legendary ghost ship that was doomed never to make port and to sail the seas forever.

Better far the good news of the apologist and the evangelist who pass out the open invitation of Jesus to "come and see." Come with us, we urge, and join the journey whose final destination is home, where the one who is waiting for us is our Father. Come with us, for the commitment of faith is not the end of all journeying, but the end of the journey toward meaning and the beginning of the journey of the rest of life. The reason is that for a seeker to find Jesus is not the end of all searching, but the beginning of the greatest search of all. It is the end of one search, but the beginning of another and even deeper one—the search to know God better and better.

Here, in shining contrast to the fate of the Flying Dutchman, is the place where the searching truly never ends. Not because of the infinity of options and the impossibility of choosing, but because of the infinity and inexhaustibility of the One in whom we have found our answer and whom we have come to know. As St. Augustine reminds us of our coming to know God, "Even when he is found, he must be sought." That lifelong search to know the One who is infinite and inexhaustible is a search "both sought that it may be found, and found that it may be sought: still sought that the finding may be sweeter, still found that the seeking may be more eager."[33]

When people take that step of committed faith and set out with us to be followers of Jesus, our task as Christian advocates is over, and from then on they join us as sisters and brothers on the long way home. The journey toward faith that is the quest for meaning is completed, though the journey of faith has only begun. The way of Jesus then means that we follow his call to the long and winding road of life, going with him, and on the road to that place where all restless hearts and minds find a place to stop, with both relief and joy. That will be the place that Jesus told us he was going ahead to prepare, in our home and with our Father—the place where the work of the apologist is over because life's search is over, and the joys of heaven and home are all that count.

Conclusion

THE WAY OF THE OPEN HAND

IN THE EARLIER DAYS OF the church there were two symbols for the art of Christian advocacy, which had come down from ancient practices in law and rhetoric. One was a *closed fist*. This represented the *dissuasoria*, the negative side of apologetics that used all the highest strengths of human reason in defense of truth. Mustering all the powers of reason, logic, evidence and argument, closed-fist apologetics had the task of answering every question, countering every objection, and dismantling false objections to the faith and to knowing God. In the words of St. Paul, "*We are* destroying speculations and every lofty thing raised up against the knowledge of God, and *we are* taking every thought captive to the obedience of Christ" (2 Cor 10:5).

The other symbol was the *open hand*. This represented the *persuasoria*, the positive side of apologetics that used all the highest strengths of human creativity in the defense of truth. Expressing the love and compassion of Jesus, and using eloquence, creativity, imagination, humor and irony, open-hand apologetics had the task of helping to pry open hearts and minds that, for a thousand reasons, had long grown resistant to God's great grace, so that it could shine in like the sun.

Today, as then, both approaches to Christian advocacy are necessary, and both are fruitful. We may each be better at one than the other, but we must never make the mistake of finally choosing one over the other. They are both essential parts of persuasion. But is there any doubt that the one we most need to recover today, both to be true to our Lord and to gain the key to reach the hearts and minds of our post-Christian generation, is the way of the heart of love that reaches out to persuade with an open hand? May all we are and all we say be worthy of the Word who was in the beginning with God, the Word who will have the last word as he had the first, the Word who was made flesh and lived among us, and the Word whose name is Love. To him alone be the glory, but let us strive as never before to witness to him in a way that is worthy of him, and so introduce others to know him as our own greatest privilege is to know him.

Acknowledgments

Life for a follower of Jesus is a matter of lifelong learning, including the lessons learned from mistakes of all kinds. This book has certainly been a part of that process for me. It is the fruit of nearly fifty years of thinking, thousands of conversations, innumerable talks and lectures, countless books read, and endless lessons learned from all my poor attempts to present the good news of Jesus—sometimes with some effect and sometimes sadly not. But over it all stands the challenge of the apologist heroes of the faith who have gone before—for me, supremely St. Augustine, Blaise Pascal and G. K. Chesterton. This book also owes everything to three great giants of contemporary faith to whom my debt will always be unpayable: C. S. Lewis, Francis Schaeffer and Peter L. Berger.

As I said in an earlier chapter, C. S. Lewis, Francis Schaeffer and Peter Berger did not know each other, they might not even have liked each other, and they might heartily disagree with what I have done with their ideas. But the creative clash of their three quite different ways of understanding has set off a nuclear explosion whose energy has fired my thinking. Indeed, I have worked for years in the light of their ideas, and my gratitude to each one of them is unfathomable.

Among many others who have been friends, examples and guides along the way, the following are those to whom I owe a special debt of thanks when it comes to apologetics: Ranald and Susan Macaulay, John and Priscilla Sandri, Dick and Mardi Keyes, Bill and Barbara Edgar, Jerram and Vicky Barrs, Barry and Veronica Seagren, Larry and Nancy Snyder, Darrow and Marilyn Miller, Richard and Jane Winter, and Andrew and Helen Fellows—

all friends and colleagues from L'Abri who have shared the same privilege and joy in pursuing the great task of Christian advocacy.

Kelly Monroe Kullberg, Dan Cho and Rebecca MacLaughlin of the Veritas Forum, whose invitations and support in lectures in many universities across the world have been a privilege beyond my wildest dreams.

Ravi Zacharias, John Lennox, Alister McGrath, Michael Ramsden, Amy Orr-Ewing, Ian Smith, David Lloyd, Vince Vitale, Tom Price, Simon Wenham, Christian Hofreiter, Sharon Dircks, Michelle Tepper, Tanya Walker and Stuart McAllister, friends and colleagues at the Oxford Centre for Christian Apologetics whose passion for the gospel and skills in presenting it are an inspiration to me and a source of strong hope for the next generation.

Bill Edgar, Douglas Groothuis, Al Hsu, Dick Ohman and Karis Grace Riley, dear friends whose careful reviews of the first draft of this book served to correct what I had written as well as encourage me in pressing on to the finishing line.

Al Hsu and his wonderful colleagues at InterVarsity Press, and Erik Wolgemuth my wise and tireless agent, to whom thanks is always customary, but whose wisdom and skill deserves a gratitude that goes far beyond the customary.

And supremely to Jenny and CJ, my family, whose support is unflagging, whose encouragement is as strong as their critique is sometimes necessary, and whose love and loyalty are an anchor in all the storm and stress of my very existence.

Notes

Introduction: Recovering the Lost Art

[1]William Edgar and K. Scott Oliphint, *Christian Apologetics Past and Present: A Primary Source Reader*, vols. 1-2 (Wheaton, IL: Crossway, 2009); Avery Cardinal Dulles, *A History of Apologetics* (San Francisco: Ignatius Press, 2005); Douglas Groothuis, *Christian Apologetics: A Comprehensive Case for Biblical Faith* (Downers Grove, IL: IVP Academic, 2011); W. C. Campbell, Gavin J. McGrath and C. Stephen Evans, eds., *New Dictionary of Christian Apologetics* (Downers Grove, IL: IVP Academic, 2006).

2 Technique: The Devil's Bait

[1]See Os Guinness, *Unspeakable: Facing Up to the Challenge of Evil* (San Francisco: HarperOne, 2008).

[2]Jaroslav Pelikan, *Divine Rhetoric: The Sermon on the Mount as Message and Model in Augustine, Chrysostom, and Luther* (Crestwood, NY: St. Vladimir's Seminary Press, 2000), p. 3.

[3]Robert Louis Wilken, *The Spirit of Early Christian Thought* (New Haven, CT: Yale University Press, 2003), p. xvi.

[4]Blaise Pascal, *Pensées* 913, trans. A. J. Krailsheimer (London: Penguin Books, 1966), p. 306.

3 The Defense Never Rests

[1]Dorothy Sayers, *Strong Poison* (London: Times Mirror Books, 1970), p. 33.

[2]Albert Camus, *The Fall* (New York: Vintage Books, 1991), p. 81.

[3]Richard Hammer, *The Court-Martial of Lt. Calley* (New York: Coward, McCann & Geoghan, 1971), p. 238.

[4]Rashi, cited by Rob Barrett, "Idols, Idolatry, Gods," in *Dictionary of the Old Testament: Prophets*, ed. Mark J. Boda and J. Gordon McConville (Downers Grove, IL: IVP Academic, 2012), p. 351.

[5]Auguste Rodin, quoted in Jacques de Caso and Patricia B. Sanders, *Rodin's Sculpture: A Critical Study of the Spreckels Collection, California Palace of the Legion of Honor* (Rutland, VT: Charles E. Tuttle, 1977), p. 133.

4 The Way of the Third Fool

[1]Edmund Burke, quoted in Paul Rahe, *Republics Ancient and Modern: Classical Republicanism and the American Revolution* (Chapel Hill: University of North Carolina Press, 1992), p. 233.

[2]Joseph Priestly, quoted in ibid.

[3]Michel de Montaigne, quoted in ibid., p. 236.

[4]Ovid, quoted in ibid., p. 283.

[5]Cesare Cremonini, quoted in ibid., p. 237.

[6]Gerald Curzon, "Paolo Sarpi," *Philosophy Now*, March-April 2014, p. 22.

[7]Ibid., p. 238.

[8]Ibid., p. 244.

[9]See Ralph Lerner, *Playing the Fool: Subversive Laughter in Troubled Times* (Chicago: University of Chicago Press, 2009).

[10]Ibid., p. 18.

[11]William Shakespeare, *King Lear*, act 5, scene 3.

[12]Desiderius Erasmus, *Praise of Folly,* trans. Betty Radice (London: Penguin Books, 1993), p. 134.

[13]Lerner, *Playing the Fool*, p. 70.

[14]Shakespeare, *King Lear*, act 4, scene 2.

[15]Viktor Frankl, *Man's Search for Meaning* (Boston: Beacon Press, 1959), p. 68.

[16]Reinhold Niebuhr, "Power and Weakness of God," in *Discerning the Signs of the Times* (New York: Charles Scribner, 1946), p. 145.

[17]Niebuhr, "Humor and Faith," in ibid., p. 111.

[18]C. S. Lewis, "Christianity and Culture," in *C. S. Lewis Essay Collection* (London: HarperCollins, 2002), p. 81.

[19]Friedrich Nietzsche, *The Birth of Tragedy* (Oxford: Oxford University Press, 2002), p. 45.

[20]Søren Kierkegaard, *Concluding Unscientific Postscript*, trans. David F. Swenson (Princeton, NJ: Princeton University Press, 1941), p. 459.

[21]Niebuhr, "Humor and Faith," p. 112.

[22]Peter L. Berger, *Redeeming Laughter: The Comic Dimension of Human Experience* (Berlin: Walter De Gruyter, 1997), p. 205.

[23]Peter L. Berger, *The Precarious Vision* (Garden City, NY: Doubleday, 1961), pp. 67, 213.

5 Anatomy of Unbelief

[1]Paul Johnson, *Intellectuals: From Marx and Tolstoy to Sartre and Chomsky* (San Francisco: HarperPerennial, 2007).

[2]Plato, *The Republic*, trans. Allan Bloom, 2nd ed. (New York: Basic Books, 1991), p. 164.

[3]Johnson, *Intellectuals*, p. 342.

[4]Aldous Huxley, "Beliefs," in *Ends and Means: An Inquiry into the Nature of Ideals* (Piscataway, NJ: Transaction Publishers, 2012), p. 291.

[5]Ibid., p. 314.

[6]Ibid., p. 320.

[7]Ibid., p. 312.

[8]Ibid.

[9]Ibid., p. 315; emphasis added.

[10]Thomas Nagel, *The Last Word* (New York: Oxford University Press, 1997), p. 130.

[11]Blaise Pascal, *Pensées*, trans. A. J. Krailsheimer (London: Penguin, 1966), p. 34.

[12]Huxley, "Beliefs," p. 316.

[13]See Evelyn Barish, *The Double Life of Paul de Man* (New York: Liveright, 2014).

[14]Friedrich Nietzsche, *Beyond Good and Evil*, trans. Walter Kaufmann (New York: Vintage Books, 1966), p. 25.

[15]Max Weber, quoted in Peter L. Berger, *Facing Up to Modernity* (New York: Basic Books, 1977), p. xiv.

[16]Søren Kierkegaard, *Attack upon Christendom* (Princeton, NJ: Princeton University Press, 1968), p. 37.

[17]Lord Acton, quoted in Roland Hill, *Lord Acton* (New Haven, CT: Yale University Press, 2000), p. 138.

[18]Ziyad Marar, *Deception* (Durham, UK: Acumen, 2008), p. 8.

[19]Douglas Smith, introduction to Friedrich Nietzsche, *The Birth of Tragedy* (Oxford: Oxford University Press, 2002), p. xxi.

[20]W. H. Auden, "Death's Echo," 1936.

[21]Pierre Nicole, *Moral Essays*, trans. anonymous (London: n.p., 1696), p. 32.

[22]Reinhold Niebuhr, *Discerning the Signs of the Times* (New York: Scribner, 1946), p. 121.

[23]John Milton, "Paradise Lost," book 1, line 263 and book 4, line 110; Jean-Paul Sartre, *Being and Nothingness*, trans. Hazel E. Barnes (New York: Washington Square Press, 1993), p. 724; Friedrich Nietzsche, *Thus Spoke Zarathustra*, trans. R. J. Hollingdale (New York: Penguin Classics, 1961), p. 110.

[24]Steven Aschheim, *The Nietzsche Legacy in Germany* (Berkeley: University of California Press, 1992), p. 17.

[25]G. K. Chesterton, *The Everlasting Man* (Garden City, NY: Image Books, 1955), p. 85.

[26]Marar, *Deception*, p. 147.

[27]N. T. Wright, *The Case for the Psalms: Why They Are Essential* (San Francisco: HarperOne, 2013), p. 120.

[28]Kierkegaard, *Attack upon Christendom*, p. 201.

[29]Nicole, "Of Christian Civility," in *Moral Essays*, p. 139.

[30]Augustine, *Confessions* 7.15, trans. R. S. Pine-Coffin (London: Penguin, 1961), p. 150.

[31]Ibid., 12.25, p. 302.

[32]Ibid., 4.8, p. 79.

[33]Ibid., 10.23, p. 230.

[34]Blaise Pascal, *Pensées (Thoughts)* 100 (Stilwell, KS: Digireads.com, 2005), p. 22.

[35]Friedrich Nietzsche, *On the Genealogy of Morals: A Polemic*, trans. Douglas Smith (Oxford: Oxford University Press, 1996), pp. 39, 42.

[36]D. H. Lawrence, *Selected Essays* (London: Penguin, 1950), pp. 44-45.

[37]Marar, *Deception*, p. 52.

[38]Reinhold Niebuhr, *Discerning the Signs of the Times: Sermons for Today and Tomorrow* (New York: Charles Scribner, 1946), p. 13.

[39]Ibid., pp. 14, 18, 49, 86.

[40]Pascal, *Pensées*, p. 44.

[41]Francis A. Schaeffer, *The God Who Is There* (London: Hodder & Stoughton, 1970), p. 122.

[42]Nietzsche, "The Joyful Wisdom," sec. 125, in William V. Spamos, *A Casebook on Existentialism* (New York: Crowell, 1966), pp. 256-57.

[43]Nietzsche, quoted in Spamos, *Casebook*, p. 4.

[44]Herbert Lottmann, *Albert Camus* (London: Weidenfeld & Nicholson, 1979), pp. 615, 99.

[45]Otto Reinert Strindberg, *Strindberg: A Collection of Critical Essays* (Englewood Cliffs, NJ: Prentice-Hall, 1971), p. 8.

[46]Pascal, *Pensées*, p. 67.

[47]Francis Bacon, quoted in Michael Peppiatt, *Francis Bacon: Anatomy of an Enigma* (London: Skyhorse, 2009), p. 203.

[48]Pascal, *Pensées*, p. 66.

[49]Ibid., p. 66.

[50]Ibid., p. 68.

[51]Ibid., p. 72.

[52]Damon Young, *Distraction* (Durham, UK: Acumen, 2010), p. 65.

[53]Pascal, *Pensées*, p. 129.

[54]Peter Watson, *The Age of Nothing: How We Have Sought to Live Since the Death of God* (London: Weidenfeld & Nicolson, 2014), p. 268.

[55]David Hume, *Treatise on Human Nature* 1.4.7 (Oxford: Oxford University Press, 2000), p. 175.

[56]Henrik Ibsen, *Wild Duck*, act 5.

[57]Kati Marton, *The Great Escape: Nine Jews Who Fled Hitler and Changed the World* (New York: Simon & Schuster, 2006), p. 179.

[58]E. M. Forster, "What I Believe," in *Two Cheers for Democracy*, ed. E. M. Forster (London: Allen & Unwin, 1969), p. 46.

[59]C. E. M. Joad, *For Civilisation* (Macmillan War Pamphlets, 1940), p. 20.

6 TURNING THE TABLES

[1]G. K. Chesterton, *Manalive* (Los Angeles: Indo-European, 2009), p. 73.

[2]Ibid., pp. 73-78.

[3]Ibid., p. 78.

[4]C. S. Lewis, "God in the Dock," in *C. S. Lewis Essay Collection* (London: Harper-Collins, 2002), p. 37.

[5]Peter L. Berger, *A Rumor of Angels: Modern Society and the Rediscovery of the Supernatural* (Garden City, NY: Anchor Books, 1969), p. 42.

[6]Berger, *Rumor of Angels*, p. 40.

[7]Vaclav Havel, *The Power of the Powerless* (New York: Routledge, 1985), p. 41.

[8]W. H. Auden, quoted in Arthur Kirsch, *Auden and Christianity* (New Haven, CT: Yale University Press, 2005), p. 9.

[9]Georg Lukács, quoted in István Mészáros, *Lukács' Concept of Dialectic* (London: Merlin Press, 1972), p. 52.

[10]Peter Brown, *Augustine of Hippo* (London: Faber & Faber, 1967), p. 345.

[11]C. S. Lewis, *Undeceptions* (London: Geoffrey Bles, 1971), p. 213.

[12]Lucretius, *On the Nature of the Universe*, trans. R. E. Latham (Harmondsworth, UK: Penguin, 1951), pp. 12, 66; emphasis added.

[13]Augustine, *Confessions* 2.2, trans. R. S. Pine-Coffin (London: Penguin, 1961), p. 44.

[14]Ibid., 3.12, p. 69.

[15]G. K. Chesterton, *Orthodoxy* (New York: Image, 1959), pp. 21-22.

[16]C. E. M. Joad, *God and Evil* (London: Religious Book Club, 1944), p. 14.

[17]George Orwell, quoted in Bernard Crick, *George Orwell: A Life* (London: Penguin, 1982), p. 428.

[18]Harry Blamires, *The Faith and Modern Error* (London, SPCK, 1964), p. 1.

[19]Blaise Pascal, *Pensées*, trans. A. J. Krailsheimer (London: Penguin Books, 1966), p. 60.

[20]Augustine, *Confessions* 1.16, p. 36.

[21]Ibid., 3.4, p. 58.

[22]Ibid., 7.10, p. 146.

[23]Pascal, *Pensées*, p. 53.

[24]Chesterton, *Orthodoxy*, p. 84.

[25]Friedrich Nietzsche, letter to Gersdorff, November 1870, quoted in Erich Heller, *The Disinherited Mind* (London: Penguin, 1961), p. 70; emphasis added.

[26]Franz Kafka, quoted in Arthur Kirsch, *Auden and Christianity* (New Haven, CT: Yale University Press, 2005), p. 20.

[27]C. E. M. Joad, *The Recovery of Belief: A Restatement of Christian Philosophy* (London: Faber & Faber, 1952), p. 82.

[28]Chesterton, *Orthodoxy*, pp. 156-57.

[29]C. S. Lewis, *Mere Christianity* (New York: Macmillan, 1943), p. 47.

[30]Michael Peppiatt, *Francis Bacon: Anatomy of an Enigma* (London: Skyhorse, 2009), p. 346.

7 TRIGGERING THE SIGNALS

[1]W. H. Auden, quoted in Arthur Kirsch, *Auden and Christianity* (New Haven, CT: Yale University Press, 2005), p. 20.

[2]W. H. Auden, "September 1, 1939," in *Another Time* (London: Faber & Faber, 1940).

[3]W. H. Auden, *Forewords and Afterwords* (New York: Random House, 1973), p. 69.

[4]William James, quoted in Edward Lurie, *Louis Agassiz: A Life in Science* (Chicago: Chicago University Press, 1960), p. 346; and James Joyce, *A Portrait of the Artist as a Young Man* (London: Penguin Books, 1992).

[5]Humphrey Carpenter, *W. H. Auden: A Biography* (Boston: Houghton Mifflin, 1981), p. 283.

[6]Auden, quoted in Kirsch, *Auden and Christianity*, p. 22.

[7]Carpenter, *W. H. Auden*, p. 283.

[8]Kirsch, *Auden and Christianity*, p. 13.

[9]Peter L. Berger, *A Rumor of Angels* (Garden City, NY: Doubleday Anchor, 1970), p. 53.

[10]Ibid.

[11]Alberto Giacometti, quoted in James Lord, *Giacometti: A Biography* (New York: Macmillan, 1997), p. 61.

[12]William Wordsworth, *Ode: Intimations of Immortality* (Boston: D. Lathrop, 1884), p. 35.

[13]C. S. Lewis, "Christianity and Culture," in *C. S. Lewis Essay Collection* (London: HarperCollins, 2002), pp. 81-82.

[14]Ibid., p. 82.

[15]Arthur Koestler, quoted in Kati Marton, *The Great Escape: Nine Jews Who Fled Hitler and Changed the World* (New York: Simon & Schuster, 2006), pp. 45-46.

[16]Robert Louis Wilken, *The Spirit of Early Christian Thought* (New Haven, CT: Yale University Press, 2003), p. 299.

[17]Augustine, *Confessions* 1.1.1, trans. R. S. Pine-Coffin (London: Penguin, 1961).

[18]Iris Murdoch, quoted in Peter Watson, *The Age of Nothing: How We Have Sought to Live Since the Death of God* (London: Weidenfeld & Nicolson, 2014), p. x.

[19]C. S. Lewis, *Surprised by Joy: The Shape of My Early Life* (Boston: Houghton Mifflin, 2012), p. 17.

[20]Ibid., p. 18.

[21]Ibid., p. 16.

[22]C. S. Lewis, *The Weight of Glory* (San Francisco: HarperOne, 1980), p. 31.

[23]Ibid.

[24]Ibid.

[25]See Berger, *Rumor of Angels*, pp. 49-75.

[26]Gregory of Nyssa, quoted in Wilken, *Spirit of Early Christian Thought*, p. 300.

[27]Ibid., pp. 300-301.

[28]Augustine, quoted in Wilken, *Spirit of Early Christian Thought*, p. 310.

[29]Thomas Nagel, quoted in Watson, *Age of Nothing*, p. 4.

[30]Philip Hallie, *Surprised by Goodness* (McLean, VA: Trinity Forum, 2002), p. 12.

[31]Philip Hallie, *Lest Innocent Blood Be Shed* (New York: HarperCollins, 1994), p. 4.

[32]Ronald Dworkin, "Religion Without God," *The New York Review of Books*, April 4, 2013.

[33]Kenneth Clark, *The Other Half* (London: John Murray, 1977), p. 108.

[34]Ibid.

8 Spring-Loaded Dynamics

[1]Friedrich Nietzsche, *The Birth of Tragedy* (Oxford: Oxford University Press, 2002), p. 30.

[2]Peter L. Berger, *The Precarious Vision: A Sociologist Looks at Social Fictions and the Christian Faith* (Garden City, NY: Doubleday, 1961), chap. 1.

[3]Ibid., p. 17.

[4]Ibid., p. 122.

[5]Ibid., p. 223.

[6]Ibid., p. 226.

[7]Peter Watson, *The Age of Nothing: How We Have Sought to Live Since the Death of God* (London: Weidenfeld & Nicolson, 2014), p. 396.

[8]Peter L. Berger, *Invitation to Sociology* (Harmondsworth, UK: Penguin, 1966), p. 152.

9 The Art of Always Being Right?

[1]Albert Camus, quoted in Herbert Lottmann, *Albert Camus* (London: Weidenfeld & Nicholson, 1979).

[2]Augustine, quoted in Peter Brown, *Augustine of Hippo* (London: Faber & Faber, 1967), p. 48.

[3]Erasmus, quoted in Roland Bainton, *Erasmus of Christendom* (New York: Scribners, 1969), p. 140.

[4]John Henry Newman, quoted in Roland Hill, *Lord Acton* (New Haven, CT: Yale University Press, 2000), p. 126.

[5]Arthur Schopenhauer, *The Art of Always Being Right* (London: Gibson Square, 2011), p. 23.

[6]Plato, *Phaedrus* 267a-b.

[7]Schopenhauer, *Art of Always Being Right*, p. 32.

[8]Plato, *Phaedrus* 257c emphasis added.

[9]Schopenhauer, *Art of Always Being Right*, p. 24.

[10]C. S. Lewis, "Christian Apologetics," in *C. S. Lewis Essay Collection* (London: HarperCollins, 2002), p. 159.

[11]Friedrich Nietzsche, *The Birth of Tragedy* (Oxford: Oxford University Press, 2002), p. 109.

[12]William Shakespeare, *Hamlet*, act 2, scene 2.

10 Beware the Boomerang

[1]Algernon Charles Swinburne, "Hymn to Proserpine," *Poetry Foundation*, accessed November 25, 2014, www.poetryfoundation.org/poem/174559.

[2]Julian, quoted in the introduction to *Julian's Against the Galileans*, ed. R. Joseph Hoffmann (New York: Prometheus Books, 2004), p. 34.

[3]Ibid., p. 32.

[4]My own attempted answer to this challenge is *Unspeakable: Facing Up to the Challenge of Evil* (San Francisco: HarperOne, 2008).

[5]Henry Chadwick, "All Things to All Men," *New Testament Studies 1*, 1954–1955, pp. 264-75.

[6]Albert Camus, *The Fall*, trans. Justin O'Brien (New York: Vintage, 1991), pp. 82-83.

[7]Harry Frankfurt, *On Bullshit* (Princeton, NJ: Princeton University Press, 2009), p. 1.

[8]Fyodor Dostoevsky, *The Brothers Karamazov*, trans. Constance Garnett (New York: Macmillan, 1922), p. 40.

[9]Camus, *Fall*, pp. 89-90.

[10]W. H. Auden, quoted in Arthur Kirsch, *Auden and Christianity* (New Haven, CT: Yale University Press, 2005), p. 16.

[11]Ibid., p. xvii.

[12]See John M. Parrish, *Paradoxes of Political Ethics: From Dirty Hands to the Invisible Hand* (Cambridge: Cambridge University Press, 2007).

[13]Pierre Nicole, *Moral Essays*, trans. anonymous (London: n.p., 1696), p. 232.

[14]Ibid., p. 383; emphasis added.

[15]C. S. Lewis, *The Four Loves* (New York: Houghton Mifflin Harcourt, 1971), p. 30.

11 Kissing Judases

[1]David W. Virtue, "Atlanta Bishop Departs from the Faith in Interfaith Comments," *Virtueonline*, January 13, 2014, www.virtueonline.org/atlanta-episcopal-bishop -departs-faith-interfaith-comments.

[2]Benjamin B. Warfield, "Introductory Note," in Francis R. Beattie, *A Treatise on Apologetics*, vol. 1 (Richmond, VA: The Presbyterian Committee of Publication, 1903), p. 26.

[3]Benjamin B. Warfield, "Introduction to Francis R. Beattie's *Apologetics*," in William Edgar and K. Scott Oliphint, *Christian Apologetics Past and Present* (Wheaton, IL: Crossway, 2011), 2:395.

[4]Karl Barth, *Church Dogmatics*, 1.1, trans. Geoffrey W. Bromiley (London: T & T Clark, 1936), p. 31.

⁵Ibid., 4.1, p. 882.

⁶Dietrich Bonhoeffer, *Letters and Papers from Prison* (London: Fontana, 1959), pp. 108-10.

⁷Jacques Ellul, *The New Demons* (London: Mowbray, 1975), p. 228.

⁸Martyn Lloyd-Jones, *Authority* (London: Inter-Varsity Press, 1958), p. 14.

⁹George Orwell, *Inside the Whale and Other Essays* (Harmondsworth: Penguin, 1962), p. 152.

¹⁰Anthony Flew, *God and Philosophy* (London: Hutchinson, 1966), p. 9.

¹¹Stephen Toulmin, Ronald W. Hepburn and Alasdair MacIntyre, eds., *Metaphysical Beliefs* (London: SCM Press, 1957), p. 97.

¹²William Cantwell Smith, *The Meaning and End of Religion* (New York: Mentor Books, 1964), p. 177.

¹³Langdon Gilkey, "Theology for a Time of Troubles," *The Christian Century,* April 29, 1981, pp. 474-80.

¹⁴Samuel Thompson, *A Modern Philosophy of Religion* (Chicago: University of Chicago Press, 1955), p. 30.

¹⁵Ninian Smart, "The Intellectual Crisis of British Theology," *Theology,* January 1965.

¹⁶Bertrand Russell, *The Scientific Outlook* (New York: Routledge, 2009), p. 72.

¹⁷See for example *Philosophers Who Believe*, ed. Kelly James Clark (Downers Grove, IL: InterVarsity Press, 1997).

¹⁸G. K. Chesterton, *Orthodoxy* (Seattle: CreateSpace, 2009), p. 45.

¹⁹Blaise Pascal, *Pensées,* trans. A. J. Krailsheimer (London: Penguin Books, 1966), p. 54.

²⁰George Tyrell, *Christianity at the Cross-roads* (London: Allen & Unwin, 1963), p. 49.

²¹Albert Schweitzer, *The Quest for the Historical Jesus* (London: A & C Black, 1954), p. 398.

²²Karl Barth, *From Rousseau to Ritschl* (London: SCM Press, 1959), p. 315.

²³Peter L. Berger, *A Rumor of Angels* (Garden City, NY: Anchor Books, 1969), p. 52.

²⁴James Hitchcock, "Does Christianity Have a Future?" *New Oxford Review,* July-August 1980, p. 12.

²⁵C. S. Lewis, "Christian Apologetics," in *C. S. Lewis Essay Collection* (London: Harper-Collins, 2002), p. 149.

²⁶Smart, "The Intellectual Crisis of British Theology."

²⁷Walter Kaufmann, *The Faith of a Heretic* (New York: New American Library, 1959), p. 32.

²⁸Walter Kaufmann, *Existentialism: Religion and Death* (New York: New American Library, 1976), p. 3.

²⁹C. S. Lewis, "Myth Became Fact," in *C. S. Lewis Essay Collection* (London: Harper-Collins, 2002), p. 141.

³⁰Peter L. Berger, "Secular Theology and the Rejection of the Supernatural," *Theological Studies* 38 (March 1977): 51.

[31]Peter L. Berger, *Facing Up to Modernity* (New York: Basic Books, 1977), p. 163.

[32]Alasdair MacIntyre, "God and the Theologians," in *The Honest to God Debate*, ed. D. L. Edwards (London: SCM Press, 1963), pp. 215-27.

12 Charting the Journey

[1]Plato, *Apology* 38a, in *Plato in Twelve Volumes*, trans. Harold North Fowler, vol. 1 (Cambridge, MA: Harvard University Press, 1966).

[2]Ronald Dworkin, "What Is a Good Life?" *New York Review of Books*, February 10, 2011.

[3]Carl Gustav Jung, cited in Peter Watson, *The Age of Nothing: How We Have Sought to Live Since the Death of God* (London: Weidenfeld & Nicolson, 2014), p. ix.

[4]Clifford Geertz, quoted in ibid.

[5]Os Guinness, *Long Journey Home* (Colorado Springs: WaterBrook Press, 2001).

[6]Francis Bacon, quoted in Michael Peppiatt, *Francis Bacon: Anatomy of an Enigma* (London: Skyhorse, 2009), p. 3.

[7]C. S. Lewis, "Surprised by Joy," in *The Inspirational Writings of C. S. Lewis* (New York: Harcourt Brace Jovanovich, 1987), p. 130.

[8]Kati Marton, *The Great Escape: Nine Jews Who Fled Hitler and Changed the World* (New York: Simon & Schuster, 2006), p. 77.

[9]Malcolm Muggeridge, personal interaction.

[10]Arthur Koestler, quoted by Martin, *The Great Escape*, p. 96.

[11]Eva Striker, quoted in ibid.

[12]Peter L. Berger, *Pyramids of Sacrifice* (New York: Basic Books, 1974), p. 201.

[13]C. S. Lewis, "Is Theology Poetry?" in *The Weight of Glory and Other Addresses*, rev. ed. (New York: HarperCollins, 1980), p. 140.

[14]John Milton, *Areopagitica*, Dartmouth.edu, accessed December 1, 2014, www.dart mouth.edu/~milton/reading_room/areopagitica/text.shtml.

[15]Maurice Merleau-Ponty, "Eye and Mind," in *The Primacy of Perception*, trans. Carleton Dallery, ed. James Edie (Evanston, IL: Northwestern University Press, 1964), pp. 159-90.

[16]G. K. Chesterton, quoted in Peter L. Berger, *A Rumor of Angels* (New York: Anchor Books, 1970), p. 3.

[17]C. S. Lewis, "Miracles," in *C. S. Lewis Essay Collection* (London: HarperCollins, 2002), p. 107.

[18]Ibid., p. 108.

[19]Francis Bacon, quoted in Michael Peppiatt, *Francis Bacon: Anatomy of an Enigma* (London: Skyhorse, 2009), p. 159.

[20]Ibid., p. 271.

[21]Ibid., p. 272.

[22]William Butler Yeats, quoted in Watson, *Age of Nothing*, p. 167.

[23]Ludwig Wittgenstein and Ortega y Gasset, quoted in ibid., p. ix.

[24]Eugene O'Neill, quoted in ibid., p. 261.

[25]G. K. Chesterton, *The Everlasting Man* (Seaside, OR: Rough Draft, 2013), p. 159.

[26]Koestler, cited in Marton, *Great Escape*, p. 98.

[27]Ibid.

[28]Lewis, "Myth Became Fact," in *Essay Collection*, p. 141.

[29]Lewis, "Surprised by Joy," p. 124.

[30]Lewis, "The Seeing Eye," in *Essay Collection*, p. 60.

[31]Augustine, *De Praedestinatio Sanctorum*, in *Nicene and Post-Nicene Fathers*, vol. 5, ed. Philip Schaff (Buffalo, NY: Christian Literature, 1887), chap. 5.

[32]Ibid.; emphasis added.

[33]Augustine, *The Trinity* 15.2, in *Nicene and Post-Nicene Fathers,* vol. 3, ed. Philip Schaff (Buffalo, NY: Christian Literature, 1887).

NAME INDEX

Subject Index

SCRIPTURE INDEX